THE AUTOBIOGRAPHY
OF
YUKICHI FUKUZAWA

Fukuzawa at sixty-three (1898).

THE AUTOBIOGRAPHY
OF
YUKICHI FUKUZAWA

Revised Translation by
EIICHI KIYOOKA

With a Foreword by
CARMEN BLACKER

COLUMBIA UNIVERSITY PRESS
New York

UNESCO COLLECTION OF
REPRESENTATIVE WORKS
This book
has been accepted
in the Japanese Series
of the Translations Collection
of the United Nations
Educational, Scientific and Cultural Organization
(UNESCO)

First published in 1899. First translation into English 1934 (published in Japan as *The Autobiography of Fukuzawa Yukichi*). New translation into English 1960. First American edition 1966. Printed in the United States of America.

Library of Congress Catalog Card Number: 66–15468

ISBN 0-231-08373-4

10 9 8 7 6 5 4

Clothbound editions of Columbia University Press books are Smyth-sewn and printed on permanent and durable acid-free paper.

FOREWORD

Here is the autobiography of a remarkable man. Fukuzawa Yukichi's life covered the sixty-six years between
1835 and 1901, a period which comprised greater and
more extraordinary changes than any other in the history
of Japan. At the time of his birth Japan was almost
entirely isolated from the outside world, with a hierarchical feudal system based on a Confucian code of morals.
Her notions of warfare were medieval, her economy
largely agricultural, her knowledge of modern science confined to the trickle of Dutch books which found their way
into the country through the trading station at Nagasaki.
At the time of his death Japan was to all effects a modern
state. Her army and navy were so well disciplined and
equipped that six years before they had defeated China
and four years later they were to defeat Russia. She had
a parliament, compulsory education, rapidly growing in-
dustries, and distinguished universities.

For these astonishing changes we can hold responsible
both the impersonal forces of history and the very personal power of certain individual men. Among the latter
Fukuzawa Yukichi was one of the most remarkable. He
is generally acknowledged to have been the leading educa-
tor of the new Japan, the man who above all others explained to his countrymen the ideas behind the dazzling
material evidence of western civilization; who insisted
that it was not enough for Japan merely to have the
"things" of civilization—the trains, the guns, the warships,
the hats, the umbrellas—in order to take her place with

dignity and confidence among the nations of the modern world. It was also necessary for her to comprehend the learning which in the West had led to the discovery and production of these things. And this would require a drastic reconsideration of some of her most ancient and unquestioned assumptions about the nature of the universe.

To explain these new and unfamiliar ideas Fukuzawa wrote voluminously over a period of some thirty years. He started a newspaper which continued for half a century as one of the great Tokyo dailies. He founded a school which is one of the largest and most distinguished universities in Japan.

The autobiography of such a man, a philosopher and a schoolmaster, might be expected to be perhaps a little dry, an abstract, inward account of ideas and conflicting principles. Not so this book. From the first page we are captivated, enthralled by both the author and the tale he tells.

He starts with his childhood in the small feudal clan of Nakatsu in Kyushu. We are shown a vanished world, a small, rigid society governed to an extent almost unimaginable today by minute distinctions of hierarchical rank. Fukuzawa tells us that he always loathed the "narrow stiffness" of the life there, indeed hated the feudal system as though it had been his father's murderer. His discontent is not difficult to understand. His family was of the samurai class, but of a low rank within that class. He was one of those "lower samurai," in fact, whose impoverishment and discontent at this time drove them a couple of decades later to become the main force behind the overthrow of the Shogunate. The strict laws of the

Nakatsu clan required that in almost every context of daily life the lower samurai should abase themselves before their superiors in feudal rank. The men of Fukuzawa's low status, besides being much poorer, less educated, and more tediously occupied than the upper samurai, were required to prostrate themselves on their faces every time they encountered an upper samurai; to address their superiors with all the resources of the honorific vocabulary while suffering themselves to be addressed in language which was habitually abusive; to speak with a more boorish accent than that used by the samurai of higher rank. The two classes of men were treated in effect like two different species of nature, for marriage between them was strictly forbidden and virtually unknown.

Most of his contemporaries, Fukuzawa tells us in another work of reminiscence, were discontented with their lot, but utterly unable to express their discontent. They would no more dream of trying to rise in the world by entering the ranks of the upper samurai than would a four-legged beast hope to fly like a bird. They accepted all the distinctions of feudal rank as though these were part of the fixed and immutable order of nature rather than the invention of man.

Fukuzawa was one of the very few who cared nothing for feudal propriety, thinking it no disgrace to go shopping in broad daylight. "Why should I not?" he asked himself. Nor had he any reverence for the things generally accounted holy. Secretly, in order to test their efficacy, he trampled on the sacred paper charms and put them to vile uses in the lavatory. The fact that nothing terrible ensued from these outrages made him a lifelong skeptic.

To escape from the tedium and petty formality of the

clan was his one thought. His chance eventually came, when he was nineteen years old, in the form of the western studies which were later to become his life's work. But in 1854 it was not from any lofty ambitions for the future that he set out for Nagasaki to learn gunnery, but simply because it was a convenient excuse for getting away. "I would have been glad to study a foreign language or the military art or anything else if only it gave me a chance to go away . . . I still remember how I swore to myself that like a bullet shot out of the gun's muzzle I would never come back." He spat on the ground as he walked away.

His pursuit of western studies eventually took him to Osaka, where he entered the school of the celebrated scholar Ogata. His account of his Dutch studies in Osaka is one of the most fascinating chapters in the book. The Ogata students were poor and unconventional. Most of them had pawned their swords. Indoors they usually went naked except at meals and at classes. In the streets they were so rowdy that the citizens were careful to give them a wide berth. Yet at their Dutch studies they worked with a fierce enthusiasm which made no distinction between night and day. "I would be reading all day," Fukuzawa tells us here, "and when night came I did not think of going to bed. . . . We could not have studied harder." The difficulties they encountered can scarcely be realized by us today. Among eighty or ninety students there was only one Dutch dictionary. The college library consisted of ten Dutch books of science, which the student, once he had mastered the rudiments of grammar, had to wait his turn to copy laboriously with a brush or quill.

What was the motive which prompted Fukuzawa and

his fellows to expend such selfless energy on the study of Dutch science? It was not the hope of fame or gain. No one at that time saw in them the future leaders of the new Japan, the pioneers of the intellectual and political movement which was to result in the momentous changes of the Meiji period. Rather they appeared to the rest of their countrymen as weird and disagreeable eccentrics, given to disgusting practices which put them on a par with the outcast *eta*. Their only incentive at that time, Fukuzawa tells us, was the pleasure of acquiring rare and difficult knowledge. Knowledge desirable not because it was likely to prove useful, but simply because it was difficult. It was as though they were swallowing a nasty medicine, not because it was likely to do them any good, but simply because they were the only people brave enough to swallow it.

Several more years were to elapse, indeed, before Fukuzawa in any way began to realize the potential importance of the studies he had undertaken. They were years, however, full of adventure and momentous events. He was summoned to Edo by the clan authorities to start a school for the study of Dutch. He visited the foreign trading community in Yokohama, to make the disheartening discovery that no one there spoke Dutch or understood anything he said. Nothing daunted, he made up his mind at once to set about the even more formidable task of learning English. He joined the first Japanese mission to America in 1860, sailing through atrocious weather to San Francisco. There, he tells us, he was bored by explanations of the process of galvanizing and the use of the vacuum in sugar refining, which he had understood perfectly for years, but utterly puzzled by such things as an ordinary carriage.   He joined the first Japanese mission to Europe in 1862, visiting the capitals of all the countries with which Japan had concluded treaties in 1858.   The mission's hosts always took pains to show them the most impressive examples of western civilization that their countries could muster, and Fukuzawa, an indefatigable note-taker, lost no opportunity of learning and marking all he could.

He returned to Japan to find that assassins were abroad ready to strike down foreigners or any Japanese suspected of pro-foreign leanings.   For many years Fukuzawa did not dare to go out at night.   Instead he stayed at home, taught in his school, and started to write the books which were soon to make him famous.

The most celebrated of these was *Seiyō Jijō* (Things Western), which in 1866 sold no less than 250,000 copies, an unprecedented number for those days.   Its immense success was due to the fact that it gave the Japanese public exactly the information about the West that it needed.   A few intrepid spirits might have studied works on western chemistry, medicine, or gunnery, but hardly anyone had any conception of how the people in the West lived their everyday lives, what they wore and ate, and how they were governed.   *Seiyō Jijō* described western hospitals, schools and newspapers, museums, the taxation system, and other ordinary social institutions.   It gave the Japanese public for the first time a picture of what the western countries were like to live in.

Its success was so great that soon all books about the West came to be called *Fukuzawa-bon*.   But even then its author could not believe that the knowledge it imparted would ever prove of lasting value and importance.   "I had no idea that the contents of [my] books would ever be applied to our own social conditions," he wrote. "In short, I was writing my books simply as stories of the West or as curious tales of a dreamland."

It was not until after the upheaval of the Restoration, when the new government had shown itself to be not the collection of ignorant fools which he had feared, but rather a group of able men determined to build up a new Japan on thoroughly modern lines, that Fukuzawa came to realize his true mission in life. This was nothing more nor less than to refashion the whole way of thinking of his countrymen. He felt, he wrote towards the end of the book, that he "must take advantage of the moment to bring in more of Western civilization and revolutionise our people's ideas from the roots. Then perhaps it would not be impossible to form a great nation in this far Orient which would stand counter to Great Britain of the West, and take an active part in the progress of the whole world."

What was it that he found so misguided in the traditional Japanese way of thinking? In an interesting passage he tells us that there seemed to be two important things lacking, science and the spirit of independence. The reason why western statesmen governed their countries so successfully and western businessmen were so successful in commerce and industry, why the people were so patriotic and their family circles so happy, was because their civilization was based on the laws of science and the principle of independence. The reason why Japan lay behind in these matters was because her traditional Confucian learning had neglected these two important principles.

For the rest of his life, therefore, Fukuzawa made it his task to promulgate this new philosophy in every way

possible—in the teaching in his school, in the policy of
his newspaper, in his voluminous writings, in his private
life.   After the tales of adventure, of foreign travel, of
the hidden assassin, which make the early chapters of this
book such compelling reading, his life following 1868
settled down to a quieter tenor of writing and teaching.
He refused all offers of government employment, for reasons we may read towards the end of the book, and devoted
himself in an entirely private capacity to the propagation
of his philoscphy.

Books and articles appeared from his pen in a steady
stream, concerned to point out the shortcomings of the
old learning and values, and to propose new principles
better suited to the position Japan must play in the modern world.   His writings cover an astonishing range.   He
wrote on ethics, on politics, on economics, on historiogra-
phy, on international law.   He wrote, of course, on the
philosophy of science, and the spirit of independent ob-
servation and criticism which had led to the rise of such
a philosophy in the West.   He showed how the old Confucian system of ethics could no longer stand in a society
which promoted science, and proposed a new set of values
to put in its place.   He attacked the old family system,
championing particularly the cause of women, and of children oppressed by too demanding canons of filial piety.

Many of his ideas we now take for granted, forgetting
the courage that was needed at the time to voice them so
clearly.   Among his most sensational words were the
opening sentences of his book *Gakumon no Susume* (The
encouragement of learning): "Heaven never created a
man above another nor a man below another."   Men
might differ in their outward circumstances and conditions,

but in the matter of their "rights," their claim to life,
property, and human dignity, all were equal. We now
take these principles for granted as fundamental to the
democratic way of life. But in Japan in 1872 they caused
a great outcry. They contradicted entirely the traditional
political philosophy which assumed that human society
was a natural hierarchy in which all men were by nature
unequal.

His stress on science and the spirit of independence we
now regard as essential to our conception of valid knowledge. But in the early 1870s in Japan it was something
unfamiliar and strange, requiring an entirely new attitude
to the things of the external world. How rare indeed
was the spirit of independence when Fukuzawa was young
we can judge from the first chapter of this book. He
seems to have been the only member of his community
who questioned the rigid conventions of the hierarchy.
The moral code based on the principles of "independence
and self-respect" which he formulated at the turn of the
century strikes us now as sound and decent common sense.
Yet when it first appeared in 1900 it was attacked as the
subversive doctrine which had led to the horrors of the
French Revolution.

As compassionate and sensible also seem Fukuzawa's
pleas for a new spirit in the family, in which the members
should live together like a "group of friends," bound by
ties not of hierarchical duty but of mutual love and affection. His call for respect for the rights of women, for a
more reasonable treatment of their position in society than
that accorded them for so long by the odious *Onna
Daigaku*, is now accepted without cavil in all civilized
countries.

We are too often apt to accept our common stock of wisdom, forgetting the vision and courage which were needed for its discovery. Fukuzawa's contribution to the wisdom of Japan does not strike us now as recondite. It is built into the whole structure of our lives. But, as the Chinese reformer Liang Ch'i Ch'ao said of him, together with Voltaire and Tolstoy, "If these men had not lived, it is doubtful whether their countries could have advanced." Had Fukuzawa not lived, the heritage of Japan would be the poorer. For, however we may choose to define greatness, we must surely include the qualities of vision beyond one's time and of the moral courage to voice what one has seen. Fukuzawa possessed both these qualities, and the extra one of lucidity. He conveyed his unfamilar ideas not in the erudite language so fashionable among scholars but in words that any housemaid could understand.

We are happy to find from this book that he was also very human. Possibly because the book was dictated to a secretary rather than carefully planned and composed, we feel as we read that we are listening to a friend talking. Relaxed and spontaneous, he reminisces of the adventures of his youth among scenes long vanished, recalls odd conversations with his friends, tells confidentially of his hopes and fears. Vignettes from the past well up in his memory, and stay for long afterwards in our own. We recall the scene in the Shōgun's castle on the eve of the Restoration, with the Shōgun's retainers, their usual strict etiquette forgotten, sprawling in the exquisite rooms talking politics as though they were mad or drunk. Or the scenes in Ogata's school, with the students, naked and dirty, poring with fierce concentration over Dutch treatises on anatomy and chemistry. Or the ferocious warrior who came to Fukuzawa's school straight from the last battle of the Restoration, girt with swords and strange trophies. Or the dissipated student whom Fukuzawa ordered to sit up all night in self-reflection, and whom he afterwards regretted having roughly shaken in anger. Or the old beggar woman whose lice and fleas Fukuzawa's mother used compassionately to catch and kill. And throughout, the figure of the author, becoming stronger as we read, more genuinely human, more three-dimensionally companionable and knowable as he speaks.

Professor Eiichi Kiyooka could have made this memorable translation from a sheer delight in the book itself. But for him there is an extra tie. He is Fukuzawa's grandson and has that special insight which comes from a true "sympathy" in the most literal sense of "feeling with" the writer of the book. Fukuzawa would certainly have been glad, as he looked back over his early struggles to learn English, to see that his efforts had borne fruit in such a felicitous command of the English language in his own grandson. Still more glad that these talents should have been used to bring *Fukuō Jiden* (The Autobiography of the Aged Fukuzawa) to the English-speaking world.

CARMEN BLACKER

Cambridge, England
July, 1965

ACKNOWLEDGMENT

It seems that a translator's work never comes to an end. Although errors had been eliminated in the past editions, the need for improving the whole translation remained. It is his great happiness that an opportunity was given him to reexamine every line of the book and to bring out what he calls the new translation. This is a rare privilege for a translator. Also, he was able to redivide the chapters and to add the marginal titles according to the newly discovered Fukuzawa's manuscript. He is very grateful to Prof. Max H. Fisch for giving him very minute criticisms on the old translation. And, in writing the enlarged notes and index, he received invaluable assistances again from Mr. Masafumi Tomita, Mr. Washichi Konno, the editing staffs of the One Hundred Year History of Keiō-gijuku, and the student members of the Keiō English Speaking Society, for which he wishes to express his very deep appreciation. Nor has he forgotten the help he had had from Mr. Charles F. Bopes and Mr. W. Bradford Smith for the first translation.

PREFACE TO THE 1899 EDITION

As it is often the custom with foreign men of learning to leave an account of their lives for the benefit of posterity, many members of our university had, for some time, wished our Fukuzawa Sensei[1] to do the same. Some of them had actually spoken of it to him, but Sensei had always been very busy and had no spare time to undertake the writing. But the year before last, in the autumn, he had occasion to tell some of his reminiscences of the period of the Restoration at the request of a certain foreigner. At that time, Sensei, on a sudden thought, called in a writer of shorthand and had the oral narrative of his life from early childhood to old age taken down. Later he made several corrections in the manuscript and had it published in a serial form in his Jiji-shimpō, beginning in last July and continuing till February of this year under the title of Fukuō Jiden (Autobiography of Aged Fukuzawa).

Since these notes are simply a narrative based on his casual memory told in order as he recalled each incident, it is more an informal talk than an autobiography. Therefore, Sensei had planned to write a companion volume so as to supply what was left out in the present one, and to make a complete account of the beginning of our intercourse with foreign nations, and also of the last phases of the diplomatic steps taken by the Shōgun's government. The general plan of this second volume had already been made, but in September of last year Sensei was suddenly overcome by a severe illness which prevented his carrying it out. When Sensei

---

[1] Note on p. 337.

recovers from his illness, he will have the second volume[2]
published and satisfy our present regret.

ISHIKAWA KAMMEI

June, 1899
Jiji-Shimpō

---

[2] Note on p. 337.

CONTENTS

ILLUSTRATIONS

THE AUTOBIOGRAPHY
OF
YUKICHI FUKUZAWA

I
CHILDHOOD

My father, Fukuzawa Hyakusuke, was a samurai[1] belonging to the Okudaira Clan of Nakatsu on the island of Kyūshū. My mother, called O-Jun as her given name, was the eldest daughter of Hashimoto Hamaemon, another samurai of the same clan. In social order, my father was barely high enough to have a formal audience with the lord. He was a few ranks above the common soldier (*ashigaru*), but he was of the lower order among the samurai. In today's society his position would probably correspond to *hanninkan*,[2] the lowest rank of government officials.

My father had been made "securer of the foundation" (*motojimeyaku*), or in other words the overseer of the treasury.[3] Consequently he had to spend much of his time at his lord's storage office and headquarters[4] in the city of Ōsaka.

Therefore all of us children were born in Ōsaka, five in all—first a boy, then three girls, and then myself, the youngest. I was born on the twelfth of December in the fifth year of the Tempō era (according to the modern calendar, January 10, 1835) when my father was forty-three years old and my mother thirty-one.

A year and a half later, in June, my father died. At that time, my brother was only eleven, and I was a mere infant,

---

[1] Note on p. 337.　[2] p. 338.　[3] Ibid.　[4] Ibid.

so the only course for our mother to follow was to take her children back with her to her original feudal province of Nakatsu, which she did.

We children did not fit into Nakatsu society What I seem to remember best about Nakatsu is the fact that we children never quite mixed with other children there. Though we had dozens of cousins, and there were flocks of children in the neighborhood, we never seemed to get along with any of them, or play with them, as we did among ourselves. There was no real reason for this, but, having a different Ōsaka dialect, we children grew self-conscious even in saying "yes" and "no" to our neighbors. Moreover, my mother, although she was a native of Nakatsu, had accustomed herself to the life of Ōsaka, then the most prosperous city in Japan, and so the way she dressed us and arranged our hair made us seem queer in the eyes of these people in a secluded town on the coast of Kyūshū. And having nothing else to wear but what we had brought from Ōsaka, we naturally felt more comfortable to stay at home and play among ourselves.

I must mention a very important characteristic of our family. My father was really a scholar. And the scholars of the time, different from the Western scholars of today, disdained to spend any thought on money, or even to touch it. My father always longed for a quiet scholarly life with his books and the noble philosophy of the ancient sages. Yet he was forced to attend to the most worldly affairs, for it was his duty as treasury overseer to associate with merchants, and to count money, and to negotiate loans for his lord. Sometimes when his lord was in difficulty, my father had to bargain with the rich men like Kajimaya and Kōnoike of Ōsaka.

In this work he was unhappy, and so when it came to

**Education ac-
cording to Con-
fucian doctrine**
bringing up his children, he tried, it
seems to me, to give them what he
thought was an ideal education. For
instance, he once sent them to a teacher
for calligraphy and general education.
The teacher lived in the compound of the lord's storage
office, but, having some merchants' children among his
pupils, he naturally began to train them in numerals: "Two
times two is four, two times three is six, etc." This, today,
seems a very ordinary thing to teach, but when my father
heard this, he took his children away in a fury.

"It is abominable," he exclaimed, "that innocent children
should be taught to use numbers—the tool of merchants.
There is no telling what the teacher may do next."

I heard of this incident later from my mother, for I was
too small at the time to be sent with the others to the
teacher.

At any rate one may easily see that he was a very strict
father who never compromised on what he felt was right.
From the writings he left, I know that he was a Confucian
to the very heart. Among the great scholars on Chinese
philosophy, my father had a particular respect for Itō Tōgai,[5]
and was literally living the old saying, "Be true and sincere,
unashamed even in the innermost privacy."

My father's ideas survived him in his family. All five of
us children lived with few friends to visit us, and since we
had no one to influence us but our mother who lived only
in her memory of her husband, it was as if father himself
were living with us. So in Nakatsu, with our strange habits
and apparel, we unconsciously formed a group apart, and
although we never revealed it in words, we looked upon the
neighbors around us as less refined than ourselves. Even

---

[5] Note on p. 338.

our cousins were, we felt, not quite like ourselves. We did not reproach them for any breach of good manners, for we were too few to assert our superiority. We simply held our self-possession deep in our hearts and stood aloof.

I still remember that I was always a lively happy child, fond of talk and romping about, but I was never good at climbing trees and I never learned to swim. This was perhaps because I did not play with the neighborhood children.

Discipline without strictness

Thus we lived apart in that alien place and had many lonely experiences, but our home life was a happy one. Though there was no father to lord it over us, we children never quarreled among ourselves or annoyed our mother. It was not that our mother was strict, or that she took particular pains in teaching us manners, but we grew up naturally to be obedient and thoughtful. It must have come from the memory of our father and the quiet influence of our mother.

As an instance of the discipline observed, we never had a musical instrument like *shamisen* in our home, nor did we ever think of hearing it, for that was an amusement unworthy of the samurai. Likewise, it was natural that it never occurred to us to go and see a play. In the summer time during a festival, there would sometimes be a series of plays lasting seven days together when the traveling actors set up their temporary stage in the Sumiyoshi temple-yard. Then there would always be a proclamation that the samurai of our clan should not attend the plays or even go beyond the stone wall of the temple.

Though the proclamation sounded very strict, it amounted to a mere formality. Many of the less scrupulous samurai would go to the plays with their faces wrapped in towels, wearing only the shorter of the two swords which all samurai wore—thus making themselves appear like common people. These disguised samurai broke over the bamboo fence of the theater, whereas the real common people paid their fees. When the management tried to stop the intruders, they would utter a menacing roar and go striding on to take the best seats.

Among the many samurai families of middle and low class, ours was perhaps the only one that did not see the plays. Though all women love the theater, my mother never let herself mention it, and we children never asked a question about it. Sometimes after a warm day we might go out together for a stroll in the cool of the evening. As we walked along, we would see the canvas of the temporary theater come into view, but we would never speak of the plays that were being staged. Such was our family.

As I have mentioned, my father was unhappy in the worldly duties which it was his lot to perform. He might have broken with his master and gone to seek his fortune elsewhere, but he did not entertain such an idea. Apparently he submitted to the distasteful position and the small stipend, and buried his discontent in his heart. Perhaps it was because he knew that it was impossible to overcome the rigid customs of the time.

There is a story that makes me sorry for him. When I was born, I was found to be a rather thin but big-boned child, and the midwife said that I would grow up to be a fine man if only I was fed plenty of milk. This made my father very glad.

When he grows up, I will make a priest of him "This is a good child," he often said to my mother. "When he gets to be ten or eleven years old, if all goes well, I shall send him to a monastery and make a priest of him."

Later, after the loss of my father, my mother often told me that she never understood why he wanted me to be a priest. "But," she would say, "if your father were still living, you would be a priest of some temple by now."

Years later, when I came to understand better, I realized that this wish of my father's was a result of the feudal system of that time with the rigid law of inheritance: sons of high officials following their father in office, sons of foot-soldiers always becoming foot-soldiers, and those of the families in between having the same lot for centuries without change. For my father, there had been no hope of rising in society whatever effort he might make. But when he looked around, he saw that for me there was one possible road to advancement—the priesthood. A fish monger's son had been known to become a Buddhist abbot.[6]

Feudalism is my father's mortal enemy

I believe I am not far from the truth in thinking that this may have been my father's reason for directing me to the priesthood. I am filled with heart-pity when I think that he should have lived the forty-five years of his life in the fetters of the feudal system, and died before any of his desires had been fulfilled. He had determined to put his son in a monastery so that he might have some wider field of thought and life which had been denied to himself. When I think of this, I realize his inward suffering and his unfathomable love, and I am often moved to tears. To me, indeed, the feudal system is my father's mortal enemy which I am honor-bound to destroy.

But despite my father's wish, I did not become a priest. Nor did I do any studying at home as he would have encouraged me to, for there was nobody to force me to do so. My brother, who had taken my father's place in the family, was still a young man; my mother was obliged to do all the house-work, feeding and clothing the five of us children by

---

[6] Note on p. 338.

herself, as she did not have enough means to hire a servant. Naturally, our education was neglected in the busy rush of daily work.

It was not unusual for the young sons of the Nakatsu clan to study Chinese classics such as Lun-yü, the sayings of Confucius, and Ta-hsüeh, a book of ethics, but such studies were never really encouraged by anyone. I suppose there is no child in the world naturally fond of study; so perhaps I was not the only one to take advantage of a parent's leniency, and to profess a dislike of books.

At fourteen or fifteen, I turn my mind to learning However, when I was fourteen or fifteen years old, I found that many of the boys of my age were studying these classics; and I became ashamed of myself and willingly started to school. It was embarrassing in the beginning, for I was a young man of fifteen beginning with the oral reading of Mencius, while other boys of my age were discussing the books of Chinese philosophy (Shih-ching and Shu-ching).

The system followed there was that the advanced students gave lessons in oral reading to the new students early in the morning, and then later they all had an open discussion of the subject. Perhaps I was somewhat talented in literature, for I could discuss a book with the older student who had taught me the reading of it earlier in the morning, and I was always upsetting his argument. This fellow knew the words well, but he was slow to take in the ideas they expressed. So it was an easy matter for me to hold a debate with him.

I changed school two or three times, but I studied most under the care of a master named Shiraishi.[7] Under his guidance I made rapid progress, and in four or five years I

---

[7] Note on p. 338.

had no difficulty in studying a good part of the Chinese
classics.

Shiraishi Sensei placed special emphasis on the classics,
and so we gave much of our time to the study of Lun-yü,
Mencius, and other books of ancient sages. Especially, as
our master was fond of Shih-ching and Shu-ching, we often
listened to his lectures on these books. Also Mêng-ch'iu,
Shih-shuo, Tso-chuan, Chan-kuo-ts'e, Lao-tzu, and Chuang-
tzu. As for historical books, we had Shih-chi, Ch'ien-hou
Han-shu, Chin-shu, Wu-tai-shih, Yüan-ming Shih-lüeh, etc.[8]

Of all the books I read at Shiraishi's
I read Tso-chuan   school, Tso-chuan was my favorite.
eleven times over While most of the students gave it up
after reading three or four volumes out
of the fifteen, I read all—eleven times over—and memorized
the most interesting passages. Thus in the course of time
I became *zenza*, or senior disciple who had the privilege of
giving occasional lectures.

Shiraishi Sensei belonged to the school of Kamei[9]; in fact,
he worshipped that master of sound philosophy, and rather
despised the delicately literary, and did not encourage the
writing of lyric poetry among us. There was, at that time,
a certain poet and satirist, Hirose Tansō[10]; of him our
master would disparagingly say that he could not write a
line of perfect Chinese and was but a trifling poet in Japanese.* Likewise, of another literary contemporary, Rai
Sanyō,[11] he would say, "If his writings are called 'literature,'
then anybody's scribblings might be literature too. A man
may stammer, but his meaning will be understood!" Following our master, we disciples soon learned to think little
of those he denounced.

My late father was like Shiraishi, for although he was in

---

* Chinese was the scholar's language in Japan just as Latin was in Europe.
[8] Note on p. 338.   [9] p. 339.   [10] Ibid.   [11] Ibid.

Ōsaka, and Sanyō lived in Kyōto, not far away, they never exchanged courtesies. My father, however, did become a friend of another scholar, Noda Tekiho. I do not know what kind of man this Tekiho was, but if my father made a friend of him while avoiding Sanyō, this Tekiho must have been a scholar of true worth. At any rate, as Kamei Sensei had established his own theory in opposition to the Chu-tzu School, his disciples were often at odds with scholars of other groups.

I was clever with my hands
Besides these studies at school, I was very clever at doing little things with my hands, and I loved to try inventing and devising things. When something fell in the well, I contrived some means to fish it out. When the lock of a drawer failed to open, I bent a nail in many ways, and poking into the mechanism, somehow opened it. These were my proud moments. I was good at pasting new paper on the inner doors of the house, which are called *shōji*. Every so often when the old lining of the *shōji* turned gray with dust, it had to be taken off and new white paper pasted on the frame. I used to do all this work for our own house, and sometimes one of our relatives hired me out to help him do the work in his house. I was proud to do all I was asked, for I was quick and clever at little jobs of every kind.

As I grew older, I began to do a greater variety of things, such as mending the wooden clogs and sandals—I mended them for all my family—and fixing broken doors and leaks in the roof. As we were poor, it was necessary that some member of the family should look to keeping the house in repair. I bought a large needle and changed the covering of the *tatami*—the thick mats that are used to cover the floors. Also I knew how to split bamboo and put hoops around buckets and tubs.

Later, I began to earn money by making wooden clogs and fitting out swords. I never learned to polish the blade, but I could lacquer the sheath, wind the cords around the handle, and somehow put on the metal fittings. I still have a short sword which I fitted out myself, though of course it is of poor workmanship as I look at it now. I learned these arts from various acquaintances among the samurai who were practising them to add to their living.

I was surprised by a saw-file   For any work in metals it is very necessary to have a good file; I had a difficult time in making one for myself.

I knew how to make an ordinary file from a steel bar, after a fashion, but the fine file for sharpening saws was beyond my art. Years later, when I first came to Yedo,* I was surprised at the sight of a boy, an apprentice to a blacksmith, making a saw-file. I still remember the place. It was at Tamachi on the right-hand side of the street as I entered the city. The boy had the file on a piece of leather on an anvil, and was chiseling away at very fine notches as if he never realized there was any wonder in it. I stopped and watched him, thinking what a great city of industry this must be where even a youngster could make a saw-file such as I myself had never dreamed of making. This was the first shock I received on coming to the city.

Thus ever since my childhood, besides my love of books, I have been accustomed to working with my hands. And even yet, in my old age, I find myself handling planes and chisels, and making and mending things. But these are only common, homely things, devoid of art. I possess little of what people call "good taste." I care nothing for the kind of clothes I wear or the kind of house I live in. I do not even see why one must wear one garment over the other

---

* The present city of Tōkyō. It was renamed soon after the Imperial Restoration of 1868.

in a certain way. Still less do I understand why fashions in dress should change every year. In this awkward, common-place life of mine, if I might claim any one taste, it would be the sword, for I do know what constitutes good workmanship in sword fitting. I believe this taste came from my early work in it though my skill was never more than that of an amateur.

I was always unconcerned with the way of society, and it was my inborn nature to act always in my own way. Since all the samurai of small means kept no servants, they were obliged to go out and do their own shopping. But according to the convention among the warrior class, they were ashamed of being seen handling money. Therefore, it was customary for samurai to wrap their faces with hand-towels and go out after dark whenever they had an errand to do.

I carry a wine bottle in broad daylight I hated having a towel on my face and have never worn one. I even used to go out on errands in broad daylight, swinging a wine bottle in one hand, with two swords at my side as became a man of samurai rank.

"This is my own money," I would say to myself. "I did not steal it. What is wrong with buying things with my own money?" Thus, I believe, it was with a boyish pride and conceit that I made light of the mock gentility of my neighbors.

When guests were expected at our house, I often cooked burdocks and radishes to help my mother in the kitchen. But as soon as the guests arrived, I disappeared into a closet. I did not like to see them lazily eating and drinking and talking nonsense. I often wished they would hurry and go away, but of course they never did. So I would take my supper early, drink my wine—for I was fond of it—and crawl into some little closet in which we kept our bedding, for that was the only refuge I had in the small house. I would stay there, lying on the pile of bedding until the guests were all gone. Then I would crawl out and spread my bed in the usual corner of the room.[12]

My brother[13] had many friends who used to come in the evening and discuss the questions of the day. Sometimes I listened to them, but being yet a youngster, I was never allowed to join in. Frequently the subject of the conversation turned to Rekkō of Mito[14] and Shungaku of Echizen,[15] two great men whom all the scholars of the nation honored. As Rekkō of Mito was a close relation of the Shōgun,[16] respect for him was very deep. In mentioning him in conversation, people did not speak his name directly. Scholars, in scholarly language, would call him "Mito-no Rōkō" (The venerable aged lord of Mito) while the unlearned would call him "Mito-no Goinkyo Sama" (The honorable retired lord of Mito), always careful to use the honorific title "Sama." Inspired by all this, I too believed that he was the greatest man in the world.

Then there was Egawa Tarozaemon,[17] also much respected as a great man. Again, as he was *hatamoto*, or an immediate retainer of the Shōgun, everybody referred to him, even in private conversation as "Egawa Sama." Once I heard my brother mention to his friend that this great man, Egawa Tarozaemon, was a hero of modern times, for his self-control was such that he was able to live through the winters in summer clothing.

"H'm, I can do that myself," I thought as I listened. And after that, without disclosing my intention to anybody, I began to sleep on the floor rolled up in only one quilt. My mother was much worried when she learned this.

"What nonsense is this?" she said. "You will take cold!"

---

[12] Note on p. 339.   [13] Ibid.   [14] Ibid.   [15] Ibid.   [16] p. 340.   [17] Ibid.

But I went on and endured the cold until spring. I was fifteen or sixteen years old then, eager to try everything that others did, and happily I had a strong constitution.

As I have suggested, Chinese classics were then the basis of all learning. Naturally, my brother was a thorough scholar in Chinese, but he was peculiar in one respect—he studied mathematics according to the teaching of Hoashi Banri,[18] a scholar of Bungo province.

This teacher, though he was a noted scholar in Chinese, had a new theory that the gun and the abacus* were to be considered important instruments for the samurai, and that it was wrong to leave the abacus, or rather finances, to lower officials, and the gun to the common soldiers. This theory had spread to Nakatsu and my brother was one of the several younger men who had studied mathematics and attained some ability in it. In this he differed from the usual scholars; otherwise, he was a strict follower of the Chinese, believing to the core in their moral teachings. One day I had an amusing conversation with him.

Conversation with my brother

"Yukichi, what do you intend to be in the future?" he asked me.

"Well, Sir, I would like to be the richest man in Japan," I answered, "and spend all the money I want to."

He made a wry face and gave me a piece of his mind. So I asked him in return: "What do you want to be?"

He answered gravely in stilted Chinese phrasing: "I will be dutiful to my parents, faithful to my brethren, and loyal to my master until death."

"H'm!" I exclaimed. And there the conversation ended. That was my brother.

---

* A simple but efficient calculating instrument with many sliding beads on a board.
[18] Note on p. 340.

He sometimes had queer ideas. "I was born the eldest son," he once said to me, "and I am now the head of the family. But I should like, if it were possible, to become an adopted son of some very difficult family with the most headstrong parents. I would prove that an adopted son can live with any parents and be good and obedient."

His opinion was that all troubles arising between parents and an adopted son came from the wilfulness of the son. But I had an entirely opposite opinion. "I should hate to be an adopted son," I said. "Why should I serve people as parents who are in truth not parents at all?"

So our ideas differed. When this conversation took place, I was sixteen or seventeen years old.

My mother was an unusual woman who thought individually on certain matters. In religion she did not seem to have a belief like that of other old women of the time. Her family belonged to the Shin sect of Buddhism,[19] yet she would never go to hear a sermon as was expected of everyone in that sect. Nor would she worship Amida Buddha, because, as she said, "I feel rather shy in worshipping before Amida Sama. I can't bring myself to do so." Yet she never missed paying respects to the graves of her husband and her ancestors on a certain day in each month, or taking a bagful of rice to the temple. The bag which my mother used for so many years is still preserved in my family.

She never worshipped Buddha, but she had many friends among the priests—not only the priest of the temple to which her family belonged, but also novices from different parts of the country who were studying at my school. Mother loved to treat these novices with tasty dishes whenever they came to visit me, and I have no reason to think that she was against religion in any way.

---

[19] Note on p. 340.

My mother was fond of doing kindnesses to all people, especially of making friends among the classes beneath her own, the merchants and farmers. She had no objection even to admitting beggars, or even the outcast *eta* (the slaughterers of cattle and dealers in leather who were a separate class by themselves[20]). My mother never showed any sign of slighting them and her way of speaking to them was very respectful. Here is an instance of my mother's charity, which I remember with both affection and distaste.

My mother's charity
There was a half-witted beggar woman in Nakatsu who called herself "Chie," but nobody knew who gave her that name. She was a miserable creature, ragged, tattered and dirty, with long filthy hair swarming with vermin. Nobody wanted to come near her. Many a time on a fine day my mother would call the beggar woman in and make her sit on the grass in the yard; then she would tie her own sleeves behind her back to keep them out of the way and bare her arms. Thus prepared, she would begin to catch the little creatures in the beggar woman's hair. I was always called on to help, and was ordered to stand by with a stone to crush the little creatures that mother pulled from the beggar's hair.

After catching fifty or a hundred or as many as could be found, my mother and I would brush our clothes and wash our hands with rice-bran. Then she would give the woman a bowl of rice for her patience in sitting still. I suppose this was a pleasure to my mother, but how I hated it! Even now it makes me uncomfortable to think of it.

One day when I was twelve or thirteen years old, I ran through the room in one of my mischievous moments and

---

[20] Note on p. 340.

I step on some papers, then on a sacred charm stepped on some papers which my brother was arranging on the floor. Suddenly he broke out in disgust:

"Stop, you dunce!"

Then he began to speak solemnly. "Do you not see what is written here?" he said. "Is this not Okudaira Taizen-no Tayū—your lord's name?"

"I did not know it," I hastily apologized. "I am sorry."

"You say you did not know," he replied indignantly. "But if you have eyes, you should see. What do you think of trampling your lord's name under foot? The sacred code of lord and vassal is . . ."

Here my brother was beginning to recite the samurai rules of duty. There was nothing for me to do but bow my head to the floor and plead: "I was very careless, please forgive me."

But in my heart there was no apology. All the time I was thinking: "Why scold about it? Did I step on my lord's head? What is wrong with stepping on a piece of paper?"

Then I went on, reasoning in my childish mind that if it was so wicked to step on a man's name, it would be very much more wicked to step on a god's name; and I determined to test the truth.

So I stole one of the charms, the thin paper slips, bearing sacred names, which are kept in many households for avoiding bad luck. And I deliberately trampled on it when nobody was looking. But no heavenly vengeance came.

"Very well," I thought to myself. "I will go a step further and try it in the worst place." I took it to the *chōzu-ba* (the privy) and put it in the filth. This time I was a little afraid, thinking I was going a little too far. But nothing happened.

"It is just as I thought!" I said to myself. "What right

did my brother have to scold me?" I felt that I had made a great discovery! But this I could not tell anybody, not even my mother or sisters.

What the god Inari really was   When I grew older by a few years, I became more reckless, and decided that all the talk about divine punishment which old men use in scolding children was a lie. Then I conceived the idea of finding out what the god of Inari[21] really was.

There was an Inari shrine in the corner of my uncle's garden, as in many other households. I opened the shrine and found only a stone there. I threw it away and put in another stone which I picked up on the road. Then I went on to explore the Inari shrine of our neighbor, Shimomura. Here the token of the god was a wooden tablet. I threw it away too and waited for what might happen.

When the season of the Inari festival came, many people gathered to put up flags, beat drums, and make offerings of the sacred rice-wine. During all the round of festival services, I was chuckling to myself: "There they are—worshipping my stones, the fools!"

Thus from childhood I have never had any fear of gods or Buddha. Nor have I ever had any faith in augury and magic, or in the fox and badger which, people say, have power to deceive men. I was a happy child, and my mind was never clouded by unreasonable fears.

Once a queer woman came to our town from Ōsaka. She was about thirty years old, a daughter of Dempōjiya Matsu-emon, the chief of the stevedores who worked for the clan's storage office where my father used to be. This woman came to our house and claimed that she knew the magic of Inari. She said that if any person would hold a *gohei*, a

---

[21] Note on p. 341.

ceremonial wand, while she prayed, the spirit of Inari would descend upon the person and the *gohei* would begin to move. I stepped forward—I think I was fifteen or sixteen then— and said: "Let me hold it. It would be fun to see what it feels like to have Inari Sama inside me."

The woman looked at me scrutinizingly and shook her head.

"No," she said, "this young man will not do."

"You said any person would do," I insisted. "Why can't you try the magic on me?" I had a good time teasing her.

My revolt a- **gainst feudalism** The thing that made me most unhappy in Nakatsu was the restriction of rank and position. Not only on official occasions, but in private intercourse, and even among children, the distinctions between high and low were clearly defined. Children of lower samurai families like ours were obliged to use a respectful manner of address in speaking to the children of high samurai families, while these children invariably used an arrogant form of address to us. Then what fun was there in playing together?

In school I was the best student and no children made light of me there. But once out of the school room, those children would give themselves airs as superior to me ; yet I was sure I was no inferior, not even in physical power. In all this, I could not free myself from discontent though I was still a child.

Reprimanded for **mere mode of** **address** Among men of official rank, the distinction was still greater. Once my brother sent a letter to the chancellor of the lord, and addressed the outside cover in the scholarly style : "*Sama Kashitsuji*," using the classical Chinese term. The letter came back with an order to change it to "*Sama O-toritsugi*

Shū," a much humbler mode of address. Seeing this I cried to myself, "How foolish it is to stay here and submit to this arrogance!" And I was determined then to run away from this narrow cooped-up Nakatsu.

Among our cousins there were some good scholars and some who took much interest in the ways of society. All of them, being samurai of low rank, would often complain of the despotic atmosphere of the clan. But I was always stopping them, for by then I had grown to understand somewhat of the world and society. "Never complain of Nakatsu as long as you stay here," I would say. "Complaining does not improve things. Better go away or stay here and stop complaining."

One day while reading a Chinese book,

Never show joy or anger in the face I came upon these ancient words: "Never show joy or anger in the face." These words brought a thrill of relief as if I had learned a new philosophy of life.

Since then I have always remembered these golden words, and have trained myself to receive both applause and disparagement politely, but never to allow myself to be moved by either. As a result, I have never been truly angry in my life, nor have my hands ever touched a person in anger, nor has a man touched me in a quarrel, ever since my youth to this old age. Only once I had a bitter experience.

Some twenty years ago—long after I had become a man, and had come to have a school of my own—one of my pupils was hopelessly dissipated; and though I gave him assistance in many ways, even in the means of living, he would not give up his dissolute life. One night—I do not know where he had been or what he had been doing—he came back drunk and gay. I ordered him to sit up all night and reflect upon his actions. But when I returned a few minutes later, he was snoring.

"Shameless wretch!" I cried, catching him by the arm and shaking him. He was soon awake, but I gave him a good shaking which I thought he well deserved. But later, as I thought of it, I was sorry, for I had allowed my hands to touch a man in rage, and my remorse was like that of a priest who broke the commandments. I have never forgotten that feeling.

Notwithstanding this priestly fastidiousness, I was fond of talking—more so than the average—and in everything I did I liked to be quick and active, and I was never behind anyone in anything. But there was one thing that I never indulged in. That was the boyish argument in which one would become excited and go on arguing until he won by out-talking the other. I was willing to discuss a subject, but when my opponent grew heated, I would evade his point, thinking to myself, "Why does this fool love to make so much noise?"

Outwardly I was living peacefully enough, but always in my heart I was praying for an opportunity to get away. And I was willing to go anywhere and to go through any hardship if only I could leave this uncomfortable Nakatsu. Happily, a chance sent me to Nagasaki.

II
I SET OUT TO LEARN DUTCH
IN NAGASAKI

I counted myself twenty-one years old (my exact age, nineteen years and three months) when in February of the first year of Ansei (1854) I set out to Nagasaki.*

At that time there was not a single one in our town who could understand the "strange letters written sideways," nor was there even a man who had looked at the forms of those letters, though in larger cities there had been students of the Dutch language for a hundred years or longer.

But it was a few months after the coming of Commodore Perry. And the news of the appearance of the American fleet in Yedo had already made its impression on every remote town in Japan. At the same time the problem of national defense and the modern gunnery had become the foremost interest of all the samurai. Now, all those who wanted to study gunnery had to do so according to the instruction of the Dutch who were the only Europeans permitted to have intercourse with Japan after the seventeenth century.

One day my brother told me that anyone who wanted to learn Western gunnery must study *gensho*.

"What is *gensho*?" I asked.

---

* The native manner of counting a man's age adds one year at the New Year instead of at his birthday. Therefore, Fukuzawa, who was born in December, had become two years old in less than a month,

"*Gensho* means books published in Holland with letters printed sideways," he replied. "There are some translations in Japanese, but if one wishes to study this Western science seriously, one must do so in the original language. Are you willing to learn the Dutch language?"

As I had had no trouble in learning Chinese, I had some confidence in myself. So I answered, "I will study Dutch or any other language. If other people can learn it, I think I can too."

And so the next time my brother had business in Naga-saki,[1] I went with him, and there began my first study of the A B C's. Nowadays the European letters are seen everywhere in the country; they are even on the labels of beer bottles, and no one sees any strangeness in them. But to me those odd looking letters were very strange. It took me a full three days to learn the twenty-six letters of the alphabet. But I must leave the account of this study, and tell something of how I lived in Nagasaki.

The true reason why I went there was nothing more than to get away from Nakatsu. And so I would have been glad to study a foreign language or the military art or anything else if it only gave me a chance to go away. Therefore, it was nothing of the homesick feeling usual to a youngster leaving home that possessed me. I still remember how I swore to myself that like a bullet shot out of the gun's muzzle I would never come back. This was a happy day for me. I turned at the end of the town's street, spat on the ground, and walked quickly away.

In Nagasaki I first lived as a sort of dependant in Kōei-ji, a Buddhist temple in the street called Okeya-machi. I was taken to this temple by one Okudaira Iki, a son of the chancellor of our feudal lord, who was a relative of the priest.

----
[1] Note on p. 341.

Okudaira Iki was also boarding in this temple as a guest, studying the Dutch language and gunnery. A little later, his teacher in gunnery, Yamamoto Monojirō, took me as an "eating guest"* in his house. This was the beginning of my activity in the world.

Beginning my strenuous life   Though I was supposed to be a kind of free boarder, I did all sorts of work in the household. The master had poor eyesight, and I used to read to him the essays of contemporary scholars on the problems of the age. I also gave lessons to his son, a youth of eighteen or nineteen. Not very bright, but as the son of a scholar, he had to be taught to read the Chinese classics.

Yamamoto was a poor man, but being a local official of the Yedo government, he lived extravagantly with many friends and followers, and he had gone heavily into debt. Because of this, I took on another duty. This was to negotiate postponement of his debts and to contract new debts. Of the man servant and the maid in the house, the man would often fall ill and I had to take his place. I would draw water from the well, sweep the house in the mornings, and wash the master's back in his bath. His wife was fond of animals; she kept many cats and lap dogs in the house, and bigger dogs in the yard. I took care of them also. I had taken in hand every kind of work from the highest to the lowest.

By and by my master began to think a good deal of me, for he had found me a youth full of energy yet very well behaved. Finally he asked me to become his adopted son.[2] However, I had to tell him that I had already been adopted by my uncle Nakamura. I might say here that ever since

---

* *Shokkaku* in Japanese, a dependent with no particular obligations. Fukuzawa's work in Yamamoto household was mostly voluntary.

[2] Note on p. 341.

childhood, before I could know anything about it, I had been promised to my uncle's family as his heir in the future.

When Yamamoto learned my situation, he said, "If that is the case, you should consider all the more coming into my family. I will do all in my power to look after your future." He used to express his wish at many different times.

Like all the specialists on gunnery of the time, Yamamoto had a collection of books as his own private property—all of them hand-written copies—and part of his income came from charges on lending out these books or from selling handwritten copies made from them. However, as he had poor eyesight, I was given the charge of all this work.

Nagasaki at that time was the only part of Japan in contact with the outside world through the Dutch compound. So naturally students of gunnery and foreign affairs came to Nagasaki from many different clans for first-hand information. If they wanted to visit the Dutch compound on the island of Dejima—the only spot in the whole country where the Dutch were allowed to reside—Yamamoto could arrange the visit.[3] Again, if any wanted instruction on casting cannon, Yamamoto could furnish diagrams and necessary directions.

Such was his business, but really I was the one who did the work. I was a mere amateur. I had never seen a gun in operation. But it was easy to draw diagrams and to write the directions. And if more information was wanted, I could go and explain as if I had been specializing in the subject all my life.

Now, it was rather strange to see that Okudaira Iki and I had exchanged places. He had placed me in Yamamoto's household as a dependent. But now I had come to occupy something of a position in the field of gunnery while Iki was

---

[3] Note on p. 341.

still the same student.   And that was the cause of the break
between us.

My chief concern was, after all, the Dutch language.   I
often went to the interpreter's house, and sometimes to the
house of the special physicians who practiced "Dutch medicine."   And little by little, after fifty or a hundred days, I
came to understand something of the Dutch language.   Iki,
on the other hand, had never really learned it, as a spoiled
son of a high official never does.   And though he was not
really a man of deep malice, he was after all a self-willed
aristocrat trained in the Chinese morality.

He must have been planning to make me his life-long
follower after helping me in my education.   Now that he had
found me flying ahead of him, he decided that I should be
sent home to Nakatsu.   He was nearly ten years my senior,
but he was like a child in his thinking, which was a great
misfortune to me.

**It became dif-
ficult to stay in
Nagasaki**

Iki's father, Yohei, was the old chancellor in our clan.   We called him with
much respect "Go-Inkyo Sama" as he
was then in retirement.   It seems that
Iki had urged his father to send an out-
rageous order to my family for my return.   My brother had
just left for Ōsaka to assume the official post which my
father had occupied twenty years before, and my mother
was living alone at home as all my sisters had married.[4]
The only relative living near was a cousin of ours, Fujimoto
Gentai, a doctor and a scholar, who had a true sympathy
for my mother.

One day Iki's father, the retired chancellor, called our
cousin into his presence and ordered him to write a letter.

"Yukichi's presence in Nagasaki hampers my son's

---

[4] Note on p. 341.

career," he told Fujimoto. "You must write him that his mother is ill and needs him at home."

Such a direct order from the chancellor could not be evaded. Fujimoto, after letting my mother know about the scheme, wrote me the letter which formally requested my return because of my mother's "illness." But on a separate sheet he explained the transaction and enjoined me to have no anxiety about my mother's health.

I grew very indignant, for what baser act could there be than to command a subordinate to tell a lie? I wanted at first to break out and challenge Iki in a great argument. But my better judgment told me that it was useless to quarrel with the son of a chancellor. I should only be the loser in the end, and it would be wiser to look out for my own safety. So I went to Iki with a show of surprise and anxiety.

"I am very much troubled," I said. "A letter has just come from home with news that my mother is ill. She has always been a very healthy woman, but it seems that one can never tell. I am quite worried because I am so far away from home." I pleaded the poor homesick boy; Iki expressed his "surprise" and "sympathy."

"You must be anxious to go home at once," he said. "It will be best for you to do so. But then, after your mother's recovery, I will see that you return here to go on with your work." He put on the most sympathetic tone, and perhaps was inwardly enjoying the smooth effect of his scheme.

"I will take your advice," I said, "and if you have any message for your honored father, or if you have anything to send him, I will gladly take it with me."

When I called the next morning, Iki gave me a letter for his father and another to Ōhashi Rokusuke, a cousin of my mother's, saying that the latter would be helpful in securing the permit to return to Nagasaki. Then as if he meant that

I should read this message, he handed me the letter without sealing it. I made the politest of leave-takings and returned to my lodging where I opened the unsealed letter. The note read: "Because of his mother's illness, I am sending Yukichi home at his own urgent request. But when his mother recovers, you are to arrange for his return to Nagasaki, as he is still in the course of his studies, and it is proper that he should continue them."

This idiot's game! I grew more indignant than ever. I called him "fool" and "monkey," and cursed him with all the vocabulary at my command.

Yedo is my destination Then I took leave of the Yamamoto family. Even to them I could not tell the truth, for if the truth were made public, and the disgrace put on Iki, I should be the one to suffer most. I simply said that my mother was ill, and took my leave. But I had not, for one moment, thought of going back to Nakatsu; I was determined to make my way to Yedo, for I believed that was the city where the young and ambitious should go to make their start.

By good fortune there was a student from Yedo, named Okabe Dōchoku, among my new acquaintances. As I believed he was a broadminded and trustworthy friend, I revealed to him all that had passed.

"I am running away," I said finally. "I am too angry to go meekly home. But I don't know anybody in Yedo. You told me your father was a practicing physician there. Couldn't he take me in as a dependent? I don't know much about medicine, but I am sure I can roll pills and do such simple work. Please send me to your father."

"Go to him, by all means!" he exclaimed, angry with sympathy for me. "I will write a letter for you. And you will have no difficulty in finding him, for he has his house in Nihombashi, Himonochō in Yedo. Don't worry but go right to him!" He wrote the letter, and I thanked him heartily.

"If the truth were found out," I continued. "I'd be sent to Nakatsu anyhow. So please keep it a secret until I get a safe distance away. It will take me perhaps ten or fifteen days to get as far as Ōsaka. About that time, you may tell Iki that Nakamura Yukichi (my name then) has gone to Yedo. That will be a good joke on him."

I part with my companion I met a merchant from Nakatsu by the name of Kuroganeya Sōbei, returning to our town, and I set out with him as if to that destination. The first day we walked about eighteen miles and reached Isahaya in the evening under a fine March moon. Here I broke my purpose to my surprised companion.

"Well, Kuroganeya, I have decided I don't want to go home now. Take my box with you, and take it to my home, will you? I don't need more than one or two changes of clothing. Now I am going to Shimonoseki for a boat to Ōsaka, and then to Yedo."

The honest merchant looked thunderstruck.

"What madness is this?" he cried. "A young master like you to think of traveling so far alone?"

"Oh, don't be excited. What's the matter with a man's moving from Nagasaki to Yedo? As the saying goes, anyone but a dumb can ask his way to the capital."

"But what will your mother say? What shall I tell her?"

"Just give her my love; I'm not going to die, or anything. If you tell her Yukichi has gone to Yedo, she'll understand."

So I gave him my box and the letters which Iki had given me to take back to Nakatsu.

"I'm going first to Shimonoseki," I went on, "to take the

boat for Ōsaka, but I don't know the place. Can you tell me a good *funayado*[5] there?"

Since he saw he could not dissuade me, honest Kurogane-ya tried no further. "You might go to Sembaya Suguemon's; I know the man very well."

The real reason why I inquired about a *funayado* was that since I had so little money—even after selling a Dutch dictionary called Yakken,[6] I had left from my expenses only two *bu* and two or three *shu*[7]—I thought Kuroganeya's name and recommendation might be of some future help to me.

I took the local ferry and crossed the sea of Amakusa[8] to Saga. The fare was five hundred and eighty *mon*. The bay was very calm and we reached the opposite shore the next morning comfortably. From Saga I went on to Kokura in entire ignorance of the road and the towns through which I was to pass. I simply kept walking to the east, asking the way as I went along. Thus following a route through the province of Chikuzen, I think I must have passed the vicinity of Dazaifu, but to this day I do not know exactly what road I took.

Three days and two nights were spent in crossing the island. It was not at all easy to find a room for the night either, as I must have made a pretty odd figure, wandering alone, seemingly poor and without an obvious purpose. The innkeepers were afraid of me; the better inns turned me down, and I had to look for less reputable places. But somehow I passed those two nights and reached Kokura on the third day.

I forge a letter On the way I made up a false letter of introduction to Sembaya, using Kuroganeya's own name, the whole in a very formal style: "The bearer of this letter is a son of the

---

[5] Note on p. 341.   [6] p. 342.   [7] Ibid.   [8] Ibid.

Honorable Mr. Nakamura, a member of the fief of Nakatsu. I have often been honored by his patronage. Serve this young master in every way possible."

In Kokura I had to walk around all over the town looking for an inn which would give me accommodation. Finally one lodging house took me in, but it was a pretty shabby one. And I was put in a room where there was already a man sleeping. During the night I found to my discomfort that this man was a helpless invalid, unable to take care of himself. He was probably not a guest but a member of the proprietor's family. I still remember vividly what an uncomfortable night it was.

Early the next day I took the ferry across to Shimonoseki where I sought out Sembaya's *funayado*, and delivered my document. It was evident that the proprietor was a good friend of Kuroganeya's, for he merely glanced at the letter and took me in with every sign of good will. The boat fare to Ōsaka was one *bu* and two *shu*, but I did not have enough to pay for the food on board. I proposed to settle my bill after reaching Ōsaka where I was to meet my brother. This, too, Sembaya gladly agreed to arrange for me. The letter proved to be a rather useful idea.

Crossing the Straits of Shimonoseki   In crossing the strait from Kokura we had had something of a narrow escape. As we were about in the middle of the channel, the wind blew up and the sea became choppy. The sailors seemed much alarmed and called on me to help them. I did join in, pulling the ropes and carrying things around, and enjoyed the excitement.

But when I told the hostess in Sembaya what had happened, and showed her how my clothes were wet with spray, she looked much concerned and said, "That was dangerous! If those men were real sailors, it would have

been all right. But they are really farmers. In this idle
time, some of them take to ferrying for side-work. But the
farmers don't know the sea. They often have sad mishaps
even in a little wind. You are lucky to have come through
safely."

I felt a belated scare, and then understood why those men
had looked so alarmed and called on me for help on the sea.

It was March, the season of sight-seeing. In the boat for
Ōsaka were all kinds of travelers—a foolish-looking son of a
rich man; a bald-headed grandsire; some *geisha*, gay and
richly dressed, and other women of questionable reputation;
farmers; priests; rich and poor; all sorts, crowded together
in the narrow boat, drinking, gambling, clamoring over any
nonsensical matter. Among them sat I, forlorn and quiet,
like a priest doing penance.

After a voyage of some days in the Inland Sea, the boat
came to Miyajima. I had no business, but as long as I was
there, I went along with the others to see the famous shrine.
All the passengers had the usual round of good times on
shore and came back drunk. I longed to drink too, but
having not even a *mon* to spare, I walked back to the boat to
eat the meal provided on board. Naturally the captain did
not feel very kindly towards me, and he stared at me as I was
eating the boat's fare. In the same way I saw the sights of
Kintai Bridge in Iwakuni without really wanting to.

We next reached Tadotsu, near which is the shrine of
Kompira. It was eight miles to the shrine from the port,
they told me. I might have gone along; but again, without
any spending money, what was the use? I stayed on board
while all the others went. They turned up the next morning, every one of them drunk and happy. I was furious, but
what could I do?

After fifteen days of this highly unpleasant voyage, early
one morning we anchored at Akashi. Although I had been

**I travel on land
from Akashi** told that the boat would sail the next day if the wind should be right, and that we would reach Ōsaka in a day or so, I thought I had put up with the company long enough.

"How far is Ōsaka from here?" I asked. They told me about thirty-eight miles.

"All right," I said. "I shall walk there. Captain, will you come to the Nakatsu Storage Office for my bill? I shall pay you there what I owe you. And will you bring my baggage with you?"

But the captain insisted on my paying the full fare on the spot, or else continuing with him on to Ōsaka. In the bundle which I carried tied in a square of cloth were two changes of silk garments and some books.

"Look here," I said. "I am leaving my best clothes and some books with you. The books may not be of much value to you, but the clothes are worth the fare I owe you. I might put in my swords too, but a gentleman can not travel without his swords. I shall be at the storage office before you arrive anyway. Come any time, and receive your money."

"I know your office all right," returned the captain, "but I don't know you. You will have to remain a passenger as was arranged till we reach Ōsaka and I can collect your fare. It doesn't matter how long it takes or how much food you eat on the way."

I humbly pleaded with him, but his voice grew louder and louder. Then a strange man, who seemed like a merchant from Shimonoseki, came up and said he would settle the question for us.

"This is not quite fair of you, Captain," he began, "to put the screws on the young gentleman. He is willing to leave his clothes with you in good faith, isn't he? As a samurai, he will be true to his word.   If not, I shall be responsible for him.   All right, young Sir," he said turning to me.   "You may walk off on shore as you wish."

At his generous interference, the captain was at last satisfied.   I thanked him heartily as if I had seen a Buddha come down into hell to rescue a victim.   I then made off into the open country, free and foot-loose.

The thirty-eight miles from Akashi to Ōsaka I walked in a single stretch, for my remaining money—some sixty or seventy *mon* in my purse—would have been barely enough to pay for food without a thought of lodging.   Somewhere on the road, I stopped at a food-stand on the left-hand side of the way, and drank some two *gō*[9] of wine at fourteen *mon* a *gō* and ate a dish of boiled bamboo shoots and five or six bowls of rice.   Then again I walked on, through what towns and by what roads I cannot tell.   I am not even sure whether I passed through Kōbe or not.

When I was approaching Ōsaka, I was ferried across many rivers.   These are somewhat recognizable to me now, for as we travel by train today, we pass over many bridges on the western side of the city.   Fortunately a samurai was exempt from toll.   But soon the day was over, and in the dark moonless night passers-by were few.   I hardly dared inquire the way anyhow, for if a man passed in a lonely spot, I was more afraid of him than eager to find out which road to take. I did feel helpless, for though the short sword I wore was a fine one by the swordsmith Sukesada, the long sword was thin and light, not of much use in an actual fight.

But then, as I learned, Ōsaka was not especially noted for murders, and I had no great cause to be afraid.   However, a lone traveler on a dark, strange road cannot well help feeling some chills run up and down his spine, and looking with a

---

● Note on p. 342.

certain security to the sharp objects on his side. But as I
think back over it, it seems to me that I was really the one
to be feared rather than the one to be afraid.

Ōsaka at last   Our storage office was in Dōjima, near
a bridge called Tamae. This I had
known since my childhood from hearing
my mother talk about our old home. So I did not have great
trouble in locating my brother's lodging. But I did have a
pair of sore feet when I reached my destination at about ten
o'clock that night.

Once in Ōsaka, I met my brother at last; I also saw many
older people who remembered me from my childhood there.
I had gone back to Nakatsu at the age of three and now I
was twenty-two, but there were some old people around the
storage office who found in me even now resemblances to
my infant features. Among them was the wife of a workman, my wet-nurse, and an old man named Buhachi, one of
the faithful servants of our family—he had served my father
before, and he was serving my brother now. The day after
I arrived I was walking with him in Dōjima Street.

"Well, Sir, I remember the night you were born. It
happened in the night, and I went for the midwife. The old
dame midwife still lives over there in that street. When
you were big enough, I used to carry you around in my arms,
and I took you sometimes over to the wrestling ring to
watch the practice."

He pointed out to me the house of the old midwife and the
wrestlers' practice-arena. It all came back to me as we
walked along and I could not keep back the tears that were
prompted by dear memories. I could not think I was on a
trip; it was just as if I had come home after a long absence.

At our first meeting my brother asked why I had come so
suddenly. I told him exactly what had taken place, for there
was nothing I should hide from my own brother. He then

assumed his guardian's right and objected to my plan: "I cannot let you go on your proposed career to Yedo, because though Nakatsu is nearly on a line from Nagasaki to Ōsaka, I see you avoided the town in your journey.

"If I were not here, your going on to Yedo without taking leave of mother might be excusable. But as I am here and I have met you, I cannot think of allowing myself to be a partner in disrespect. She herself might not think much about it, but I cannot permit myself. Therefore, stay in Ōsaka. I am sure there will be just as good a teacher here as in Yedo."

So I stayed with my brother in Ōsaka and in a little while found out that there was a good teacher of the Dutch language named Ogata.[10]

Some episodes from Nagasaki days

My own particular talent seems to be in doing all kinds of humble work. While I was in Yamamoto's house, I did all kinds of work in his household. I do not recall ever saying, "I cannot do this," or "I don't want to do that." When the great earthquake occurred in that district, I happened to be drawing water at the well just after finishing a lesson in Chinese with Yamamoto's son. I was carrying a pair of large water-buckets swung from the ends of a pole across my shoulder. I remember just as I made a step towards the house, the ground began to move, and I was much shaken as my foot slipped under the heavy weight.

The Buddhist temple called Kōei-ji, where I first stayed when I went to Nagasaki, was one of the largest in the town, with three minor temples connected with it. The head priest had just returned from Kyōto and he was going to pay his formal respects to the local officials of Nagasaki.

---

[10] Note on p. 342.

Among my odd duties I was hired out to be his attendant. The priest was wearing an enormously long robe, and when he alighted from his palanquin at the gate of the magistrate's office, I picked up the train of his robe and followed him slowly as he walked in all his dignity. It must have been a funny sight. When the priest went on his round of New Year calls among the parishioners, I again followed him. While he was being received indoors I waited at the entrances, and a kindly host would often send out a tray of *zōni* (rice-cake soup) and different delicacies which I enjoyed heartily.

Once I took part in a strange prank. On the evening of the spring equinox, by an old custom of Nagasaki, the mendicant friars walked around the streets blowing conch shells and reciting some kind of incantation. This corresponds to Tōkyō's "bad luck expelling" at the New Year. People would bring out money or rice to these mendicants whenever they stood at the door to pray away bad luck and pray in happiness.

There was a neighbor next door to Yamamoto's by the name of Sugiyama Matsusaburō (brother of Sugiyama Tokusaburō) who was fond of practical jokes. He came to me on the day of the equinox and said, "Let's go around to-night. What do you say?" I was ready for it at once. So we borrowed a shell somewhere, and hiding our faces in hoods, we started out. He would blow the conch as we passed along and when we came to a house entrance, we would stop while I broke into a droning chant of some odd phrases from Mêng-ch'iu and other Chinese books I had memorized in school.

"*Ō-jŭ-kan-yō! Ten-chi-gen-kō!*" Our "prayer" worked. We found that offerings came freely, and once back home again, we took the contents of our bowl and bought rice-cake and duck and feasted at ease.

Teacher and pupil change places In Nagasaki my first teacher of the Dutch language was a certain Matsu-zaki Teiho. He was one of the medical students sent there by his master, the lord of Satsuma,[11] who was a foremost advocate of Dutch culture and especially of the study of Dutch medicine.

Matsuzaki gave me first the letters of the alphabet with the pronunciation of each in Japanese ideograph. It was bewildering. I could hardly believe these ABC's to be signs of a language. But after a while I began to be familiar with them, and found myself able to understand something of the language. I realized then that my teacher was not overly brilliant in his strange subject. I thought: "He hasn't much of a brain. If it were Chinese instead of Dutch, our position would be reversed. If I learn Dutch as well as I know Chinese, I would not have to bow to this fellow. Some day I shall turn on him, and teach *him* Dutch."

Such was a mad dream of the young beginner. When I entered the student household of Ogata in Ōsaka, I had already had a year's start in the Dutch language. So in two or three years I had passed the eighty or ninety school-mates and become one of the senior students. The chances of life are very strange. The same Matsuzaki came about this time from Nagasaki and entered the Ogata school.

I was conducting one of the lower classes then, and Matsu-zaki was ordered to join it. So the teacher and the student had exchanged places in these few years, and my mad dream had come true. Of course I could not tell this to anyone, but I could hardly suppress my sudden delight. I took it out in drinking to myself in honor of the secret exultation.

The soldier's passion for fame, the politician's coveting of high office, and the rich man's accumulation of wealth: these

---

[11] Note on p. 343.

may seem, philosophically speaking, worldly and foolish
vanities.   But these vanities are not to be made light of, for
the very scholar who ridicules them may have the same vain
ambition himself.

III

I MAKE MY WAY TO ŌSAKA

In accordance with my brother's decision, I gave up all thought of going to Yedo. It was in March of the second year of Ansei—the year of the Rabbit (1855)—when I entered Ogata's home-school.

In Nagasaki my manner of studying had necessarily been irregular. I studied under many teachers—indeed, under anyone who was kind enough to help me. One of them was an interpreter named Narahayashi; another a doctor of the same name. I also went to an affluent physician named Ishikawa Ōsho, but he, being a very noted doctor, would not teach a humble student like myself. I went to his medicine room and asked one of his assistants to give me help in the foreign writing. So it was here in Ōsaka that I really began my systematic study of the Dutch language; and my progress was fast, for with so much spirit and interest I believe I was one of the best students.

Brother and I both fall sick   A year passed quickly, but at the following New Year time a great misfortune befell my family. My brother on his duty as official of the feudal headquarters in Ōsaka was taken with severe rheumatism. For a long time his ailment dragged on. Sometimes he seemed to grow better, then he would again come down with the pain. He grew worse until he was not able to use his right hand at all, being forced to do his writing with the left.

At the same time a friend in the school, Kishi Naosuke, became ill with typhoid fever. As he had always been very kind to me, I thought I must help him at a time like this. Another student, Suzuki Giroku, came in also to take care of the sick fellow, for they were from the same province. Together we nursed him day and night for three weeks, but his case was a particularly hard one. He was not to recover. We decided to have the body cremated in accordance with the Buddhist rites of his own Shin sect and later sent the ashes back to his home.

When this extra care and work was all over, one day I suddenly became ill. I had a high temperature and felt very badly. It was certainly not like an ordinary cold. As all my school friends were students of medicine, one of them examined me and said I had contracted Kishi's typhoid fever. Then our teacher, Ogata Sensei, heard of it, and came to visit me in my brother's quarters in the storage office where I lay. He decided that I had really developed typhoid fever, and a bad case of it.

Ogata Sensei's great kindness   I shall not forget his kindness, for he said, "I will come every day to see you and give you as much advice as possible. But I am going to ask some other doctor to direct the use of medicine, because when a doctor knows his patient too well, he is apt to be anxious and do too many things, trying one medicine after another, and then suddenly remembering some other medicine, giving that too; and in that way he may miss what should be the proper treatment. You cannot escape this fault as long as you are human."

It will be seen that the relation between teacher and student of the time was of the intimate, father-and-son kind. When Ogata Sensei felt it difficult to treat my illness, his was the same feeling that he would have felt toward his own son. This has changed nowadays with the increase of students and the teacher-student relation has turned into something of a public affair; and I fear even the little regard for each other will grow less and less as the new school system progresses. But when I was in Ogata's school, I could not but feel that I was a member of his family.

So a doctor named Naitō Kazuma was called in, and he with Ogata Sensei gave me every treatment known to medicine then, but my illness proved to be very serious. In a few days I became unconscious, and for a week I was in a dangerous condition, but fortunately I was able to overcome it. When the crisis had passed, I recovered quickly, and in April I was well enough to be out again in the streets. I had the vitality of a strong young man.

Brother and I go home together All this while my brother was still suffering from his rheumatism. With two invalids in the quarters, we were in a sad plight. But happily my brother's term of office came to an end, and we were both happy to take advantage of it to go home by the Inland Sea boat and recuperate.

A few weeks in Nakatsu, and I was regaining my strength daily. My brother was not entirely well yet, but on the way to recovery. And so I decided to go again to Ōsaka to continue my study there. I arrived in August, full of life and spirit again. I rented a section of the officer's quarters in the storage office, cooking my own food in the earthenware boiler all by myself, and resumed my attendance at the Ogata school every day. I had started a regular routine again when the great blow fell.

On about the tenth of September, as I recall, a letter from home reached me with the sudden news of my brother's death on September third, and with instructions to return home at

once. I was shocked, but *shikata-ga-nai* (it had to be). I took
passage in all haste and, with a favor-
Brother's death– ing wind, reached home quickly. By
I am obliged to the time I arrived, however, everything
stay home had been concluded: the funeral services
and the arrangements for the future.
My relatives had taken me back from my uncle Nakamura's family and had made me the head of our own branch.

My brother had left a daughter, but as a woman cannot
be the heir, it had been decided that the logical thing was for
me to succeed in the Fukuzawa family. I was not asked for
my consent. They simply told me when I returned that I
was the master of the house.

In thus becoming the head of the house, I had legally
become a son to my brother. Therefore I had to follow the
rule of fifty days of mourning. Besides, I owed certain duties
to our lord according to the position of my family in the
feudal system. But my mind was thinking of things many
thousands of miles away, and I could never think of keeping
myself in Nakatsu. Yet the orders of the clan were strict. I
obediently carried out every act of filial and feudal obligations.

I had determined to go to Ōsaka again, but in the atmosphere of Nakatsu, it was difficult even to reveal my wishes
openly. All the men in town, including my near relatives,
hated anything Western.

One day when I was visiting one of my uncles, I intimated
my wish to continue my studies in Dutch. He broke out in
a fury, thundering over my innocent head:

"What crazy thoughts are these in your mind! Now that
you have become responsible in the honorable service of
your family, your duty is here—to serve your lord with all
fealty and banish all other thoughts. Outrageous that you
should think of studying *Ran-go* (Dutch)!"

Then he took an insinuating tone and said something about a pretentious wrestler who falls under the first blow, which I understood as meaning I should know where I belonged.

Though I tried not to let people know my inner intentions, when they were so often in my thoughts, I would let hints slip out of my mouth. In the small town with its circulating talk, all of our neighbors came to know of my purpose. An elderly friend of my mother who lived a few doors away from us—I still remember her well, a Madame Yae—came one afternoon, and in the way of neighborly gossip, she said, "I have heard that your Yukichi is going to Ōsaka again. But you would not let him go away, would you? If you do, it would be madness!"

So it was told everywhere, and in all Nakatsu there was no one who had any sympathy with my view. Truly I was like the "deserted boat on a desolate shore," which may sound like a line from a theatrical romance. But I did not see any romance in my situation then.

I thought it over many times and **Mother's perfect** decided that there was but one hope for **understanding** me: to go to my mother with my wish. If she alone would consent to my going away to continue my studies, I need fear nothing. I would go. So one day I went and talked over with her all that was in my mind, saying, "Now that I have already studied Dutch both in Nagasaki and in Ōsaka, I am confident that if I go on with it, I can make something of myself. If I stay here in Nakatsu, I shall never be able to distinguish myself. And I do not wish to let myself rot away in this Nakatsu. Now, Mother, will you not give me your permission to go to Ōsaka again? You told me that my father intended to make me a priest. Can you not imagine that I have become a priest and have left home?"

At this time all my sisters were married,[1] and now that my elder brother was no more, my mother—now over fifty—had only a little granddaughter of three years, left by my brother. My leaving home then would take away the last of her family except this little girl who would share the home. But my mother was quick to resign herself to all circumstances.

"Well, Yukichi," she said, "you may go."

"If you say so, Mother, I have nothing to fear. I don't need to care what people say."

"Well," she went on, "your brother now is gone, but that is beyond our help. Anyone might be taken—you, too, while away. But we shall not talk about death. I shall wait here, so you may go wherever you wish."

She understood perfectly.

A debt of forty ryō; we sell everything But the problem on hand was how to pay the debts left by my brother. The amount that had accumulated during his illness was about forty *ryō*,[2] which was an enormous amount for the meager means of our family. Unless we paid this by some drastic measure at once, we would probably never pay it. So we decided to sell everything in our household. And my father's large collection of books was something, we thought, we could fall back on.

There were over fifteen hundred volumes in the collection, among them some very rare ones. For instance, there were Chinese law books of the Ming dynasty, entitled Shang-yü T'iao-li, or in Japanese pronunciation, Jō Yu Jō Rei, in sixty or seventy volumes. These books which my father had been wanting for a long time were acquired on December the twelfth in the fifth year of Tempō. On that same day while he was still happy in the glow of his new acquisi-

---

[1] Note on p. 343.   [2] Ibid.

tion, a boy was born in his household, and that was myself. My father took the second syllable of the title, Jō Yu Jō Rei, and named me Yukichi. This story I knew from its frequent repetition by my mother.

But my mother and I had decided to sell everything. We began with the paintings and *kakemono** which were the easiest objects to sell. A small *kakemono* with Rai Sanyō's calligraphy was sold for two *bu*. Taigadō's painting of a man under a willow tree was sold for two *ryō* and two *bu*. There were other specimens of calligraphy by Sorai and Tōgai, but they brought in only a very little sum. Then we sold the swords. One of them, a good sword by Tenshō Sukesada, two and a half feet long and very well fitted, brought us four *ryō*. Finally we came to the books.

However, there was nobody in Nakatsu who would give anything much for rare books. Then I remembered my old teacher, Shiraishi, now a household scholar of the lord of Usuki in the province of Bungo. He had been driven out of Nakatsu after a quarrel.[3] I went then to Usuki with our books, and through my old teacher's intervention, I was able to sell the entire collection to the clan of Usuki, and acquired the large sum of fifteen *ryō* in one block. Then we disposed of our trays, cups, and drinking vessels. All of them were mere odds and ends, not of much value, but we had to bring out everything under the roof to make up for the required forty *ryō*. At last we were able to pay off our debts entirely.

There were a few things that we did not sell. My father had treasured his series of Chinese ethics (I-ching), thirteen volumes, which Itō Tōgai, the scholar he most respected, had annotated carefully in his own hand. In the catalogue of his books, my father had written, "These thirteen

---

* A hanging scroll of a picture or of calligraphy.
[3] Note on p. 343.

volumes of Ethics with Tōgai Sensei's notes are a rare treasure.   My descendants shall preserve them generation after generation in the Fukuzawa family."   When we saw this inscription, standing out like a testament in his writing, we had no heart to sell them.   They remain today preserved in my household.

Then there is a pair of china bowls which were left unsold. A second-hand shop-keeper said he would take them for three *pun*.   This *pun* was a unit of the paper money issued by our clan.   Three *pun* in hard cash was only eighteen *mon*.   That was too little.   I thought that eighteen *mon* would not help us much anyway, and we kept the bowls. Now, forty years afterwards, the bowls are still among my possessions; I use them to hold water for my brushes.

I am tempted to literary thieving While in Nakatsu, I was tempted to do a piece of literary thieving.   Okudaira Iki, the son of the chancellor, had just returned from Nagasaki.   I called on him to inquire after his *go-kigen*, honored health, as a matter of duty.   While talking with me, he brought out a Dutch book and said it was a recent work on fortification that he had brought from Nagasaki.   I was much impressed by it, for while books on medicine and physical sciences had naturally been used in Ogata's school, I had never seen any work of this kind.   Moreover, it was only a few years after the coming of Perry, and the paramount issue of the nation then was national defense.   I wished I might have a chance to read the book, but of course Iki would never lend a book to me to read.

"I bought it cheap," said Iki, "only twenty-three *ryō*."

What a price!   It made me feel forlorn.

Suddenly a scheme came to my mind.   "This is a wonderful book, Sir." I said as if casually.   "It would not be possible for anyone to read much of it in a few days, but would you mind letting me keep it for a little while—for three or four days? I should be very happy if you would let me go over the table of contents and the illustrations."

"All right," said the unsuspecting Iki. "You may take it for a few days."

Fortune from Heaven! I took the book home, made ready an ample supply of paper, ink and birds' quills, and began copying the text from the very title page. It was about two hundred pages long. Of course, all was done in secret in a room in the rear portion of our house where people seldom came. I kept on, day and night, as fast as my strength allowed.

At that time I had the duty of guarding the gate of the lord's castle. My relief came every second or third day after being at the post for twenty-four hours. On duty, of course, I had to give up the copying during the day service, but when night came and the gate was closed, I took out the book and set to work in the guards' house all through the night until the time came to open the gate in the morning.

Though I was careful, "the walls have eyes and ears," as the ancient proverb says. I was constantly afraid of being discovered. Iki might send for his book. If my procedure should be exposed, Iki, as the chancellor's son, would not stop with simply demanding his book back, but might put me in a difficult position. The suspense was unbearable. I had never been a thief, but then and there I understood and had sympathy for their feelings.

Finally, after twenty or thirty days, the copying was done—illustrations and all. But I needed to check it for accuracy with the help of someone who could read the original with me. Curiously enough, there was one man in Nakatsu who knew the Dutch alphabet, and he was an acquaintance of my family. When we lived in Ōsaka, this man, Fujino Keizan, then a young student of medicine, had lodged with us. So I went to him, believing that he could be trusted.

"I am telling you a great secret," I said, and told him all about how I came to copy the foreign book. He was glad to help me.

"It would be nicer," I went on, "to work in the day time. But if our work should be discovered, it would be a calamity to both of us. So I am coming in the evening. It is going to be hard work, but will you watch the book while I read my copy to you, and tell me whenever there is a mistake in my copy."

So we spent three or four nights together and finished the work.

I was having the sensation of carrying off some treasured jewel from a legendary castle. I took back the book to the good gentleman, thanking him for his kindness. I had taken good care of the book, so there was no possibility of his suspecting anything. I said with all my heart: "This is a wonderful book, Sir. Because of your generous 'shadow,' I was able to have a glimpse of the wonders it contains. If this were to be translated into Japanese, how much it would mean to our coast defense. I bring it back with my heartiest thanks. A poor student like me can never hope to own such a book."[4]

The incident was closed, and I breathed relief. I do not remember exactly how long it took me to finish the work, but it was over twenty days and not quite a month. Within this period I had made the essence of the treasure my own, and the owner had not the least suspicion. It was quite like a thief stealing unseen into some vault of treasures.

All the while my mother had been anxious about my

---

[4] Note on p. 343.

health. "What are you doing?" she often would ask. "You will take cold if you go on working like that without having any sleep at all. There is a limit to things even if hard work is a virtue."

"No, Mother," I would reply. "I am just copying a book. I won't get sick by this much work. I know how much I can do."

A petition to study gunnery under a physician Now I was ready to go to Ōsaka. And in applying for a permit to leave home, I was to use a most ridiculous subterfuge. While my brother was living, I could go anywhere at any time with only his sanction, but now that I had become the head of the family with certain duties to the lord, I had to obtain a permit for going "abroad."

I wrote my petition without consulting anyone, for I knew better than to talk to my relatives. When I submitted the petition, the friendly secretary spoke to me privately.

"This will not be accepted," he said gravely, "because in this clan there has not been any precedent of a samurai leaving his duty for the purpose of studying *Ran-gaku* (Dutch learning)."

"Then what shall I write?" I inquired.

"Well, you might say that your purpose is the study of gunnery. That has a precedent."

"But," I added, "I am going to Ogata's school. And O-gata is a practicing physician. I am afraid it is rather out of the course of things to go to a medical man for gunnery."

"But we cannot do anything without precedent," kept on the friendly secretary. "It does not matter whether your statement is true to fact or not. It has to be gunnery."

So I rewrote my petition, and in due course, was formally permitted to leave for studying "gunnery" under Master Ogata of Ōsaka. From this may be guessed the state of

things at the time.   And I am sure my clan was not the only
one to grant such a roundabout permit.   Any other clan of
the time would have done the same.   It was still the age of
Chinese studies and anything Western was to be frowned
upon.   But since the Perry expedition, one subject in the
culture of the West, the gunnery, came to be recognized as
a necessity.   This was my one way of escape to study the
civilization of the West.

Mother's illness   The permit granted, I was preparing
to sail on the coastal boat when sud-
denly my mother was taken ill.   I was
much alarmed.   I consulted several doctors of the town and
did all I could to nurse her.   Finally we traced her illness
to "worms," and for that ailment, doctors said, semencina
was the best remedy—at that time santonin was not known.
It was a costly medicine and there was but one shop in Nakatsu where it was sold.   But it was no time to think of the
cost even though it was not easy for us, after paying our
debts, to give up two *shu* or one *bu* for the prescribed
medicine.   I could only trust in Heaven for her recovery and
nurse her day and night.   Whether the medicine was effective or not—for it was only a country remedy—in about
two weeks' time my mother was well again.

At last I had to decide the day of my departure.   When
the day came, only my mother and sisters bade me farewell
and prayed for my safe journey.   No other relative or
acquaintance paid any attention to my leaving.   I went on
board the boat feeling like an outcast.   My home broken
up, my brother dead—there in the nearly empty house like
an old temple, all its familiar objects sold away, and with no
friends to visit her, my mother was to live alone with her
little grandchild in the worst poverty.   As I thought of all
this, I, the usual happy-go-lucky fellow, was for once broken
by the sorrow of leaving home.

Ogata Sensei's   As soon as I reached Ōsaka, I made
great kindness; my way to Ogata Sensei, and told him
I become his all that had passed since I had left his
dependant household three months before. And
as I would not hide anything from him
any more than I would from my own
father, I told him of my brother's death, how we had paid
our debts by selling our belongings, and finally I showed
him the copy of the book on fortification, and confessed
how cleverly I had got away with it.

Sensei laughed and said, "Well, you perhaps did do
something which may be thought reprehensible, but at the
same time it certainly is a useful piece of work." Then
looking at me kindly, he went on, "You have grown much
stronger, haven't you? You look much better than you did
when you left."

"Yes, Sensei, last spring I did give you much cause for
anxiety, but I am well again now. No more signs of any
trouble."

"That is good," he replied. "Now I think I judge rightly
that you are without means to pay your expenses. I wish
to help you, but I do not want to appear to be partial to
you." Then taking up my copy of the book, he went on,
"I shall give you the work of translating this book."

So from that time I was taken into Ogata's household as
a translator. In a physician's household it is quite customary to keep apprentices for the medical work, but to keep
a translator of a foreign book was certainly not very usual.
It really meant that I was to be a free boarder, or "eating
guest," through the kindness of Ogata Sensei and his wife.
Therefore it was not very important whether I really did
this translating or not. But as the old saying puts it, "a
truth is often born of a lie." I really translated the whole
book.

Student ways;
my
shameful habit

It was in November of the third year of Ansei (1856) when I joined Ogata's student-household. This was really the beginning of my school life, for until then I had come as a day student while living in our feudal headquarters. Ogata Sensei's school was the most progressive one of the time, and its students were all active and promising men. But on the other hand they were a pretty rough and reckless crowd, or, as was often said, they were of the kind "not to be stopped by one or two strands of rope." Into this free-living set I plunged with all the vigor in me and soon adapted my life to their reckless ways. I must say at the same time that in many respects I was somewhat different from the rest of the students.

To begin with the shortcomings, my greatest weakness lay in drinking, even from my childhood. And by the time I was grown enough to realize its dangers, the habit had become a part of my own self and I could not restrain it. I shall not hold back anything, for however disagreeable it may be to bring out my old faults, I must tell the truth to make a true story. So I shall give, in passing, a history of my drinking from its very beginning.

My use of the rice-wine was not a formed habit; I was born with it. Though very faintly, I still remember how I used to cry whenever my mother shaved my head, because it hurt when she scraped the top of my head. Then she would say, "I will give you a little sip of the wine, so let me scrape you a little more." Then I kept still and let her go on. Thus began my early taste for wine.

As I added more years to my age, I was pretty well behaved in most respects, but in drinking I was a boy without any conscience. I would do anything for the sake of having a taste of it. I have no excuse to make even if I should be called a coward on this point.

When I went to Nagasaki at the age of nineteen, I was already an accomplished drinker. Yet I gave up drinking entirely for a year. Though I was ever quivering with the desire, I could not by any means allow myself to indulge in it, for then my long-cherished wish had been fulfilled and I was there to pursue my studies. For a whole year I was a man dead to all indulgences.

It would have been easy to steal a nip in the kitchen when the master, Yamamoto, was having a party, or I could have run out to one of the cheap drinking-shops and taken my drink from a corner of the "square measure."* But I never allowed myself to do so, for I knew that this wrong-doing on my part would some day be discovered. When I left Nagasaki the next year, however, I stopped at the first town on the road and drank till my one year's thirst was satisfied.

My Nagasaki master, Yamamoto, had, of course, believed that I was a teetotaller. Some years later, on my way to Europe, when our ship called at Nagasaki, I visited my old master in the harbor city. After expressing my gratitude for his kindness to me as a young student, and telling him about my new venture abroad, I confessed that my being a teetotaller was a lie. Then I showed him my true self, for we drank together, and I heroically, till he and his good wife were thoroughly surprised.

Do not turn red by touching blood So I admit my love of drinking, and realize that I fell into many bad habits through it, and have often abused my health by an excess of it. But otherwise I may claim to have been a pretty clean man. In my life with the boisterous and free-living students, and after I was married, even in associating with

---

* Proper way is first to warm the rice-wine and drink it from a cup. But a lowly workman would sip it right out of the measuring vessel as the wine is poured from the barrel.

various men of the world, I always kept myself within the prescribed limit of the well-behaved man. Yet I was not "puritan" or moralist—I knew quite well the inside life of the hidden quarters of our society. By simply listening to my friends talking together, I could easily learn about things I had never seen.

For instance, although I do not know how to play the game of *go*, Japanese chess, yet whenever my friends in the school would begin to play it, I was always sitting near the *go*-board, criticizing their moves like a seasoned expert— "There! That move of your black was wrong. You see you lost again, and don't you see your next move? Ah, you are a fine player!"

My remarks flowed on despite my blissful ignorance. This was safe as long as I was on the winning side and finding fault with the loser, which was not difficult to determine from the expressions of the players. But I never let myself get drawn into an actual game. Whenever I was challenged, I would say, "I haven't any time to waste in a game with you." My reputation as a *go* player became greater all the time, but after nearly a year, by some little chance, my "skin of pretence" was once pulled off, and I was left to the mercy of their oaths and execrations.

So in this way I had learned all about the gay quarters, but I myself was of "iron and stone." In short I was one who "did not turn red by coming in contact with blood." I am convinced that I was brought up to be like this in my family. In Nakatsu we as a family of five children were reared by our mother alone, inmune from the knowledge of anything that was not reputable, and we had a world of our own. Even when I left home, I carried the self-respect learned there, and it remained with me. I was not restraining myself particularly; I was thinking that my attitude toward life was what it ought to be.

There are people whom we call *kunshi*, "bigoted saints," who are good through fear and the stupid inability to act. They, of course, resent the immoral behavior of others who give free play to their desires. These persons complain when no one is present to refute them, but they are too afraid to come near any actual encounter with the less virtuous world. So they go around frowning on life and shunning friendships. On the contrary I never hesitated to talk on any subject with my friends, and often made fun of their follies.

"You are the dullest bunch of fellows I have ever seen," I would tell them. "You go out to make love to the professional love makers, and come home a failure! I don't go at all, but once I should go there, I could show you I would be a hundred times more of a success than you ever could be. You aren't made to be gallants anyway. This trying to learn the ABC's of gallantry at your age makes me suspect you will never be much of men after all."

While my friends had to accept my hits, their foolish pastimes were a continual source of amusement to me. My love of drinking brought many experiences in the course of my life.

I put down a fellow student The very day I entered the Ogata school, a student approached me and asked me where I was from. That was the beginning of our conversation. "Let's have a drink together," he said, "to mark our new friendship."

"Gladly," I replied. "I am a pretty good hand at drinking myself, though I shouldn't say so perhaps on the first occasion. But I have to tell you the truth; I can't spare any money just now. I've just come from Nagasaki, and it's even doubtful whether I have enough to pay my expenses here. But it certainly is kind of you to ask me."

"Don't talk nonsense," he returned. "You know very well that you need money to drink with. You must have something to spare."

"If I haven't, I haven't."

The fellow walked away with an angry glance. The next day when I saw him, I spoke to him.

"I'm wondering what became of your invitation yesterday. I am more thirsty this morning."

He muttered something in a bitter tone and walked away.

I waited two or three months till I learned the way of things at the school and made some friends. Then one day I stopped that same fellow and had it out with him.

"You remember," I began, "when you first met me, you tried to get a drink out of me. I knew very well you were trying to take advantage of a new student, for a new student usually has some money. So I didn't let you fool me. And the next day I reminded you. What did you say then? Remember? Because it was I, Yukichi, I was able to turn it off. I was ready then, if you had been as insolent as you were before, to knock you down and drag you to the master's presence. Perhaps you noticed my determination; you backed off like a coward. You are a disgrace to the school! You are the kind people call 'the worm in a lion's belly.' I tell you right now, don't try that trick of yours again on a new student. If you do, I'll consider it my own affair. I'll drag you right away to our master and ask him to judge you. Remember now!" I think I broke down his bullying for the rest of the school.

I become *Juku-chō* Later on, by the time I had advanced in my studies, many of the older students had gone back to their homes, and I was left to become *jukuchō*,[5] monitor of the students.

---

[5] Note on p. 343.

However, this highsounding title did not mean any authority. According to the custom of the school, the *jukuchō* was to preside in the upper class when they read the most difficult texts. But in daily life I was just one of the students, studying the foreign texts and, between studies, joining the others in all sorts of activities which were apt to go too far to be commendable.

So it was quite natural if I rarely stopped to think that I should lead an exemplary life in order to inspire the rest of the student-body, or imagine that any act of mine in raising the moral standard of the school would be an act of loyalty to my master. No such sage-like idea ever existed in my head then. But I was the sort who never took advantage of the weak or coveted the possessions of others, clean in behavior, never ashamed of myself in the "face of Heaven and earth." So while I was leading a rough and tumble life, there was in me something different from the rest of the crowd. I wanted all the students to be like myself, to think and act as I did. That was my youthful pride, and I believe it did bear fruit. It might have done harm also, because after all I was merely an active young man with no very definite purpose. So whatever good I may have done in the Ogata school was an incidental by-product, hardly to be credited to myself.

IV

STUDENT WAYS AT OGATA SCHOOL

I was still very poor after I had been made the monitor, but I was beginning to find my living somewhat easier. My mother and little niece back at home were living on the small stipend that our family received from the clan, and I was able to board openly in my teacher's household as I was now the monitor of the students. Moreover, there was the rule that each new student should give two *shu* to the monitor besides presenting the usual gift of money to the teacher. So if it happened that there were three new students in a month, my income would amount to one *bu* and two *shu*; if there were five, two *bu* and two *shu*—a neat sum for a student's pocket money. And most of this went to drinks. Then, as my mother sent me clothing of homespun cotton from time to time, I did not need to buy any. Therefore whenever there was any money in my purse, I thought first of drinking. I am afraid many a young student learned because of me to spend his allowance in drinking.

Our way of drinking was very crude. When we did not have much money, we would be contented to buy three or five *gō* of wine and have it in the dormitory. When we felt rich—which meant we had as much as one or two *shu* to spend—we would go to a restaurant for a carouse. That was a great luxury which did not happen often. More frequently we went to the chicken-restaurants. Still oftener we went to the cheapest place—the beef-stand.

There were only two places where they served beef; one was near Naniwa Bridge, and the other near the prostitute quarters of Shinmachi—the lowest sort of eating places. No ordinary man ever entered them. All their customers were *gorotsuki*, or city bullies, who exhibited their fully tattooed torsos, and the students of Ogata's school. Where the meat came from and whether it was of a cow that was killed or that had died, we did not care. They served plenty of boiled beef with wine and rice for a hundred and fifty *mon*. Certainly this meat was often tough and smelled strong.

Although the majority of the students were samurai who could have worn the two swords of their rank, most of them, about fifty or sixty students, had pawned their swords so that there were perhaps only two or three pairs in the whole dormitory. Among these were my own, because I had not then, nor have I since, pawned any of my property. Yet we had no difficulty, for the few pairs of swords were like our common property, and anyone wore them who wished to appear in formal dress. On ordinary days we went around with only one sword so as not to lose entirely the dignity belonging to samurai.

The unclothed students

Ōsaka has generally a warm climate, and there was no difficulty for poorly dressed students in the winter time. In the summer, indeed, we found it almost necessary to live without clothes. Of course, in class and in the dining room, we wished to appear somewhat respectable, so we wore something—usually the *haori*, or loose overgarment, next to the bare body. That was an odd sight—how a person of today would laugh to see it!

The floor of the dining hall was of bare boards. So it was out of reason for us to kneel on these at dinner. We wore our sandals in on the floor and ate standing. At first we did pass around the rice tub like well-mannered people, but that did not last long. Gradually we were all pressing around the big rice container, helping ourselves like so many devils at an infernal feast.

Our food was very simple. On the days of the month containing the numerals one and six—that is, on the first, the eleventh, the twenty-first, and on the sixth, the sixteenth, and the twenty-sixth—we had boiled onions and sweet potatoes; on the days with numerals five and those formed with ten, bean-curd soup; on the days of threes and eights, shell-fish soup. Therefore we generally knew what was coming for dinner.

Nudeness brings many adventures I recall some of the incidents of our nakedness in those summer days. One evening five or six of us had obtained a generous amount of wine. One of the group suggested that we take it out on the roof-porch, the open porch on the housetop used for drying laundry. But just as we were climbing out, we discovered our teacher's maids already there enjoying the evening breeze. If we went out while they were there, certainly talk about us would be circulated later on. Then Matsuoka Yūki, bolder than the others, stepped out and declared he would get those women off the porch. He climbed up, without one stitch of clothes on.

"A warm evening, isn't it?"

With these words he stretched himself out on the floor. This was too much for the maids. A bit confused, they scurried away. As soon as they were out of sight, Matsuoka called down to us in Dutch that all was well. "Come on up, old chaps, and take care of that wine."

There is another incident in connection with our nudity, and it was a terrible blunder on my part. One evening I heard a woman's voice calling my name from the lower floor. "What could the maid want at this ungodly hour?" I thought, for I had just lain down after a hearty bout. But if I was called, I could not very well lie quietly. I jumped up, and without stopping to put any clothes on, I strode downstairs and stood before the woman.

"What do you want?" I shouted.

Before I could get the words out of my mouth, I froze to the spot. It was not the maid, but our teacher's wife! I could not run, nor could I kneel or bow before her, naked as I was. I was helpless. Madame Ogata then perhaps felt sorry for my plight. She walked away without saying anything. I could not bring myself to call on her the next morning to say how sorry I was for my misdeed the night before. So the incident passed without an apology, but I have never forgotten it. A few years ago when I had occasion to be in Ōsaka again, I visited the old Ogata house, and recalling what had once happened at the foot of that same staircase, I felt again the shame of forty years before.

Sanitation is all but disregarded I am afraid I cannot easily make real the disorder and the careless slovenliness of the school. In our dormitory we had such unexpected articles as small braziers and boilers, and we used to do much informal cooking about our desks. But being always short of utensils, we often used the wash-basin and other such things for the preparation of food. If, for instance, a friend were to give us some noodles on a summer day, we would ask our teacher's maids to cook them for us in the kitchen, and then we would cool them in our wash-basin with water from the well. As for a sauce, why, with some of the white sugar stolen from the medical supply room where it was especially kept, we could make a pretty good flavoring. And so, for washing vegetables, for dressing fish, for any purpose, the one faithful wash-basin came in. We never thought it strange.

There were other things to give the fastidious qualms. Lice, along with the students, were permanent residents of the dormitory, and no one could escape their intimacy. Whenever a man took off his clothes, he could easily catch five or ten of them. In warmer weather, we sometimes felt them crawling out from under our collars. Once a fellow made them the subject of his discourse:

"The louse resembles the roast potato," he said, "because both of them have prosperity in the winter season and decline in the spring. They disappear entirely for two months in summer with the flea taking their place. So in September, when the new potatoes come, again appears the louse."

I once tried a new method of killing the pest. I said that the method the laundresses used often—that of pouring boiling water on the clothes—was too trite; I would show how to kill them off with one single operation. So I took my underwear to the roof-porch one frosty winter night, and let both the creatures and the eggs freeze to death in the cold. But I could not claim the invention; someone had suggested this to me.

As may be easily imagined, there were few among us who dressed decently. Yet at every festival time, when a street fair was held, we all sauntered out as we were. The crowd, especially the girls in it, would cry out, "Here come the students!" and hurry back out of our way. They looked upon us as if we were *eta** or some unclean people. And certainly we often did what no one but the *eta* would think of doing.

A pig is slaughtered

One day the proprietor of our favorite beef-shop bought a pig, but the man,

---

* Slaughterers of cattle and dealers in leather who belonged to the lowest stratum of the social order, an outcast. See note on *samurai* on p. 337.

being a softhearted fellow, could not force himself to kill it. So he came to us.

"All right," said our spokesman. "But what will you give us if we do it?"

"Well, Sir, er—"

"Will you give us the head?"

"Yes, Sir."

So the crowd set out. Being medical students, they knew that the easiest way of securing death was by suffocation. They tied the pig's four legs together and threw it into the river nearby. And for their reward, they did bring back the decapitated head, and borrowing an axe, cut the head up into sections. Then the would-be medical men had a fine time studying the brain, eyes, and so forth. After the scientific investigation was over, they cooked up the pieces and ate them. No wonder the beef-shop keeper and others thought we were like the *eta*.

A bear is dissected
One day a druggist of Dosho-machi came to us with an introduction from a doctor of Chinese medicine. He requested us to demonstrate the dissection of a bear which he had just received from the forest of Tamba. This was a lucky chance, and seven or eight of the students interested in anatomy went. I did not go as I was not a medical student, but I heard what happened at the dissection.

The students were making their dissection with gusto— "This is the heart"; "Here are the lungs"; etc. When they came to the liver and took it out, someone made way with it. And both the druggist and the doctor suddenly left with a simple "Thank you." Then the crowd understood that the druggist's only desire was to secure the bear's gall-bladder intact, as that had been an old staple of healing, and knowing that the Ogata students were most skillful in dissecting, he had come to them to have this done under the guise of general anatomical study. Therefore he and the old doctor left as soon as the liver was taken out from the carcass.

When this imposition was reported in the dormitory, the crowd, eager for a rumpus, decided to make something out of it. Among us was a ready talker and stubborn debater, named Tanaka Hatsutarō (who now lives in Kanazawa). So he was made the chief speaker. I was appointed to draft the letter. Another student, Numata Umpei, because of his good handwriting, copied the letter. Then the other officers, such as one to escort the messenger, another to intimate his preference for quicker method than quiet argument, were chosen. So six or seven men prepared to present our protest to the druggist and the doctor.

Not naked as we usually were, we dressed ourselves formally for the occasion in *haori-hakama*, full skirt and overgarment, and wore our two swords. Our argument was based on the honor of the medical profession, such as that was, and to that none could make a rejoinder. The result was that the druggist and the doctor were completely humiliated; we got not only their apology but five *shō* of wine and a chicken and a fish; another feast of victory made lively our sleeping hall.

Theater going in disguise

However, we did not always carry our side through. Once we were caught in an embarrassing corner. Every so often the police officials went to inspect the playhouses in Dōtombori. They were always shown to the best places in the loges, and ushers would bring tea and cakes immediately.

Knowing about this privilege, some of my fellow students got the idea of seeing the plays without paying for it. They put on dark hoods that partially hid their faces, and wearing pairs of swords, proceeded to the theaters to put their hoax into effect. No samurai, other than these police officials, were supposed to show themselves in public places of amusement like the playhouses, so the trick was effective.[1]

The managers, assuming the aristocratic visitors to be authentic, received them in all cordiality in hope of official favor. The clever students then would accept the welcome with silent dignity, take the best places, and sit through the evening's entertainment in double enjoyment.

This passed off quite well for a time, but one day, while they were there, the real inspectors appeared. And this was no laughing matter—a counterfeit of government office. Fortunately one of the students knew someone in the police offices. To him we went in all humility and pleaded with him to intervene. We were able finally to make a private settlement, but we had to send gifts of much wine and fish. I believe it cost our poor rascals three *bu* or so in all.

I was not actually involved in this affair, because I did not care for theaters at all then, and was opposed to such a dangerous escapade.

"This isn't safe. Suppose you are caught—?" I used to say. But the crowd—Takahashi Juneki being the leader of it—would return, "Trust in our wits. There are more tricks than one if the emergency comes."

It was funny to see them caught after such a boast, but for a while I too was seriously concerned over the consequences.

Street fights for laughs   The rough and tumble life of those days is quite beyond the imagination of anyone today. We were free to take our own course, as there were no police at that time. The Ōsaka people are timid, for at a street

---

[1] Note on p. 344.

fight the passers-by would run away, although in Tōkyō the crowd would gather around the fight and break it up.

On warm summer evenings we often went out after supper in two parties, and having selected the busiest and most crowded part of the city, we would come together and break out in a furious show of fisticuffs, roaring at each other, swinging our arms around, but in reality striking gently so as not to hurt each other. Then would the amazed crowd run in all directions, the shop-keepers rush the goods indoors to protect them behind the shutters, and the once busy street in a few minutes be entirely deserted. The fight then stopped and the fighters went home together. This gay pastime we indulged in frequently, but not in the same area too often. Its nature might become obvious. So we changed our battleground from day to day, from Dōtombori to Junkei-machi, and so on. Numata Umpei from Shinshū was particularly good at this fighting.

Unreasonable bullying
I had another experience of my own which had a rather pathetic result. I went out one evening with a school-mate, Matsushita Gempō, to the night-bazaar in the temple grounds called Goryō. We were looking at a flower-and-plant stand when the proprietor spoke warningly: "Master, please don't do any mischief."

Of course we took this as hinting that he thought we were going to steal something from his stand. So I yelled out in an angry tone, much amused at the idea of frightening the man out of his wits: "I am going to kill this fellow. Don't stand talking, but get hold of him!"

Then Matsushita, pretending to soothe me, said, "Oh, no. This case isn't bad enough for killing a man, is it?"

"Don't stop me!" I retorted. "I'll kill him quicker than I can say it. Watch me! I'll show you how to kill him with one blow of my fist."

By this time the crowd had gathered around us. I was, thereupon, more amused than ever and began to talk more loudly. Suddenly a big fat man emerged from the throng. He was a professional wrestler.

"Please forgive the poor fellow this time," he addressed me. "I'll be responsible for this accident, so let me handle him."

"All right," I replied. "I'll let him go tonight, because this big man came in and apologized for him. But now, you, look here, if you open this shop here again tomorrow, I'll kill you the minute I find you."

The next evening I went again to the street fair. The honest proprietor of the flower-and-plant stand was not in his place, leaving one open space in the row of stands. Without any supervision of police, we were at liberty to do all the mischief we wanted. But strangely enough, we never did anything actually harmful. This affair with the flower-stand keeper was about the only one which had something of a serious outcome.

A cry of "Thief! Thief!" In one escapade I had a very narrow escape. There was a religious procession called Sunamochi in which one or two hundred young men of the city took part, each carrying a lighted lantern on his head, making much noise. I was viewing it with three or four friends when, for no good reason—perhaps under the effect of wine—I knocked a lantern from the head of a man with my stick. Then some of the men in the procession began to yell, "*Chibo! Chibo!*" (Thief! Thief!) It was a general custom in Ōsaka that when a street-thief was caught, he was beaten to death by the crowd and thrown in the river. I was truly frightened. I kicked off my clogs and ran barefoot toward Dōjima where my lord's storage office was located. If I had been overtaken, I should have had to draw my sword and defend myself though I had no desire for any bloodshed.   I ran as I had never run before in my life, and did not draw a free breath until I found myself safe in the feudal head-quarters.

In the northeast section of Ōsaka, **No god, no Bud-** there is a bridge called Ashiya-bashi. **dha for students** Near it at that time was a group of **of Dutch** houses of ill fame.   At the entrance to the section, there was a small shrine dedicated to Jizō, or Kompira, or some such popular deity. It seemed that this deity was enjoying much trust from the people, for often we noticed various framed pictures offered before the shrine.   Sometimes it was a picture of a man, or of a woman; sometimes there were sealed envelopes pasted on them; sometimes a lock of hair tied to the frame.

We often went at night to steal these offerings in order to enjoy their contents.   One swore to the god to give up gambling; another swore temperance; another offered a picture of a ship for coming through a storm at sea in safety; still another was of a man who had had much too much experience with women; still another from a young woman who had not had enough experience with men.   We stole quite a number of these offerings, for they were too amusing to resist.   Perhaps it is a sacrilege to make fun of people's sincere prayers, but it was *shikata-ga-nai* (easy come—easy go) with us students of Dutch who believed neither in gods nor in Buddha.

It was customary then for a doctor of **I fake a woman's** the old school to have his head shaved **letter** like a priest, or else to wear his hair very long in the style called *sōhatsu*. Since most of the students in the Ogata household were sons of doctors, they themselves usually followed one or the other of these styles when they came.   But after being in

Ōsaka a while, they either let their hair grow, or had their foreheads shaved and tied up the long back locks in samurai fashion, as being decidedly more swagger. So it is quite like the modern vogue of the Buddhist priests who let their hair grow and wear it parted as men of fashion.

An amusing anecdote of one young man's hair occurs to me. We had a student from Yedo, named Tezuka, the son of a household physician in a Tokugawa family. He wore an overgarment with the Tokugawa crest of hollyhocks—a special gift to his father from the head of the great family. He also wore a pair of fine swords, and he had plenty of spending money. And proudly, above all, he had a head of beautiful hair, worn in the fashionable way. Truly a handsome youth, but a rather loose fellow, he frequented the gay company of the pleasure-quarter more than the sober one of his studies. So one day I spoke to him.

"Now, Tezuka," I said to him, "if you will promise me to put your mind on your work, I will help you and read with you every day. But first, you have got to stop going to *Shinchi*."

He seemed suddenly to repudiate his licentious life. "I have no taste for *Shinchi* any more. I hate even to think of it," said the penitent.

"All right," I said. "I'll teach you then every day. But I want to be very sure. Write me your promise."

So we drew up a little agreement to the effect that Tezuka would sacrifice his hair if he were ever found to have gone to the *Shinchi* quarter again. I made him sign it and I kept it.

From that day he began to study very faithfully, I of course helping him as I promised. But after a while his continued goodness grew boring. Of course it was wrong on my part to think his goodness boring, but his adopted virtue was too unromantic. I began to contrive with two

or three friends to entice him again to the abandoned
Shinchi.

First, we had to find out the name of the woman he had
been with. That was easily found. Then I forged a letter
using all the terms of endearment which women of that kind
use. Guessing that she might once have begged some
perfume from him, I mentioned this with repeated emphasis,
using incorrect writing so that one had to puzzle over
the reading of it. When it was written, one of the accomplices, Matsuoka Yūki, copied it in his clever womanish
style. For the address we used the name "Tetsukawa,"
an idea suggested by another accomplice. In Ōsaka people
pronounce Tezuka "Tetsuka" which in turn is very much.
like another name Tetsukawa. Hence our clever invention.

We then told a school servant to take the letter to Tezuka
and tell him that a messenger from *Shinchi* had brought it.
We threatened to beat him if he betrayed us. But all went
well. The servant unwittingly said that since there was no
gentleman in the school by the name of "Tetsukawa," he
thought it might be meant for Mr. Tezuka.

We watched unseen the reaction of our victim. For a
long time Tezuka puzzled over the letter. I don't know
whether my reference to perfume hit him or not, but the
catch in the personal name may have been what turned the
trick. We had succeeded. After three days of hesitation,
the flattered youth made his way out to *Shinchi.*

The delighted little band watched for his return the next
morning. When the fellow came into the dormitory, I fell
upon him, brandishing a pair of scissors.

"What are you going to do?" cried Tezuka, now scared.

"Don't ask any questions. I'm going to remove that hair
of yours—that's all. It will take two years to grow such
nice hair again. Get ready!"

I took hold of his well-dressed top-knot and rattled the scissors. He was well frightened and began to plead seriously, his hands clasped as if in prayer. Then some of the accomplices came in to intercede.

"What's the matter?" they asked me as though in perfect innocence of it all.

I straightway told all about our agreement, and added, "There is no question about it. Now watch me make a shave-pate out of this fellow."

"Wait a minute," one of them called out. "You are too rash."

Then the others joined in and after a long argument, we decided to let Tezuka off with a bottle of wine and a chicken supper for all of us instead of his penal hair-cutting. Another big feast. In fact, we enjoyed our spread so much that we taunted poor Tezuka: "Do go again to *Shinchi*. We want another party."

Pretty rough perhaps, but after all this was good medicine for the poor fellow.

I make fun of superstitions Many different kinds of students made up the school. One Yamada Kensuke from Higo province was a believer in luck and omens. He would not pronounce the syllable *shi*, for it has the identical sound of the word for "death". At that time the great actor, Ebizō, father of the present Danjūrō, was giving a series of plays in Ōsaka. Speaking of the plays (*shibai* in Japanese), Yamada would say, "I am going to see the *yobai*," thus avoiding the syllable *shi*. Yamada was a good student and a genuine fellow, but his superstition did not take with the boisterous crowd of students.

One day he said to me, because I more often teased him, "Suppose you were on your way to pay some New Year's calls on the first of the year with all the resolutions in mind,

and you met a funeral. Wouldn't you feel badly? But
suppose you met someone carrying a crane (the bird of good-
luck, said to live a thousand years), wouldn't you feel good?
Now, tell me, which would you rather meet on New Year's
—the funeral or the crane?"

"That's easy to answer," I replied. "I should prefer the
crane, because I could eat it while I couldn't eat the dead
man. But if they wouldn't let me eat the crane, it wouldn't
make any difference which it was."

And so, he was the butt of many practical jokes. One day
I planned with another boy (it was Nagayo Sensai,[2] I think)
to put a really stiff one over on him. While Yamada was
out, we took his ink stone and wrapping a piece of paper
around it, we made an *ihai*, or a "death tablet", on which
was written the "death name" of the one deceased to be
placed in the family shrine as a memorial. We made up an
appropriate "death name" for Yamada and wrote it on the
improvised tablet. Then taking his rice bowl, we filled it
with ashes from the brazier and placed it before the tablet
with incense burning in it.

When Yamada came back and saw what had been done,
he turned pale and took on an expression I cannot describe.
As I watched him from the next room, I really was afraid,
because if he had not been so self-possessed a man, he might
have drawn his sword in indignation.

I trick him into eating "poison fish" On another occasion I thought I had
gone almost too far in the joke. This
was when I tricked a friend into eating
some globe-fish, which is thought by
many of the country folks to be fatally
poisonous. I had never been afraid of eating it, for in my
native province it is thought to be a delicacy instead of a

---

[2] Note on p. 344.

danger.* One day I asked Mitō Genkan from Nigata of Aki province to have a dish of "preserved seabream." He enjoyed it, saying, "This is good. Seabream is my favorite fish." And he ate up the entire dish.

I waited about two hours and then said, "Poor chap! You thought you were eating seabream, but really what you liked so much was a globe-fish which my friends at the Nakatsu storage office gave me. I suppose you know how long it takes to digest such fish. If you can dispose of the poison now, try it."

Poor Mitō was pretty angry and ready to fight me. I laughed at him then, but on thinking it over later, I came to wonder if the joke was not a bit overdone. Suppose a serious mishap had occurred . . . .

We were capable of petty stealing

As I have related, once a comrade and I were taken for thieves by the flower-and-plant stand keeper. He was not far wrong. We really were capable of petty stealing, not of very valuable objects like a bolt of cloth, but of lifting trays and cups and things conveniently carried off from a restaurant. We took great pride in getting away with the more bulky ones. One of us came back with a large round fan in the back of his overgarment; another got away with quite a large tray hidden at his breast. A less daring one slipped a cover of the lacquer soup bowl into his sleeve. One night, after the farewell party for a student returning home, one fellow surprised us by saying, "You are all still greenhorns. Look what I have this time," and he thereupon produced a complete set of ten trays, tied up in a towel. But I am sure the proprietor knew all about it and had added the price of the stolen objects to our bill.

Another story is brought back to me by the mention of

---

* The globe-fish has severe poison in its internal organs which may be removed by a skilled cook. Nowadays some cooks are specially licensed to prepare it.

Barrage of trays from the bridge

these trays. One summer night after ten o'clock one of the boys suddenly said he was thirsty. He did not lack company; four or five of us decided to go out to satisfy this general thirst. The gate of the grounds was already closed according to rule, but we threatened the gatekeeper and made him open it for us. We looked for one of those little eating-stalls with woven rush canopies, put up for summer stands. There we had dishes of devil-fish and cheap wine and started homeward after midnight, bringing along a few trays as usual.

When we came to Naniwa Bridge, we saw a pleasure-boat moored underneath the piers. In it some men were having an obviously jolly time with their attendant *geisha* playing and singing.

"Look at them!" I exclaimed. "Here we've had our poor spree for a mere hundred and fifty *mon*—all we could afford. But look at them down there! Because they spend so much, we stay poor!"

And into the boat I threw the trays before I knew it. The singing stopped at the last tray. We did not wait to see if anyone might be hurt, for we disappeared on the run. Curiously, a month afterwards, I learned the sequel of the incident.

One of my friends told me that at a party he met a *geisha* and heard from her a "funny story." She had been entertaining her guests-of-the-evening one night in a boat near Naniwa Bridge; several dark figures suddenly appeared on the bridge and threw some trays at her. One of the trays shot into her *shamisen*, breaking through both faces of the instrument. "Fortunately I wasn't hurt," she concluded, "but think what rough people there are in the world!"

Full well I knew who the "rough people" were, but I kept it a secret even from my intimate friend.

The habit of drinking has always been a drawback in my life and I have not yet rid myself of its effects. But once, while at Ogata School, I tried to reform myself, for I began to think of it as a sin. As if by an inspiration, I suddenly gave up drinking. To my surprise my temperance became notorious in the dormitory—rather, I became the laughing-stock of the whole school.

From temperance into smoking

"Imagine Fukuzawa a teetotaller! How interesting—how funny! He won't last ten days. He may be a three-day teetotaller. He will be drinking tomorrow—"

I persevered stubbornly for ten or fifteen days. Then a friend, Takahashi Juneki, gave me a calling-down.

"You shouldn't give up all pleasures," he argued. "I admire your perseverance. It's a wonder how you do it. But it is not good for you to break a habit entirely even if the habit is not a good one. You simply cannot do it. If you will cut out drinking, begin smoking. One cannot live without some natural indulgence."

I knew that Takahashi was half teasing me when he suggested smoking, because I had been a severe opponent of smoking, calling it useless, unhealthy, the least reasonable of habits. "Anyway don't smoke while I am around, for I won't stand that choking, dirty smoke," I used to say. So it was not at all pleasant now to take it up, but I was won over by Takahashi's apparent logic.

"Perhaps I'll try smoking," I said.

As soon as I started smoking, friends gathered around to encourage me. One gave me tobacco; another lent me a pipe; one brought a special kind of mild tobacco said to be good for the beginner. I realized they were only making a fuss over me and having a good time at my expense, because they knew that until a few days before I had been a terrible hater of smoking. But since my stand against drinking was firm, I went on puffing the irritating smoke until, in ten or fifteen days, the smelly tobacco ceased to be smelly or irritating, and I began to like its flavor. And in a month I was a steady smoker.

But my old love of wine—it would not be forgotten. I knew the weakness, but I would take a sip, and irresistible! Then another sip. Even if I swore it would be my last cup, when I shook the bottle and heard the bubbling inside, my restraint would not last. I drank three *gō* the first time. The next day, five *gō*, and then I was the old drinker again. By now I was a regular smoker—it was impossible to stop either. After my resolution, I fooled myself for a month in every way and came out a full-fledged "two-sworded" man, drinking and smoking. Even now, at the age of sixty, I have not been able to stop smoking although I have managed to deny myself the drinking. I have no excuse to offer for all the damage brought upon my health by my weakness.

Most of us being poor, it was seldom that we could enjoy the taste of good fish in a restaurant. However, when we were hungry for a fish, we could go to the night market near the Tenjin Bridge where the left-over fish were sold. We could buy them there and wash them in our wash-basin and dress them on a carving board of a broken desk with our *kozuka* (a little throwing knife attached to a samurai's sword). This was our usual way of having a feast, and often the work of dressing the fish was given to me as I was clever with my hands.

Flower viewing and fire fighting In March of one year, when the peach trees were in bloom, we heard that the trees on Momoyama, or "peach-mountain" to the east of Ōsaka Castle, were among the finest to be seen. So we all decided to go

out for a flower-picnic one day.   Since having our lunch in
one of the tea-houses was out of the question, we bought, as
usual, some left-over fish and some bean-curd and vegetables
the night before.   On the day of the picnic we got up early
and prepared our lunch.   Then we took some wine and set
out for Momoyama, some fourteen or fifteen in the party.

There under the peach blossoms we were making merry
with the lunch and wine cups when suddenly we noticed in
the distance the smoke of a big fire.   It was exactly in the
direction of Dōtombori where one of us, Nagayo, had gone
that day to see a play.   The fire was of no great concern to
us, but of course we thought of going to rescue Nagayo.   So
we ran all the way from Momoyama to Dōtombori, a
distance of some six or seven miles.   But by the time we
reached there, all of the three theaters in that district had
burned to the ground and the fire was extending to the
north.   We were anxious about Nagayo, but there was
hardly any way of locating him.

Soon it grew dark.   "Well, Nagayo must have gotten
home already.   Let's go and see the fire."   So we went right
into the burning area.   People were running about, carrying their goods to safety.   "Let's help them," we said.   And
we carried bundles of bedding tied in large squares of cloth
and the family chests and heavy things.   Gradually we
worked our way right to the very edge of the fire.   There
were firemen pulling down houses with ropes tied to the
pillars.   The firemen asked us to help them, so we fell in
and worked with the ropes among the burning houses.
Then they gave us rice balls and wine.   It was irresistibly
fascinating.   We worked, ate, and drank all we wanted.   At
about eight in the evening we came back to the dormitory.

But the fire was still burning.   Some of the more vigorous
boys wanted to go back and have more fun.   Back went
several to the scene.   It happened that the onlookers at

fires in Ōsaka were quite different from those in Tōkyō.
Large crowds would gather making plenty of noise, but
not too near the burning area. Once we shouted loud
enough for gangway, we could easily push our way through
the outer crowd into the heart of the fire, where there was
nobody except the professional firemen. So the Ogata
students, alone with the firemen, had the most lively diver-
sion of fighting the fire.

Although it may seem that we led a pretty rough and
lawless kind of life as students, among ourselves we were
very friendly and genuine, and never was there a quarrel
among us. Of course we got into numerous debates, but we
rarely let these congenial disputes turn into actual "rows."
I was naturally not given to any quarrelling, but I did enjoy
trying my wits on some interesting topics. If the theme of
the Forty-Seven Ronin came up, I would challenge my
comrades, "I will take whichever side you are against. If
you say the Forty-Seven Ronin were loyal, I will prove they
were disloyal. Or if you want to prove the contrary, I will
take the opposite side, for I can make them loyal men or
disloyal men at the twist of my tongue. Now, come, all of
you together."

Such were our innocent debates; sometimes I won, sometimes I was beaten; and our voices often were loud, but that
made it all the livelier. Never did our debates grow so
serious that the debaters had to decide the absolute right or
wrong of the problem.

**How our studies
were done**
Still it may appear to the reader that
in all this happy-go-lucky life of the
Ogata students, there was rather little
time given to the actual pursuit of learn-
ing. But really that is a wrong impression. In the practical
end of our study, I am sure there was no other group of
students anywhere at that time who could compare with us

in hard work. As an instance of our intensity, I remember that when I was recovering from typhoid fever in my brother's apartment in the feudal headquarters, I told a servant to bring me a pillow.

I had found that I had been using a rolled up kneeling-mat for my pillow all the while I was ill. Now I wanted to have a real one, but when I ordered the servant to bring it, he returned to tell me he could not find mine anywhere. I realized suddenly that I had not used one for the whole year that I had been there. I had been studying without regard to day or night. I would be reading all day and when night came I did not think of going to bed. When tired, I would lean over on my little desk, or stretch out on the floor resting my head on the raised alcove (*tokonoma*) of the room. I had gone through the year without ever spreading my pallet and covers and sleeping on the pillow. So obviously the servant could not find *my* pillow, for it did not exist anywhere in the apartment. This incident may illustrate our intense manner of studying. In this I was not unusual; all my friends lived in this way. We could not have studied harder.

So after entering the dormitory, I continued in much the same routine. When we happened to have some wine at supper time, I would drink it and go to sleep. I would wake up about ten o'clock, and sitting at my little desk, would begin reading and go on through the night. In the early morning hours when I heard the commotions of boiling rice in the kitchen, I took that for a signal to fall asleep again. Just in time for breakfast, I would wake up and go out to the bath house for a morning plunge. Then on coming back I would fall to at my "morning-rice" and back to reading again. Such was my almost fixed régime.

As it was a school of medicine, one might think that our institution would have been more particular in matters of hygiene. But we were left to lead our carefree life all our own way. We were generally healthy, however, perhaps because we were naturally strong, or it might have been because we thought that if we paid too much attention to hygiene we would become weaklings.

Text copying and reading competition

Then as to our manner of study: In the beginning, each new student, who usually knew nothing of Dutch, was given two books of grammar. These were texts that had been printed in Yedo, one called Grammatica and the other Syntaxis.[3] The new student began with Grammatica, and was taught to read it aloud by the help of some explanatory lectures. When he had studied this through, he was likewise given Syntaxis. And that was the end of his instruction in Ogata academy. Whatever in addition to this he might accomplish was through his own independent study.

For those who had finished these two texts, there were held what we called "reading competitions" (*kaidoku*), or class recitations. Several pages from various Dutch texts would be assigned to a class. There being seven or eight classes, each consisting of ten or fifteen students, the members of a class would draw lots to decide on the order of reading. The monitor of each class would take the text on the day assigned and call on the student whose lot it was to read first. If he recited successfully, he would receive a circular mark; if he failed in his passage, a black dot. When a student could not make his translation, the next one by lot would take up the passage, and so on through the class until it was rendered. Whoever made a perfect recitation without a hitch would receive a triangle which had three times the value of the circle.

Our rule was that if a student received the highest mark

---

[3] Note on p. 344.

of his class for three months in succession, he would be promoted to the higher class. This competition was held on the days of the months containing ones and sixes, or threes and eights. It may easily be seen that it was really like having examinations six times a month.

The Dutch texts that the school owned were a few on medicine and physical sciences, in all about ten books.[4] Each student was, therefore, obliged to copy every word of his reading material when he had passed the elementary stage of the grammar and syntax. Again we drew lots to decide who should take the text for copying first and who next.

There were then no steel pens in use in Japan, and our only paper was the coarse Japanese kind. Some students used to rub this paper with a porcelain bowl to smooth it first, and then they would copy the Western writing on it with a fine brush. This was a slow process and most of us soon learned to size the paper with alum coating, then to use the quill pen.

There were several stores that sold birds' quills, usually of cranes or goose, cut about three inches long, quite cheap. Fishermen were said to use them for catching bonito. We would shave down the quills and they served for pens very well. For ink—of course as yet no foreign ink had been brought in—we rubbed the native ink blocks with water and kept the liquid in a pot.

As this method of copying was obligatory in order to have a foreign text, we became quite skilled in it. The older students could write without error while some friend read out the original. The amount of copying varied from three to five pages on the Japanese paper (*hanshi*) before a reading contest.

Though we were all really good friends—the older ones

---

4 Note on p. 344.

By one's own effort

helping the new students in every way —this assistance did not extend to the preparation for the class recitations.

Then it was a point of honor never to expect or receive any help; each student had to depend on his own ability with the grammars and the one big dictionary the school possessed.

This was the work of Doctor Doeff[5] who had formerly resided in the Hollanders' compound at Nagasaki. It was a translation of a German-Dutch dictionary known as the Halma.[6] This was venerated as the one treasure of all Dutch language students in the country, being hand-copied by various Japanese scholars, and our Ogata school possessed one of its few copies. As it was a huge thing of six thousand pages in many volumes, it would have been impossible for each student to make a copy for his personal use. So always three or four men would be found around this big dictionary taking turns for a word.

Then there was another dictionary: Weiland's[7] Dutch lexicon in six volumes. Whenever a word was not to be found in Doeff, we turned to Weiland; but as the text was entirely in Dutch, it was beyond the reach of a beginner. So on the day before our contests, there was always a big crowd in the "Doeff room" silently taking turns in looking up words. It was a precious aid, and there were no idle students on that evening, nor was there scarcely a one who took a nap through the night.

Gradually the number of books in the Ogata collection would be exhausted, and the advanced students would have to utilize the prefaces or introductions which had no practical use. Sometimes these men would form a little class for reading out-of-the-way material, or sometimes they

---

[5] Note on p. 346. [6] Ibid. [7] Ibid.

would go and request Ogata Sensei to give some lectures. I was among this group during my stay there. I remember how impressed I was by the minuteness of his observations, and at the same time by the boldness of his conclusions. How many times, on returning to our dormitory, we young men talked together about the lecture and expressed our admiration of Ogata's learning and ability, feeling ourselves petty and unlearned by comparison. Certainly both in reputation and in actual accomplishment Ogata Sensei was a foremost scholar of his time in the new Western studies.

Our wandering out in the streets for our prank-playing was, the reader may be sure, confined to the evenings after the reading competition or to the next day when we had several days of freedom ahead of us. Before the ordeal we worked desperately. Of course what each student learned depended upon his own native ability, but most of them were well skilled in reading foreign texts, for in this school no student was ever promoted or graduated automatically after a number of years in residence. Each one was obliged to work his way up by his own hard labor.

One could make a living by copying books

There is another thing about Doeff's dictionary that I wish to tell in passing. Often certain *daimyō*, the lords of feudatories, in their wish to obtain it, would order copies made by some students of Dutch. This gave a source of income for some of us. One page of Doeff had thirty lines. A copy of the Dutch section would bring sixteen *mon* a page, the Japanese half eight *mon*, which was much better than the pay one got for copying ordinary books in Japanese. A copy of the whole dictionary of some six thousand pages would therefore bring in a substantial sum for a needy student.

From a modern point of view, the amount would seem very small, but then, a *koku*, or about five bushels, of rice was only three *bu* and two *shu*; one *shō*, or about half a gallon, of wine, between one hundred sixty-four and two hundred *mon*. A student's expenses in the dormitory were in all about one *bu* and two *shu* a month, or less than a sum of one hundred *mon* a day. If he could copy ten pages of Doeff a day, he could earn more than his cost of living. This was a privilege for students of Dutch alone; no ordinary copyist could think of earning his living and studying in a school at the same time.

In Yedo where the *daimyō* had their official residences, there was much demand for copying various Dutch books, as might be expected. So the wages for copying were disproportionately higher in Yedo than in Ōsaka. A certain student named Suzuki Giroku from Kanazawa went to Yedo penniless, but he earned his living there by such copying, and moreover saved some twenty *ryō* in a year or two. With this saving, he came to Ōsaka for more study, and he returned home an accomplished doctor. Once he told me that Yedo was a good place to make a living, but as for real study, it could not be done except in Ōsaka. So he had determined to make his way there with the saving.

We tried every new scientific technique

Of course at that time there were no examples of industrial machinery. A steam engine could not be seen anywhere in the whole of Japan. Nor was there any kind of apparatus for chemical experiments. However, learning something of the theories of chemistry and machinery in our books, we of the Ogata household spent much effort in trying out what we had learned, or trying to make a thing that was illustrated in the books.

I had known since my residence in Nagasaki that iron could be tin-plated if we had zinc chloride. In Japan the art of plating copper with tin by the use of pine pitch had been known, for all copper or bronze cooking vessels were tin-plated. We students decided that we would plate iron by the modern method. There was no standard chloric acid to be purchased in a store, so we had to find out a way of preparing it ourselves. After laboring over it from the description in the text, we finally made the acid, and melting some zinc in it, we succeeded in plating iron with tin—a feat beyond the practice of any tin craftsman in the land. Such was the irresistible fascination of our new knowledge.

Next we sought to produce iodine. Having worked out its chemical formula together, we went to the market at Temma and bought a quantity of seaweed. We roasted this over a fire, applied other processes, and worked till we were black with the smoke, but by no means were we able to get a satisfactory result.

Then we tried ammonium chloride. The first requisite for this experiment was bone, but we learned that horse-hoof would serve as well. So we went to a store where they sold tortoise-shell ware to get some fragments of horse-hoofs. It was quite cheap; we could have it for the asking. I had heard that horse-hoof was used for fertilizing, but that was of no concern to us. We took a large quantity of the hoofs and covered it in an earthenware jar with a layer of clay; then placed it on a charcoal fire in a large bowl. As we fanned the fire vigorously, a smelly vapor came out; this we condensed in an earthenware pipe.

Our experiment was going very well, and the condensed vapor was dripping freely from the pipe, but the disadvantage proved to be the awful stench of the vapor. It can easily be imagined what the result of heating bones and horse-hoofs would be, especially in the small back yard of the dormitory. Our clothing became so saturated with the gas that when we went to the bath house in the evening, the street dogs howled at us. Then we tried the experiment

naked; our skins absorbed the smell. The young men were
so keen on their experiment that they stood the smelly
ordeal without complaint. But all the neighbors objected
and the servants in the Ogata household wailed that they
could not eat their meals on account of the sickening gas.

After all our hardships and the complaints and apologies,
a strange powdery thing was the result—not very pure, nor
the correct crystals of ammonium chloride. At this stage
most of the young men, including myself, decided they had
had enough. But others, more stouthearted, would not give
up the search; they insisted that to give up a work unfin-
ished was a disgrace to their profession. And so ammonium
chloride was pursued.

They hired a cheap boat on the Yodo River, and placing
their brazier and utensils on board, continued the odorous
experiment in midstream. Still the vapor penetrated the
nearby shores, and the people would come out and yell to
them to get out of the way. Then the young men would
have the boat rowed upstream, keeping on with the experiment until they were urged to move again downstream. So
up and down from Tenjin Bridge to Tamae Bridge they
went on for many days. The chief of these determined
students was Nakamura Kyōan from Kompira in Sanuki
province.

Besides such experiments in chemistry, the Ogata students
were interested in dissecting animals, stray dogs and cats,
and sometimes even the corpses of decapitated criminals.
They were a hardened, reckless crowd, these aspirants for
Western learning, but they were also studious and earnest
in many ways that escaped the general notice.

I recall another episode in the manufacture of chemicals.
One day we worked hard to obtain sulphuric acid. We
produced some—very black and impure. But the time was
late in the day, and a student, Tsuruta Senan, put the acid

in a rice bowl and placed it on his shelf to keep until the next day. He forgot all about it, and by some chance, he knocked the bowl from the shelf and received a shower of the sulphuric acid all over himself. Fortunately he was not much injured, but the double layer of his clothing—for it was in the cool early spring—was burned to shreds.

Of course, we needed many bottles in our chemical works. The earthenware wine bottles were exactly right, and we used to order wine from our favorite shop, Kometō, and keep the bottles for other uses after drinking the contents. Thus we kept so many of them that the wine merchant began to wonder, and secretly inquired the fate of his vessels from the servants of our dormitory. He learned that the bottles were being needed more than the contents. Much surprised, he refused to send wine to our dormitory after that much to the mortification of the students.

We copied off Ogata Sensei was a doctor to Lord **Lord Kuroda's** Kuroda of Chikuzen, the grandfather of **book on physics** the present nobleman of that name.[8] It was not that he went to Chikuzen or to Yedo to serve him, but he was simply the lord's favorite doctor in Ōsaka. Whenever Lord Kuroda passed through Ōsaka on his annual journey to Yedo, Ogata would present himself to pay his respects in the feudal headquarters on Nakano-shima.

One year—the third or fourth year of Ansei (1856–1857)— Ogata Sensei had returned from this visit of state to his lord when he sent for me in his own room and showed me a new volume of Dutch print.

"Today on my visit to his lordship, he showed me this book, saying he had recently acquired it. So I asked for permission to look it over during his stay here."

---

[8] Note on p. 346.

I took in the book with devouring eyes. It was a new text
on physical science recently translated from English into
Dutch with the name of Vanderbilt(?). The contents
seemed to hold much that was new to us, especially the
chapter on electricity.

All that we knew about electricity then had been gleaned
from fragmentary mention of it in the Dutch readers. But
here in this new book from Europe was a full explanation based on the recent discoveries of the great English
physicist, Faraday, even with the diagram of an electric cell.
My heart was carried away with it at first sight.

"This is a wonderful book, Sir!" I exclaimed. "How
long do you think we might keep it?"

"Well," he replied, "I was told that my lord will stay in
Ōsaka for two days. I suppose he would not mind our keeping it until his departure."

"I should like to have my friends share in seeing the
book," I explained, and bore the volume back to the
dormitory.

"Look at this!"

All the young men rose up as one and crowded around me
and the book as eager as I was. Two or three of the older
students and myself decided, on talking it over, to make a
copy of it.

"See here," we said. "Just looking at the book won't do
you any good. We must get together and copy it."

But then, to copy a volume of a thousand pages! We
decided to do just the final chapter, the one on electricity.
If we could have broken the book up and divided the copying among the thirty or fifty "ready-quill men," the entire
contents might have been kept. But of course injuring the
nobleman's possession was out of the question. However,
we worked at full speed, and the Ogata students could work
expertly. One read aloud; another took down the dictation;

when one grew tired and slowed down, another was waiting with his quill, and the exhausted one would go to sleep regardless of time, morning, noon or night.

Thus, working day and night, through meal hours and all, we finished the whole chapter in the time allotted, and thus the section on electricity, about three hundred pages including its diagrams, remained with us in manuscript. We finished reading it against the text for correction and regretted that we had no more time for the other parts. But to have retained so much we counted fortunate, and when the evening of Lord Kuroda's departure came, we all handled the book affectionately in turn and gave it a sad leave-taking as if we were parting with a parent. When we heard from Ogata Sensei that Lord Kuroda had paid eighty *ryō* for the book, we were dumbfounded. Such a cost was so far beyond our conception that we should never have had even the desire or ambition to acquire such a treasure.

This event quite changed the whole approach to the subject of electricity in the Ogata household. I do not hesitate to say that my fellow students became the best informed men on the new science in the entire country. I dare say I owe to the copy of this book much of the knowledge which enables me to understand something of the electrical industry today. Many years later I remembered the book and wished to see the original again. A number of times I called at the Kuroda residence—for the times had changed and I had become a personal friend of the lord—but I was always told that since the great upheaval of the Restoration (1868), the book had been lost. I have always regretted this, feeling its loss like separation from an old friend.[9]

I think this incident will prove that the young men around Ogata Sensei were, as a group, as zealous for foreign culture

[9] Note on p. 346.

**The spirit of
Ōsaka students**
as any students in the world.   Every
now and then a student came from Yedo
to Ogata's school to study, but never
did anyone leave it for that purpose.
If any went to Yedo, it was for teaching and not for more
study.   We often talked about this fact among ourselves,
and said proudly that we, the Ōsaka students, were above
any in the country.   But it could not have been that all the
good students gathered in Ōsaka and no able ones lived in
Yedo.   It seems to me that the situation of the country then
created this contrasting standard of scholarship in the two
cities.

In Yedo, though the country's intercourse with foreign
lands was yet at its beginning, there were constant demands
for the Western knowledge from the government offices
and from the various feudal nobility resident there.   Consequently anyone able to read foreign books, or make any
translation, secured the reward of this patronage.   There
was even the possibility of a poor language student being
made a high salaried samurai of several hundred *koku* overnight.

Ōsaka, on the contrary, was a city of merchants devoted
to internal commerce; it was hardly to be expected that
anyone there wanted to be informed on Dutch gunnery or
Western arts.   Therefore, however much we studied, our
work and knowledge had practically no connection with the
actual means of gaining a livelihood or making a name for
ourselves.   Not only that, but the students of Dutch were
looked upon with contempt by most men.   Then why did we
work so hard to learn Dutch?   It would seem that we were
simply laboring at difficult foreign texts for no clear purpose.

However, if anyone had looked into our inner hearts, he
would have found there an untold pleasure which was our
consolation.   In short, we students were conscious of the

fact that we were the sole possessors of the key to knowledge of the great European civilization. However much we suffered from poverty, whatever poor clothes we wore, the extent of our knowledge and the resources of our minds were beyond the reach of any prince or nobleman of the whole nation. If our work was hard, we were proud of it, knowing that no one knew what we endured. "In hardship we found pleasure, and the hardship was pleasure." To illustrate, our position was like that of someone taking bitter medicine without knowing exactly what it was good for. We simply took it because nobody else could take it—the more bitter it was, the more gladly we took it.

Our hostility against Chinese learning Though we often had discussions on many subjects, we seldom touched upon political subjects as most of us were students of medicine. Of course, we were all for free intercourse with Western countries, but there were few among us who took a serious interest in that problem. The only subject that bore our constant attack was Chinese medicine. And by hating Chinese medicine so thoroughly, we came to dislike everything that had any connection with Chinese culture. Our general opinion was that we should rid our country of the influences of the Chinese altogether. Whenever we met a young student of Chinese literature, we simply felt sorry for him.

Particularly were the students of Chinese medicine the butt of our ridicule. There was a noted doctor of Chinese medicine, named Hanaoka, in our neighborhood. The students in his academy appeared to be all very well-to-do. We could never have compared our poor clothing with theirs. We often met each other on the streets, but we never exchanged greetings; rather, some severe glances passed between us. After we had gotten out of the range of their hearing, we would break out in our usual execrations.

"Look at them!" one of us would begin. "They have good clothes on, but that is about all there is to them. They think they are learning something; they listen to those crazy lectures of their master, but he simply repeats the same old mouldy theories handed down for how many centuries! Poor things! And the one who stores the greatest amount of rubbish in his head becomes the monitor of the school! Isn't it sad that these 'doctors' are going to begin killing people pretty soon? Wait till the time comes; our medicine will put an end to their practice. Pretty soon you will not be seeing those foolish 'doctors' any more."

We studied with-out hope in the future

So we often indulged ourselves in this kind of happy boasting, but none of us had any definite idea how the future was to be brought about.

To conclude, most of us were then actually putting all our energy into our studies without any definite assurance of the future. Yet this lack of future hope was indeed fortunate for us, for it made us better students than those in Yedo. From this fact I am convinced that the students of the present day, too, do not get the best results from their education if they are too much concerned about their future. Of course, it is not very commendable either, to attend school without any serious purpose. But, as I say, if a student regulates his work too much with the idea of future usefulness, or of making money, then he will miss what should be the most valuable part of his education. During one's school life, one should make the school work his chief concern.

V

I GO TO YEDO; I LEARN ENGLISH

In the fifth year of Ansei (1858) when I was twenty-five years old, it came about that I left Ōsaka for Yedo. I received an order through the headquarters of my clan in Yedo that there was some work for me to do there. An official in service there, Okami Hikozō, was an ardent advocate of Dutch culture. He had been endeavoring to use his influence in opening a school of the Dutch language in the estate of our clan in Yedo. Already he had gathered together under himself several students, and had secured the services of such scholars as Matsuki Kōan and Sugi Kōji for their instruction. Now that he had learned I was completing my studies in Ōsaka, he decided that I, rather than the scholars of other clans, should be employed as teacher.

The presiding officer of our clan then in Yedo was none other than Okudaira Iki. I have much to be proud of in the relations between Iki and myself, for though there had been some hard feelings between us from the time when we both lived in Nagasaki, we never let the feeling grow into a quarrel.

He must have found out later that while I was bowing politely before him, taking his letters for my return to Nakatsu with apparent good will, I was thumbing my nose at him and sticking out my tongue behind his back. However, no one ever was told of this affair—nor did I ever reveal by word or expression my feeling against him. On the contrary, I had been repeating my gratitude for whatever good he had done for me. There was also my secret copying of his valuable book. Perhaps we had evened up our scores against each other. But then, he was, after all, a good-natured son of a high official. He took things easily when I showed no sign of my old feeling. And when the question of calling me to Yedo came up, he raised no objection, although, as the presiding officer in the Yedo office, he might have prevented it. When I come to think of this, I feel that I am the more guilty of the two.

Before leaving Ōsaka for my new post in Yedo, I first made a visit to my mother. It was at the time of a great epidemic of cholera; many victims were dying even in the neighborhood of our home. While the epidemic was still raging, I took passage again by the Inland Sea vessel and returned to Ōsaka where I was officially to leave for Yedo.

According to the rule of our clan, when a man with my social rank held an office or traveled in an official capacity, he was to have one follower with him. So I was given the expenses for one man, but a serving man was quite beyond my present need. However, there was the money. Well, I could take some friend who wanted to go to Yedo with me. I announced this in our Ogata dormitory, and one Okamoto Shūkichi, a Hiroshima man who later changed his name to Furukawa Setsuzō, spoke up and said he would like to go.[1]

"All right," I replied. "But you understand, when we reach Yedo, you have to boil the rice for me. We shall have our quarters provided, and the rice also. And they will lend us a stove and a kettle. But if I am to take you along instead of a servant, you will have to boil the rice for me. Will you do that?"

---

[1] Note on p. 347.

"Boiling rice won't be a hard work. I shall do that for you."
"Well then, come along."

So off we started for Yedo. Another
A party of three student from the Ogata dormitory happened to be leaving also for Yedo; so we
had a party of three intimate friends, this third fellow being
Harada Raizō from Bitchū.

Needless to tell, we walked all the way—three hundred
miles—from Ōsaka to Yedo along the old Tōkaidō highway.
It was late in October and growing somewhat cold, but a
good season for walking. We were fortunate enough not to
be stopped for even a day at the river crossings.[2]

On reaching Yedo, we first reported at the Okudaira
residence at Kobikichō, Shiodome, and were told we would
find our quarters in Teppōzu[3] where lesser officials had their
apartments. So Okamoto and I took up our lodgings there
and began bachelor's house-keeping. Harada, who had
been our fellow-traveler, took up his abode in the household
of the great doctor, Ōtsuki Shunsai, at Neribei in Shitaya.
We found several acquaintances of ours in the city and made
many more soon; our life in the feudal capital grew more
interesting daily.

Shortly after I was settled in our clan headquarters, three
or four sons and brothers of the officials came to me for
instruction in Dutch. Later five or six men of other clans
began to attend, and my little apartment took on the air of
a small school.

We came to   As I have said, a student from Ōsaka
teach, not to   came to Yedo always to teach—not to
learn   study. So I took my share of pride in
                          illustrating this fact. However, at times
I felt some misgivings in not knowing surely what ability

---

[2] Note on p. 347.   [3] Ibid.

the scholars in Yedo had. One day I had an occasion to visit
Shimamura Teiho, a physician from Ogata's school and an
old friend of mine. He was then in Yedo engaged in translating foreign books. Whenever we met, our talk always
drifted to the subject of foreign culture.

On that day he brought out a book on physiology which
he was then working on, and said that he could not by any
means understand a certain passage in it. And truly it
seemed a difficult one when I looked at it. I asked him
curiously if he had shown this section to any of his scholar-
friends.

"Of course," he replied. "I have worked over it with five
or six of my friends, but we could make nothing of it."

"That's interesting," I exclaimed. "I shall show you I
can get it."

I read over the passage several times. It was hard. But
after I had studied it silently for half an hour, I got it.

"Now I have it!" And I gave my translation. "It seems
easy, once you get it, doesn't it?" And I laughed with my
grateful friend.

The passage, as I recall, dealt with the relation between
light and the human eye. When you lighted two candles
and did something to one of the lights, something happened.
I do not remember exactly, but it will be found in Shimamura's translation entitled Seiri Hatsumō.

After this incident I felt safer; I secretly decided that
there were few scholars of Dutch in Yedo who could surpass
me in the work of translating.

Even further than this, I sometimes took a difficult passage
of a book to various senior scholars to test their ability. I
sought out passages which in Ogata's school many of the
students had mistranslated, and pretended that I was unable
to interpret them. Then it sometimes happened that these
dignified gentlemen would again mistranslate the passage

to my secret exultation. Certainly not very commendable, yet for a young man of high spirit, this secret joy was tantalizingly sweet. After all, it was necessary for me to know something of the standard of the Yedo scholars, for without some tangible proof, I could not wisely uphold our boast in Ōsaka. I had thus satisfied myself and felt relieved, but something else occurred to upset my tranquility.

New revelation, the English language   The year after I reached Yedo—the sixth year of Ansei (1859)—there was established the so-called "Treaty of the Five Nations,"[4] and the port of Yokohama was formally opened for trade with foreign countries. One day I went to Yokohama for sight-seeing. There was nothing of the town of Yokohama then—a few temporary dwellings had been erected here and there by the foreigners, and in these the pioneer merchants were living and showing their wares.

To my chagrin, when I tried to speak with them, no one seemed to understand me at all. Nor was I able to understand anything spoken by a single one of all the foreigners I met. Neither could I read anything of the signboards over the shops, nor the labels on the bottles which they had for sale. There was not a single recognizable word in any of the inscriptions or in any speech. It might have been English or French for aught I knew.

At last I came upon a shop kept by one Kniffer.[5] He was a German and did not understand much of what I said to him, but he could somehow understand my Dutch when I put it in writing. So we conversed a little, I bought a few things from him, and returned to Yedo.

What a self-imposed labor it was on my part! Because of the closing hour of the gate of our compound, which was

---

[4] Note on p. 347.   [5] Ibid.

midnight, I had to leave home just before the closing hour and return before the same hour of the next day. This meant that I had been walking for twenty-four hours, a distance of some fifty miles, going and coming. But the fatigue of my legs was nothing compared with the bitter disappointment in my heart.

I had been striving with all my powers for many years to learn the Dutch language. And now when I had reason to believe myself one of the best in the country, I found that I could not even read the signs of merchants who had come to trade with us from foreign lands. It was a bitter disappointment, but I knew it was no time to be downhearted.

Those signs must have been either in English or in French —probably English, for I had had inklings that English was the most widely used language. A treaty with the two English-speaking countries had just been concluded. As certain as day, English was to be the most useful language of the future. I realized that a man would have to be able to read and converse in English to be recognized as a scholar in Western subjects in the coming time. In my disappointment my spirit was low, but I knew that it was not the time to be sitting still.

My daily pilgrimage to a teacher of English On the very next day after returning from Yokohama, I took up a new aim in life and determined to begin the study of English. But, needless to say, there was no teacher of English then in Yedo. I did not know how to begin. I found, after inquiring around, that there was an interpreter named Moriyama Takichirō who had been called from Nagasaki to help in the negotiation of the new treaty. I heard that this man knew some English though his specialty was Dutch. I went at once to Moriyama's house and implored him to teach me English.

He was very kind and said that, though he was very busy
in his duties, he would do what he could to help me if I was
so anxious to learn. He decided that I should come to his
house early in the morning before he went to his office. I
lived in Teppōzu then and his house was in Koishikawa, a
distance of about five miles, but every morning I rose be-
times and walked to Moriyama's residence. I never had the
luck of having a single lesson with him. One day I would
be told that it was already time for his office—I should come
earlier tomorrow. When I went earlier the next morning,
he had an unexpected visitor. It was not any unkindness
on his part. It was but natural that he should be so en-
grossed at the critical period of the treaty negotiations.

At length he said it was too bad that he had been making
me come to no avail so many times—so would I mind coming
in the evening? I began, then, and called in the evening,
leaving my place at about sunset. My route lay near Kanda
Bridge and Hitotsu-bashi, where the Higher Commercial
School now stands. At that time it was a desolate region,
called Gojiin-ga Hara, full of huge pine trees, a perfect
setting for highwaymen. I can still remember how fearful
it seemed to pass through it on my way home at eleven or
twelve at night.

Again all my patience and exertion went for nothing.
Moriyama would have a caller one evening; on another
night he would be called out by the foreign bureau. I had
been going to his residence every evening for two or three
months, and the interpreter had not been able to give me
any of his time. Then, too, I began to hear that Moriyama did not really know very much English; he knew the
pronunciation of a few words. But it was with great
reluctance that I gave him up as my teacher-to-be.

I had bought two volumes of a small English conversation book at Kniffer's store in Yokohama. It contained

sentences in Dutch and English.   Therefore, with the aid of
a Dutch-English dictionary, I thought
I enter a govern-   I would be able to use it for my own
ment school   study.   Yet no store in Yedo or Yokohama had a foreign dictionary for sale.
By good luck I learned that in the government school of
foreign culture, known as Bansho Shirabesho, there were
many dictionaries.

To have access to these books, I had to enter the school as
a student.   But since it was an institution of the central
government, it would not admit any member of outside clans
without much formality.   I had to go to the highest official
of my clan in Yedo and get his seal on my petition.   Then
putting on formal dress, *kamishimo*, with elaborate shoulder-
guards and divided skirt, I took my application to the school,
located at the foot of Kudan Hill.   At that time Mitsukuri
Gempo, grandfather of Mitsukuri Rinshō,[6] was director; he
at once permitted me to enter as a student.

Once registered, I could borrow the dictionary.   I asked
for it right away, sat in the reading room for day-students,
and looked through it for some time.   Then taking out my
cloth for parcels, I began to wrap it up to take it home.   An
attendant stepped up.   "There is no objection to your using
that here, but you cannot remove a book from the building."

"Well," I thought, "it isn't very practicable to come all
the way here from Teppōzu every day to look up some
words."   So I gave up the school on the very first day.

While I was wondering what could be done, by a stroke
of luck I obtained a dictionary for my own use.   I had asked
some merchants trading with the foreigners in Yokohama
to be looking for a Dutch-English dictionary.   One day I
heard there was a small one in two volumes, called Holtrop,[7]

" Note on p. 347.   [7] p. 348.

which contained phonetic notations. The price was five *ryō*. I petitioned my clan to buy it for me.

Once with these at my command, I felt there was hope for my endeavor. I made firm my determination to learn the new language by my own efforts. So day and night I plodded along with the new books for sole companions. Sometimes I tried to make out the English sentences by translating each word into Dutch; sometimes I tried forming an English sentence from the Dutch vocabulary. My sole interest then was to accustom myself to the English language.

Search for a companion in the study Then I realized that I ought to have a friend to work with me. But I found it was going to be difficult to find a companion in this study. All the students of Dutch were now facing the keen disappointment of finding out that Dutch was not a universal language. Naturally not one of them wanted to admit that all his work had come to naught, or that he had to drop all he had acquired in Dutch and begin the study of another language. It would be hard for any foreign-language student to reach this resolution.

Such was the thought of my friend Kanda Kōhei[8] when I approached him. He honestly confessed: "Yes, I have thought of what you say for a long time. And I really tried to learn English myself, but it was beyond me. I don't see how to make anything of it. If you have the spirit, I wish you'd try, and if you make a good start in it, I will join you. But for the present, I haven't the courage."

I went also to Murata Zōroku (later Ōmura Masujirō[9]) and sought his aid, but this fellow had an entirely different idea.

---

[8] Note on p. 348. [9] Ibid.

"Don't try to get me into such useless labor," he exclaimed. "What is the use of learning English? All the important books will be translated by the Dutch. You can read *them*. And what more do you want?"

"Yes," I replied, "that's one side of the argument. But do you think the Dutch will translate everything? The other day I went to Yokohama and what happened? Dutch alone is not enough. English is going to be necessary."

"All right. If you insist on it, go ahead and study it. But I am going to read the Dutch translation whenever I need anything."

I had to give up any more arguing with him. I went to Harada Keisaku.[10] He was enthusiastic and promised to join me whatever others might do.

"Fine," said he. "We will accomplish something together, whatever happens." So we two began.

At that time a young lad had come to Yedo from Nagasaki. We heard that he knew some English, and we tried to get some pronunciation from him. Then occasionally there were ship-wrecked Japanese fishermen who were brought back by foreign ships. These poor men had formerly, by government decree, not been permitted to reenter this land, but after the new policy of "open ports" came into effect, they were allowed to return home. Whenever we heard of any such men, we called on them at their lodgings, and asked them to give us any English they knew.

The pronunciation was naturally the most difficult part of all in the new language. The meaning and construction of a sentence was not so difficult. When, with the help of a dictionary, we replaced every word in the English sentence with a Dutch word, most of the sentences could be understood. So for the purpose of pronunciation, any child or

---

10 Note on p. 348.

uneducated fishermen who had been thrown with Englishmen or Americans could fill the place of teacher very well. And this pronunciation too did not prove to be so very difficult when we had gone through the initial stage.

After a while we came to see that English was a language not so entirely foreign to us as we had thought. Our fear in the beginning that we were to find all our labor and hope expended on Dutch to have been spent in vain, and that we were to go through the same hardship twice in our lives proved happily wrong. In truth, Dutch and English were both "languages written sideways" of the same origin. Our knowledge of Dutch could be applied directly to English; our one-time fear was a groundless illusion.

VI

I JOIN THE FIRST MISSION
TO AMERICA

The year after I was settled in Yedo—the sixth year of Ansei (1859)—the government of the Shōgun made a great decision to send a ship-of-war to the United States, an enterprise never before attempted since the foundation of the empire. On this ship I was to have the good fortune of visiting America.

Good ship Kanrin-maru Though it had been called a warship, the vessel was a very small sailing craft equipped with an auxiliary steam engine of one hundred horsepower, which was used for manœuvring in and out of harbors. In the open sea she must depend entirely on sail. The government had purchased her from the Dutch for 25,000 *ryō* a few years before, and had named her the Kanrin-maru.[1]

Since the second year of Ansei (1855), after the opening of the ports, officers had been studying navigation and the science of steamships under the Dutch residents of Nagasaki. By now, their skill and practice had made them able to venture; so the council of the Shōgun had decided that Japanese officers and crew should take a ship across the Pacific to San Francisco at the occasion of our first envoy's departure to Washington.[2] The Kanrin-maru was to act as

---

[1] Note on p. 348. [2] p. 349.

The KANRIN-MARU, first Japanese ship to make the trans-Pacific voyage to America. As a member of Kimura Settsu-no Kami's staff, Fukuzawa was able to join this expedition. Pencil sketch by Captain John Mercer Brooke, with inscription by Katsu Rintarō, from Katsu's notebook (1860).

The KANRIN-MARU. By Suzufuji Yūjirō, a member of the crew (1860).

a kind of escort to the envoy who was sailing on an American warship.

The captain of our ship was Kimura Settsu-no Kami[3]; next in command was Katsu Rintarō[4]; other officers were Sasakura Kiritarō, Hamaguchi Okiemon, and Suzufuji Yūjirō; the navigators were Ono Tomogorō, Ban Tetsutarō, and Matsuoka Bankichi; the engineers Hida Hamagorō and Yamamoto Kinjirō. Acting as purser and assistant were Yoshioka Yūhei and Konagai Gohachirō. The interpreter was Nakahama Manjirō.[5] Among the junior officers were Nezu Kinjirō, Akamatsu Daizaburō, Okada Seizō, and Kosugi Masanoshin. There were also two doctors and sixty-five sailors and stokers. The entire crew, including the captain's personal servant, amounted to ninety-six men—a larger number than usual for the ship. I recall many things of this voyage worthy of being set down.

This voyage of Kanrin-maru was an epoch-making venture for our nation; every member of the crew was determined to take the ship across unassisted by a foreigner. At about that time Captain Brooke,[6] an American officer, had come to Yokohama. He had been engaged in taking soundings in the Pacific Ocean on board a small sailing vessel, the Fenimore Cooper, which was wrecked on the southern coast of Japan. The captain and another officer of the ship with a doctor and several sailors, also saved from the wreck, were being kept under the protection of the Japanese government. Now, on learning that a Japanese ship was going to San Francisco, they wished to be carried across.

The government officials agreed to this and were about to grant the permit for the Americans when the staff of the Kanrin-maru protested strongly, the reason being that ·if the American navigators went along, the Japanese staff

---

[8] Note on p. 349.   [4] Ibid.   [5] p. 350.   [6] Ibid.

would feel an implied slur on their own ability to sail. Their opposition grew out of the sense of honor for themselves and for their country, so the Shogunate officials were much concerned for a while. But they finally ordered out right that the ship should take Captain Brooke and his men on board. Probably the elder officials of the government were in reality uncertain of the ability of the Japanese crew and thought Captain Brooke would be of use in case of emergency.

My greatest wish was to sail somehow **Captain of the** or other on this voyage. I thought that, **ship, Kimura** as Captain Kimura was a person of high **Settsu-no Kami** rank—the real head of our navy—he would need some personal servants with him as befitted his rank. I had to find some method of access to him and ask him to let me serve as his personal steward on the voyage.

Fortunately there was a near relative of Captain Kimura whom I knew. He was a physician in service of the Shōgun, Dr. Katsuragawa who was looked up to as the patriarch of Dutch learning in Japan by all the students of the country. When I reached Yedo the year before, I had taken the first opportunity of paying my respects to him, and since then I had been in his home many times. I, therefore, begged Dr. Katsuragawa for a letter of introduction, went to Captain Kimura's house, and begged him to take me along as his servant. Luckily he responded to my request and agreed immediately that I might join the ship.

It seems to me now that his reason for granting my wish so readily must have been that for such an unusual enterprise as the voyage was to be, there were not many volunteers. Even among his own followers, there would not have been many eager to risk themselves on this strange adventure. Therefore he must have been struck by my volunteering and accepted me gladly.

It was in January, the first year of
An interlude in   Manen (1860), when our ship, the Kan-
Uraga   rin-maru, left Yedo from the shores of
Shinagawa. The envoy was to sail on
an American warship, the Powhatan, sent over specially
for the official journey of the embassy. The Kanrin-maru
sailed first, and coming to Uraga, stopped there for a while.
All the officers of the ship were young men. When one of
them suggested a party to celebrate our leave-taking of our
country, everybody agreed, put off for shore, and quickly
made for a neighboring restaurant. As we were breaking
up from our party, which had been quite lively, I chanced to
spy a large china bowl on a shelf in the hallway of the
restaurant. My former spirit of souvenir collecting came
back as I thought the bowl might be useful on the voyage.
I picked it up and carried it back to the ship.

No sooner did we get out into open sea than we ran into
storms, and continued to have rough weather all the way
across. In the rocking ship a quiet meal was impossible, so
I used to pile my rice in my purloined bowl and pour soup
and everything over it, take it to the side of the cabin, and
eat standing up. That bowl proved to be about the most
convenient article I brought along on the voyage. I used it
daily until we reached America, and furthermore, I found it
useful on the return trip. Finally I took the bowl home and
it remained in my household for a long time. At a later
time I heard that the place where we had celebrated our
leave-taking was a place of rendezvous for prostitutes with
their customers. I did not suspect it at the time, but very
probably my bowl had once held a mouth wash for the gay
women of the house. That made me squirm a bit when I
learned it, but the joke was how useful the dish had been—
the one treasure I had on board.

Now our small ship, having gotten on her way out of the

Avalanche of silver coins

bay of Yedo, sailed far to the north. In winter, on the rough seas, with her diminutive steam engine of one hundred horsepower, which was to be used only in manœuvring about ports, she had to face the voyage under sail. And so hard was the weather on the voyage that we lost two of the four life-boats overboard.

One morning I went in pursuit of my usual duties as steward to the captain's quarters in the stern. On opening the door, I found the whole floor covered with dollar coins. I could not tell, but there seemed to be hundreds of thousands of them lying around. Evidently they had broken out during the night from the bags stored in his closet, and had scattered over the floor. At once I ran back to the purser, Yoshioka, and told him. He hurried in, and together we gathered up the layer of coins and restored them to the closet.

The samurai officials had no knowledge of foreign credit or money-orders at that time. They must have thought that, as money would be necessary on the voyage, money should be carried along. So a huge amount of coins had been placed in the captain's locker, and they had broken loose during a storm. Such was the mind of our professional warriors forty years ago.

Storm followed storm. Waves broke over the decks continually. I remember that whenever the ship keeled over on her side, I could look up through the skylight from below and see the tops of great waves in the distance. A list of thirty-seven or thirty-eight degrees was not uncommon; we were told that if she went over forty-five degrees, she would founder to the bottom. Still, she kept her course, and fortunately had no serious mishaps. For a whole month we saw nothing but the waves and the clouds. Once we sighted a sail boat, said to be an American vessel carrying

Chinese workmen over to America. That was the only thing we saw during the voyage.

In jail with earthquakes every day I seemed to be physically fit and did not suffer from seasickness at all. I kept on joking with friends: "This isn't anything. Just imagine you are in a jail and having earthquakes day and night. I haven't been in such a predicament myself, but I don't think this could be any worse than that." I had no feeling of fear. Probably it was that I trusted in Western science through and through, and as long as I was on a ship navigated by Western methods, I had no fear.

Our supply of water began to run low. There was a question of making port at the Hawaiian Islands. If we had been very cautious, we should have called there for more water, but it was finally decided to sail straight on to San Francisco. As it could be done by strictly conserving the water, an order was issued that no water should be used except for drinking. A poignant episode occurred in this connection.

The four or five American sailors on our ship were found to be using more water than they were supposed to. One of the officers told Captain Brooke about it, and the latter replied instantly: "You may shoot any seaman found wasting water. Any such person is guilty of treason to the ship. No admonition or inquiry is necessary. You may feel free to shoot him at once."

This was certainly logical. Our officers, calling the American seamen together, warned them of the penalty for wasting water. Our water supply was thus made to hold out, and we with the entire crew of ninety-six men reached land at San Francisco after thirty-seven days. Of these thirty-seven days, perhaps four or five had been fine; all the others had been stormy and rainy. The conditions on board became very bad since the weather made cleaning and drying impossible. Our Japanese sailors wore semi-foreign clothing, but had straw sandals on their feet. There must have been a supply of hundreds of pairs of these sandals on board. In America, by the generosity of our captain, each sailor received a pair of boots, and their appearance was much improved.

Great daring of the Japanese people I am willing to admit my pride in this accomplishment for Japan. The facts are these: It was not until the sixth year of Kaei (1853) that a steamship was seen for the first time; it was only in the second year of Ansei (1855) that we began to study navigation from the Dutch in Nagasaki; by 1860, the science was sufficiently understood to enable us to sail a ship across the Pacific. This means that about seven years after the first sight of a steamship, after only about five years of practice, the Japanese people made a trans-Pacific crossing without help from foreign experts. I think we can without undue pride boast before the world of this courage and skill. As I have shown, the Japanese officers were to receive no aid from Captain Brooke throughout the voyage. Even in taking observations, our officers and the Americans made them independently of each other. Sometimes they compared their results, but we were never in the least dependent on the Americans.

As I consider all the other peoples of the Orient as they exist today, I feel convinced that there is no other nation which has the ability or the courage to navigate a steamship across the Pacific after a period of five years of experience in navigation and engineering. Not only in the Orient would this feat stand as an act of unprecedented skill and daring. Even Peter the Great of Russia, who went to Holland to study navigation, with all his attainments could not have equalled this feat of the Japanese. Without doubt, the famous emperor was a man of genius, but his people did not respond to his leadership in the practice of science as did our Japanese in this great adventure.

American wel-come ; firing a salute As soon as our ship came into the port of San Francisco, we were greeted by many important personages who came on board from all over the country. Along the shores thousands of people were lined up to see the strange newcomers. It had been decided that the Americans on shore should fire a salute. If this were done, our Kanrin-maru would have to respond with a return salute. There is an amusing anecdote in this connection.

Second in command under Captain Kimura was Katsu Rintarō, but Katsu proved a very poor sailor—he did not leave his cabin during the whole voyage across. But now that we were in port, he appeared again to take charge of various operations. When the question of the salute came up, Katsu demurred: "That will be difficult. If we should not fire it off properly, it would bring shame on us. I think it wiser not to attempt it."

To this the First Officer, Sasakura Kiritarō, replied: "Who says we cannot fire our ordnance properly? I myself will take charge of it, if you won't."

"Don't be a fool!" returned Katsu. "You don't know anything about firing a cannon. If you can do it, I'll pledge you my head."

Thus taunted, Sasakura was roused. He swore he would fire off a salute. He ordered the sailors to make ready and load the gun. Then using an hourglass for timing, he brought off a salute beautifully. Sasakura naturally swelled with pride. He declared that the head of the sub-captain was his, but that, as long as the voyage lasted, the head had better remain on the man as it would be needed. It made a big story all over the ship.

Our welcome on shore was certainly worthy of a friendly people. They did everything for us, and they could not have done more. The feeling on their part must have been like that of a teacher receiving his old pupil several years after graduation, for it was their Commodore Perry who had effected the opening of our country seven years before, and now here we were on our first visit to America.

As soon as we came on shore, we found we were to be driven off in carriages to a hotel. While we were resting in the hotel, city officials and various dignitaries came to offer entertainment. We were given quarters in the official residence of the Navy station on Mare Island. Our hosts knew that we Japanese were accustomed to a different diet, so they arranged that our food, instead of being served, should be prepared by our own cook. But the officials being very kind, and desiring to satisfy the Japanese love for seafood, sent fish every day. Also, on learning the Japanese custom of bathing frequently, they had baths prepared daily. Our ship had been damaged by the passing storms, so it was put in dry dock to be repaired—all expressions of American hospitality. This generous treatment in every way brought to mind an old expression of ours—"as if our host had put us on the palm of his hand to see that we lacked nothing."

On our part there were many confusing and embarrassing moments, for we were quite ignorant of the customs of American life. For instance, we were surprised even by the carriages. On seeing a vehicle with horses attached to it, we should easily have guessed what it was. But really we did not identify our mode of conveyance until the door had been opened, we were seated inside, and the horses had started off. Then we realized we were riding in a carriage behind horses.

Precious carpet for floor cover!

All of us wore the usual pair of swords at our sides and the hemp sandals. So attired, we were taken to the modern hotel. There we noticed, covering the interior, the valuable carpets which in Japan only the more wealthy could buy from importers' shops at so much a square inch to make purses and tobacco pouches with. Here the carpet was laid over an entire room—something quite astounding—and upon this costly fabric walked our hosts wearing the shoes with which they had come in from the streets! We followed them in our hemp sandals.

Immediately bottles were brought in. Suddenly an explosion—the popping of champagne. When the glasses were passed around, we noticed strange fragments floating in them—hardly did we expect to find *ice* in the warm spring weather. Some of the party swallowed these floating particles; others expelled them suddenly; others bravely chewed them. This was an adventure—finding out that they were ice.

I wanted to have a smoke, but seeing no "tobacco tray" such as in Japan is placed before the smoker to hold the burning charcoal brazier and the bamboo ash-receiver, I took a light from the open fireplace. Perhaps there was an ash-tray and a box of matches on the table, but I did not recognize them as such. I finished my smoke, but finding no ash receiver, I took out some of the tissue paper which we carry in place of handkerchiefs, and wrapping the ashes in it, crushed them very carefully, and placed the ball in my sleeve. After a while I took out the paper to have another smoke; some wisps of smoke were trickling from my sleeve. The light that I thought I had crushed out was quietly setting me afire!

After all these embarrassing incidents, I thought I could well sympathize with the Japanese bride. Her new family welcome her and do everything to make her comfortable.

I have become a "blushing bride" One laughs with her; another engages her in conversation—all happy with the new addition to the family. In the midst of all this the bride has to sit trying to look pleasant, but in her efforts she goes on making mistakes and blushes every time.

Before leaving Japan, I, the independent soul—a care-free student who could look the world in the face—had feared nothing. But on arriving in America, I was turned suddenly into a shy, selfconscious, blushing "bride." The contrast was indeed funny, even to myself.

One evening our host said that some ladies and gentlemen were having a dancing party and that they would be glad to have us attend it. We went. To our dismay we could not make out what they were doing. The ladies and gentlemen seemed to be hopping about the room together. As funny as it was, we knew it would be rude to laugh, and we controlled our expressions with difficulty as the dancing went on. These were but a few of the instances of our bewilderment at the strange customs of American society.

Women are high, men are humble A certain Dutch physician was living then in a place called Vallejo near Mare Island. Since he knew that Holland had maintained the earliest and longest association with Japan, the doctor wished to show some courtesy towards the captain and officers of our ship. The home of the Dutch doctor was a fine dwelling showing his success in that region, but the strange behavior of the household puzzled us. While the mistress of the house stayed constantly in the drawing-room entertaining the guests, the doctor, the supposed master, was moving in and out of the room, directing the servants. This was the reverse of the domestic custom in our country. How strange, we thought. Then, when the dinner was served, came a real shock. On a dish was brought in a whole pig, roasted—head, legs, tail and all. We at once thought of the fabled land of Adachiga Hara where lived a cruel witch who indulged in gruesome feasts. Still, it tasted very good.

When we were taking leave, our host and hostess kindly offered us horses to ride home on. This pleased us, for a chance to ride horseback again was a relief. Especially did Captain Kimura enjoy this, for he was an accomplished horseman who used to ride every day in Yedo. We touched whip to the horses and rode back to our quarters at a trot. The Americans watched us and exclaimed at the Japanese ability in riding. So neither of us really knew much about the other after all.

Their explanations miss the point Our hosts in San Francisco were very considerate in showing us examples of modern industry. There was as yet no railway laid to the city, nor was there any electric light in use. But the telegraph system and also Galvani's electroplating were already in use. Then we were taken to a sugar refinery and had the principle of the operation explained to us quite minutely. I am sure that our hosts thought they were showing us something entirely new, naturally looking for our surprise at each new device of modern engineering. But on the contrary, there was really nothing new, at least to me. I knew the principle of the telegraphy even if I had not seen the actual machine before; I knew that sugar was bleached by straining the solution with bone-black, and that in boiling down the solution, the vacuum was used to better effect than heat. I had been studying nothing else but such scientific principles ever since I had entered Ogata's school.

Rather, I was surprised by entirely different things in American life. First of all, there seemed to be an enormous waste of iron everywhere. In garbage piles, on the seashores—everywhere—I found lying old oil tins, empty cans, and broken tools. This was remarkable to us, for in Yedo, after a fire, there would appear a swarm of people looking for nails in the ashes.

Then too, I was surprised at the high cost of daily commodities in California. We had to pay a half-dollar for a bottle of oysters, and there were only twenty or thirty in the bottle at that. In Japan the price of so many would be only a cent or two.

Where are the descendants of George Washington? Things social, political, and economic proved most inexplicable. One day, on a sudden thought, I asked a gentleman where the descendants of George Washington might be. He replied, "I think there is a woman who is directly descended from Washington. I don't know where she is now, but I think I have heard she is married." His answer was so very casual that it shocked me.

Of course, I knew that America was a republic with a new president every four years, but I could not help feeling that the family of Washington would be revered above all other families. My reasoning was based on the reverence in Japan for the founders of the great lines of rulers—like that for Ieyasu of the Tokugawa family of Shōguns, really deified in the popular mind. So I remember the astonishment I felt at receiving this indifferent answer about the Washington family. As for scientific inventions and industrial machinery, there was no great novelty in them for me. It was rather in matters of life and social custom and ways of thinking that I found myself at a loss in America.

A certain officer at the naval base on Mare Island, a Captain McDougall, was a collector of coins, and he one day requested our commanding officer to show him some Japanese coins. Captain Kimura must have been anticipating just such a request, for he had a number of both new and old coins arranged in sequence.   These he sent to Captain McDougall.   In expressing their gratitude, both the officer and his wife were emphatic over their uniqueness, but they showed no sign of having received a gift that had monetary value.   The next morning the wife of the officer brought some flowers to Captain Kimura, thanking him again for the uncommon gift she had received the day before.   As I received the lady and carried her message to my commandant, I was much moved by her act which had a touch of nobility.   I wished that everyone could be like this American lady who thanked one for the gift of gold and silver with a bouquet of flowers.

No charge for the repair of the ship I have already described the generosity of our hosts and the people in San Francisco.   Not only did they repair the damaged parts of our vessel, but they were thoughtful enough to build lockers in convenient places on board for the use of the crew. When the ship was ready and we were preparing to sail on the homeward voyage, we inquired how much we should have to pay for the repair of our ship and other expenses. We were met with a kindly smile.   And we were obliged to sail away with our obligations unpaid.[7]

The first Webster's Dictionary in Japan Before we sailed, the interpreter, Nakahama, and I each bought a copy of Webster's dictionary.[8]   This, I know, was the very first importation of Webster's into Japan.   Once I had secured this valuable work, I felt no disappointment on leaving the new world and returning home again.

Eight years afterwards, being in America again, I had a

---

[7] Note on p. 351. [8] Ibid.

chance to meet our former companion, Captain Brooke. He then confided to me an incident of our first arrival in San Francisco. It seems there was some debate on the nature of our reception among the civil and military officials. Captain Brooke wanted to have the welcome made a gay festive event. So he went to the headquarters of the army and tried to arrange a military escort. But the officers replied that they could not do anything of that kind until they obtained permission from Washington. Captain Brooke argued that it was up to the San Francisco headquarters to act on this occasion, as no official permission could be got from Washington in time. But the army officers could not be persuaded to act.

The San Fran- Captain Brooke, indignant, declared
cisco Militia that he knew what to do if the army would not comply, and went to the city militia. This militia was composed of volunteers, their commander being a doctor and his lieutenant the proprietor of a dyeing business. But they were well equipped with uniforms and rifles with which they drilled on holidays and on moonlight nights. Having no wars, they had but few occasions to appear in public with their full regalia. Captain Brooke told me as a joke how much the welcoming of Japan's warship meant for the young militiamen of San Francisco.

To the solemn explosion of a naval salute, we sailed out of San Francisco on our return voyage, during which we made a call at the Hawaiian Islands. This time our commandant enlisted a few American sailors among the crew, but Captain Brooke was not with us; we sailed entirely under the direction of the Japanese navigators and successfully sought out the small Hawaiian Islands. We lay in port there for several days and took in a supply of coal; then again we hoisted sail for the home land.

I do not believe there is much that I
A visit in Hawaii   should tell about the people of Hawaii,
for I do not think they have changed
much since my visit thirty years ago.   The natives were
pretty miserable and I must say, on first sight, they seemed
to be what we would call "barbarians."   We met the king,
as he was then.   This may sound rather pretentious, but
actually when they came out to meet us—the king and the
queen—we saw only a native couple, the only sign of royalty
being that the monarch wore a European wool suit.   Their
residence was not different from any ordinary European
house seen in Japan.   They showed us their native treasure,
but it turned out to be a rug made of innumerable feathers
of birds.   There was in their dwelling a man said to be the
king's brother.   We saw this prince going out to market
with a basket on his arm.   So the king of Hawaii seemed to
me more or less the headman of a village of fishermen.

It was as we sailed away from Hawaii
I have my picture   that I caused a little stir among the
taken with an   young men of our crew.   As I have
American girl   heretofore admitted, I am naturally free
from amorous ties, nor would I allow
myself to join in gossip on such affairs.   So some of the men
of our ship regarded me as a rather strange kind of human.
But on the day we sailed from Hawaii, I produced a photograph and showed it to my companions on board.   Here it
is!   (And the narrator here exhibited to the shorthand
writer a photograph of himself of forty years ago with a girl
fifteen or sixteen years of age standing by him.)   What do
you think of it?

Now, none of the men could tell just what the girl really
might have been—whether a daughter of a respectable
family or a girl of the streets or a professional entertainer.
"You all talk a lot about your affairs," I said, chiding the

surprised seamen. "But how many of you have brought back a picture of yourselves with a young lady as a souvenir of San Francisco? Without any evidence, what good is it to boast of your affairs now?"

The girl was really the daughter of the photographer; she was fifteen, as I remember hearing. On the day I went to the photographer's, where on a previous day we had been for some pictures, it was raining, and I went all alone. As I was going to sit, I saw the girl in the studio. I said suddenly, "Let us have our picture taken together." She immediately said, "All right," being an American girl and thinking nothing of it. So she came and stood by me.

You may be sure the young officers of the Kanrin-maru were taken aback. Some of them showed extreme envy, but all too late. I knew that if I had showed my photograph in San Francisco, many would have followed my trick, so I kept it unseen until our boat had left Hawaii and there was absolutely no more chance, before I produced it. It was the joke of the day on board.

On our southern route homeward, the sea was very calm. We arrived at Uraga on the morning of the fifth of May. Japan was still using the Lunar calendar which adds an extra month to every leap year, so we were actually away fully six months, although according to our calendar we left in January and returned in May.

As it was the rule that every ship coming in must anchor first at Uraga, we disembarked there for the first call on our own shores. We had gone without bathing for many days since the water supply had again run so low that it was rationed off for the merest mouth wash. We were quite disheveled and unkempt. We rowed ashore with the eager anticipation of shaving our foreheads and of bathing to our hearts' content. The official welcoming party for Captain Kimura had been waiting there in Uraga for nearly a month.

Fukuzawa with an American girl in San Francisco (1860).

Fukuzawa in St. Petersburg, Russia (1862).

As I first set foot on land again, the first person I met was
Shima Yasutarō, a steward of Kimura's household. During
our absence, no news from home—not
The assassina- even a rumor of any happening at home
tion of Lord Ii —had reached us, for there was then no
mail service nor even the passage of a
ship between Japan and America. The actual six months had
seemed six years to us. On meeting Shima as I came ashore,
I besought him: "How are you after our long separation?
And has anything happened at home while we were away?"

"Anything! Indeed! Something outrageous has happened!" he exclaimed, and the smile of welcome disappeared
from his face.

"Wait, don't tell me," I said. "I'll guess it. It must be
something like an attack on our chancellor. Was it that
the *rōnin* of Mito[9] made a raid on our chancellor's residence?"

Shima showed extraordinary astonishment. "How did
you know it? Who could have told you?"

"I should have known it all along," I returned, "whether
I heard it or not. By the art of fortune-telling, I guessed
the world was moving towards that end."

"You do surprise me more and more," my informant came
back. "It wasn't just a raid on the residence. . . ." And
he told me then what had taken place on March the third at
Sakurada-mon, where the Chancellor to the Shōgun, Ii
Kamon-no Kami, had been assassinated.

I had realized long before we sailed on the American
voyage that there were signs of some disturbance. I proved
to be right in my estimation, and Shima's great surprise
amused me very much.

For a year now, previous to this time, the slogan gradually

---
[9] Note on p. 351.

had been gaining currency: "Expel the foreigners!" The cry was raised and the public of Japan became conscious and perturbed. A little incident of our visit in America may indicate the tide of opinion. In San Francisco Captain Kimura bought an umbrella as a curiosity—we called it *kōmori-gasa* (bat-umbrella) because of its shape and to distinguish it from the Japanese umbrella. The officers of the ship had gathered around to look at it, and were discussing what might be the result, should the captain carry this strange object out in the streets of Yedo back in Japan.

"There is no doubt about it," said one of them. "He would be cut down by a *rōnin* before the captain could reach Nihombashi from his home in Shinsenza." So we generally decided that the only thing the captain could do with his new possession was to open it and look at it in his home. Such were the times. Any person who showed, by any will or deed, any favor towards admitting foreigners into Japan —indeed, any person who had any interest in foreign affairs —was liable to be set upon by the unrelenting *rōnin*.

In spite of this and the general public dislike of all foreign studies, however, students in my school gradually increased after my return from America. During my stay in San Francisco, I had come in contact with foreigners, had heard their language, and made a special effort to improve my knowledge of English. After my return, I tried to read English books as much as I could and, for the benefit of the students, I taught them all English instead of Dutch. But as yet my knowledge was not sufficient; I still had to have much recourse to my English-Dutch dictionary. Though I called myself a teacher, I was still a student along with those I was instructing.

A little later I was taken on by the government to become a translator of messages from foreign legations. There were still none among the Japanese who could read or write

English or French; so it was customary
I am hired by the   for all the foreign legations to add a
Shōgun's govern-   Dutch translation to each formal mes-
ment   sage addressed to the Japanese government. Yet there was no one among the
immediate retainers of the Shōgun who could understand
Dutch. Therefore they were obliged to employ members
of different clans, like myself, to interpret the foreign messages.

The chief advantage in my holding the position under the
Shogunate government was that I had the opportunity to
practise English. Whenever a message was received from
the American or British legation, I would attempt to read
the original text. Ir it happened to be difficult, I would look
up the Dutch version to make my translation. This was
excellent practice. There were also some books in the
offices that I was privileged to take home. So my connection with the central government brought with it a very
fortunate advantage for my studies.

VII

I GO TO EUROPE

Soon after my return from America, in the first year of the Manen era (1860), I brought out my first publication, an English-Japanese dictionary which I called "Kaei Tsūgo,"[1] and which made a beginning for my series of later books. For the next two or three years, I was more occupied with my struggles in studying English than in teaching. Then, in the second year of Bunkyū (1862), a happy opportunity came my way, and I was able to make a visit to Europe with the envoys sent by our government.[2]

Before the American visit, I had asked the captain of the ship to take me as his personal servant, but for this embassy to Europe I was ordered by the government to go as an official translator. I received an allowance of some four hundred *ryō*,[3] and as our expenses on the tour were to be borne entirely by the ministry, this income was entirely for my own use. And so, being a man who did not need much money, I thought of using some of it elsewhere.

I took one hundred *ryō* of the amount and sent it to my mother back in our native town. I had really been trying to my mother, causing her much anxiety, as I had not been to see her since my return from America. And here I was about to set out again, this time for Europe. Moreover,

---

[1] Note on p. 352. [2] Ibid. [3] Ibid.

while I was away in America, the officious people of Nakatsu had been giving vent to rumors about me. One had coolly reported that I was dead in the foreign country. Another, a relative at that, had come to my mother and gossiped: "I am so sorry to tell you what I have heard. Your son, Yukichi, has died in America. They brought his body, preserved in brine, back to Yedo."

It is hard to tell whether these interfering neighbors were merely tormenting my mother or simply making a fool of her for their own enjoyment. In the full swing of the anti-foreign sentiment, there was nothing we could do but to keep quiet. I was really very sorry for my mother. Sending her some money would not make up for my long absences; but still, a hundred *ryō* was an enormous sum of money for both of us, never seen in all our previous lives. So I sent it to her with the best intentions.

We sailed in December, still the first year of Bunkyū (1861), on an English war vessel, the Odin, sent over for the purpose of conveying our envoy. We called at Hongkong, Singapore and other ports in the Indian Ocean. Then through the Red Sea to Suez where we landed for the railway journey to Cairo in Egypt. After about two days there, we went by boat again across the Mediterranean to Marseilles. From there we continued by the French railways to Paris, stopping a day at Lyons on our way. We were in Paris for about twenty days while our envoys completed negotiations between France and Japan. Next we crossed to England; then to Holland; from Holland to Berlin, the Prussian capital, and then to St. Petersburg in Russia. The return journey was made through France and Portugal, then retracing our course through the Mediterranean and the Indian Ocean, at length we reached Japan after nearly a year of traveling. It was almost the end of the second year of Bunkyū (1862) when we returned.

On this tour I was at last somewhat able to use English, both in speaking and reading. I also had the convenience of some money at my disposal. As there were few ways of spending any money beyond the needs of my traveling clothes, which cost very little at a time when such things were cheap, I used the balance of my allowance to buy books in London. This was the beginning of the importation of English books into Japan; it is only since my first large purchase in London that our students have had free access to English in print.[4]

There were about forty men in the party. They were: Takenouchi Shimotsuke-no Kami, Chief Envoy; Matsudaira Iwami-no Kami, Second Envoy; Kyōgoku Noto-no Kami, *Ometsuke* and Third Envoy; Shibata Teitarō, *Kumigashira*; Hitaka Keizaburō, *Okanjō*; Fukuda Sakutarō, *Okachi Metsuke*; Mizushina Rakutarō, *Shirabe-yaku*; Okazaki Tōzaemon, *Shirabe-yaku*; Takashima Yūkei, Physician (Chinese Medicine); Kawasaki Dōmin, Physician; Mashizu Shunjirō, *Gofushin-yaku*; Ueda Tomosuke, *Jōyaku Motojime*; Mori Hachitarō, *Jōyaku*; Fukuchi Genichirō, Interpreter; Tachi Hirosaku, Interpreter; Ōta Genzaburō, Interpreter; Saitō Dainoshin, *Dōshin*; Takamatsu Hikosaburō, *Okobito Metsuke*; Yamada Hachirō, *Okobito Metsuke*; Matsuki Kōan, Translator; Mitsukuri Shūhei, Translator; Fukuzawa Yukichi, Translator. Also, there were two or three personal attendants for each of the three envoys and six or seven cooks and men of general work. Among these men of general utility there were several respectable samurai from various clans who had privately requested to be taken along as servants. The translators, Matsuki, Mitsukuri and myself, were rated as officials, but being members of outside feudal clans, we were the lowest in that rank. We all wore

---

⁴ Note on p. 352.

our Japanese dress with a pair of swords in our girdles, and appeared on the streets of London and Paris in such attire. A sight indeed it must have been!

All the baggage for the journey Before our departure, the organizers of the embassy had decided that we should carry along all the necessary food, because agreeable food would not be available in foreign lands. So hundreds of cases of polished rice were put in our baggage. Likewise, for our use in the hotels, they had provided dozens of very large lamps (a frame-work, two feet square, for an oil-burning wick with paper sides and wire coverings). Then they ordered smaller lamps, portable lanterns, candles—all the necessities of travel customary in our native country. Indeed, our traveling accessories were planned on the basis of what a feudal lord would carry on his yearly journey along the highways of Japan to the capital.

When we reached Paris and had been formally received by the welcoming French officials, the first request we had to make was that as many of our party as possible be quartered near the chief envoy's hotel because of our number and the amount of our baggage. The heads of the mission were evidently anxious, because if different members of the party were scattered in remote hotels, it might be inconvenient and unsafe in the strange land. The host of the welcoming committee nodded his approval and asked the number of our party. When he was told it was forty, he replied, "If you are only forty, why, one of our hotels could accommodate ten or twenty of such parties." We did not comprehend what he meant, but on reaching the hotel assigned to us, we found that he was not jesting.

Our headquarters were the Hotel du Louvre, opposite the entrance to the imperial palace. It was really a huge edifice of five stories with six hundred rooms and over five hundred employees. More than a thousand guests could be accommodated at one time. So the large party of our Japanese envoys was lost in it. Instead of our anxiety lest the party might have to be separated in distant hostelries, our real anxiety became the possibility of losing our way in the maze of halls and corridors in the one hotel.

No stove or steam radiators were necessary in our rooms, for heated air circulated through them. Numerous gaslights served to illuminate the rooms and halls so that we could not tell the coming of darkness outside. In the dining hall there was such a spread of food, delicacies of "both the woods and the sea," that even those who professed their dislike of "foreign objects" could not maintain this aversion in the choice of food. The joke was in the stock of Japanese supplies brought along in our baggage. We could not cook our rice in the kitchen of the hotel; nor was it possible within reason to use the oil-wick lamps in the halls. Finally, disgusted with all these useless impedimenta, we piled them up in an apartment and offered the entire store of rice, oil-lamps and all to one of the lesser members of the welcoming committee, M. Lambert (?), and asked him to take it gratis.

As we were unfamiliar with Western life and customs, there was naturally no end of farcical situations occurring among our party. A servant brought *sugar* when ordered to go for *cigars*. Our doctor of Chinese medicine had intended to buy some powdered carrot, but instead he had come away with *ginger*, as he found later.

When one of the lord-envoys had occasion to use the toilet, he was followed to the doorway by one of his personal attendants carrying a lighted paper lantern. The attendant in his most formal dress was to be seen squatting patiently outside the open door, holding his master's removed sword. This happened to be in the bustling corridor of the hotel where people were passing constantly, and the gas was burning as bright as day. But unperturbed sat the faithful guardian. I happened to come along and see the incident which I ended by shutting the doors. Then turning to the man, I told him quietly of the etiquette of Europeans on such occasions, but my heart was fluttering with consternation.

The people and the politics of Europe Of political situations of that time, I tried to learn as much as I could from various persons that I met in London and Paris, though it was often difficult to understand things clearly as I was yet so unfamiliar with the history of Europe. However, I find now, as I look in my diary, the mention of Napoleon III as a very powerful figure, said to be the greatest statesman of all Europe at that time. Then I find mention of a great growing power—Prussia—with her influence spreading like a rising sun. The wars with Austria and the problem of Alsace-Lorraine were constantly discussed, and I remember they were made the subject of prophecy by many men.

While we were in London, a certain member of the Parliament sent us a copy of a bill which he said he had proposed in the House under the name of the party to which he belonged. The bill was a protest against the arrogant attitude of the British minister to Japan, Alcock,[5] who had at times acted as if Japan were a country conquered by military force. One of the instances mentioned in the bill was that of Alcock's riding his horse into the sacred temple grounds of Shiba, an unpardonable insult to the Japanese.

On reading the copy of this bill, I felt as if a load had been lifted from my chest. After all, the foreigners were not all

[5] Note on p. 352.

"devils." I had felt that Japan was enduring some pointed affronts on the part of the foreign ministers who presumed on the ignorance of our government. But now that I had actually come to the minister's native land, I found that there were among them some truly impartial and warm-hearted human beings. After this I grew even more determined in my doctrine of free intercourse with the rest of the world.

The country in Europe which gave us the kindest welcome was Holland. This was a natural outcome of the very special relationship which Japan had enjoyed with Holland for the last three hundred years. Moreover, all the members of the mission who knew any foreign language at all had studied Dutch before any other language. So it made Holland, so far as the use of language **Are people free** was concerned, seem like our second **to sell or buy** homeland. There was, I recall, an **land?** episode which was rather significant. One day in Amsterdam, during a conversation with some merchants and other gentlemen, our envoy chanced to ask the question: "Is the sale and purchase of land in Amsterdam freely permitted?"

The reply was "Certainly it is free."

"Do you sell land to foreigners also?"

"Yes, as long as a foreigner is willing to pay for the land, we would sell any amount of it to any person."

"Then, suppose a foreigner were to put down a large sum of money to purchase a great tract of land in order to build a fortress, would you allow that too?"

The Hollanders looked puzzled at this, and replied, "We never had occasion to think of such a case. Even though there are many rich men in England and France and other countries, we do not believe any merchant would spend money on such a venture."

Neither side understood the other. We interpreters were much amused by this conversation. It is not to be wondered at that Japan was going through a hard struggle when the control and handling of foreign affairs was in the hands of men who exhibited such reasoning in their contact with the West.

All the wonders to see; and the restrictions again In America, on my previous journey, I saw no railway, for there was none as yet constructed in California. But on this expedition I was to ride frequently in trains—first across Suez, and later throughout Europe. Then I was given opportunities to visit the headquarters and buildings of the naval and military posts, factories, both governmental and private, banks, business offices, religious edifices, educational institutions, club houses, hospitals—including even the actual performances of surgical operations. We were often invited to dinners in the homes of important personages, and to dancing parties; we were treated to a continual hospitality until at times we returned exhausted to our lodgings.

One ridiculous idea held by our embassy was that its members should not meet the foreigners or see the country any more than they had to. We were under the seclusion theory even while we were traveling in foreign territory. Among the three envoys, Kyōgoku had the office of *ometsuke* (eye fixer), or conduct officer of the party. He had many retainers with him, and consequently during our entire journey we were under the constant eye of the chief or of a lesser "eye." This particularly applied to us three translators.

While most of the party were feudal retainers of the central government, we three translators belonged to different clans; moreover, we three could read the "strange language written sideways," and we were eager to see and learn everything foreign that we could. These facts were all causes of concern to the high officials.

Every time we wished to go out, one of the *ometsuke* went curiously along. We were not out to smuggle, nor could we possibly impart any national secret. So the "eye fixer" following us was simply a nuisance. But we could put up with this nuisance; the greater inconvenience was that when all the *ometsuke* were occupied elsewhere, we could not go out at all.

I once remarked for the merriment of us three that this practice was like carrying the policy of seclusion all around Europe on the very tour of friendship. In spite of all these restrictions, however, we were able to see or hear pretty much everything that we wished.

I faint at the sight of blood Here, by the way, I have to admit a weakness of mine. I have always been lively and rather inclined to boasting. But the truth is I am of a timid nature when it comes to putting a living thing to death or seeing any kind of injury. While I was a student in Ogata's school, the letting of blood was a common method in treating illnesses. But whenever I had to undergo or be near that operation, I would close my eyes for fear of seeing the blood flow. I would grow pale at the sight of a minor injury; even when I had an infection, I would hesitate to lance it. At the report of an accident on the street I always ran the other way.

So, while we were in Russia, this faint-hearted human was to be taken to see a major surgical operation. My friends, Mitsukuri and Matsuki, were eager to go, because they were both physicians by profession. They induced me to go along.

In the operating room of the hospital, the surgeon in a kind of raincoat was giving the patient chloroform on a table, which looked to me like a carving board. Then he took a shining knife and pierced the side of the patient. A tremendous burst of blood shot out on the raincoat of the surgeon. The operation was for a "stone." I kept on looking until he inserted an instrument like a pair of pliers in the wound to lift out the stone. Then I grew faint. One of my companions, Yamada Hachirō, helped me out of the room and gave me water which brought me around.

Some time before this incident, I had attended an operation in Berlin on the cast eye of a child. I saw half of that operation and escaped from the room before I grew faint. Matsuki and Mitsukuri said I was a coward and laughed at me often, but it was my nature. I shall probably die without overcoming my weakness.

My efforts at understanding commonplace things

During this mission in Europe I tried to learn some of the most commonplace details of foreign culture. I did not care to study scientific or technical subjects while on the journey, because I could study them as well from books after I had returned home. But I felt that I had to learn the more common matters of daily life directly from the people, because the Europeans would not describe them in books as being too obvious. Yet to us those common matters were the most difficult to comprehend.

So, whenever I met a person whom I thought to be of some consequence, I would ask him questions and would put down all he said in a notebook—like this. (Here, the narrator exhibited an old oblong notebook.) After reaching home, I based my ideas on these random notes, doing the necessary research in the books which I had brought back, and thus had the material for my book, Seiyō Jijō (Things Western).[6]

---

[6] Note on p. 352.

All the information dealing with the sciences, engineering, electricity, steam, printing, or the processes of industry and manufacture, contained in my book, I did not really have to acquire in Europe.   I was not a specialist in any of those technical fields, and even if I had inquired particularly into them, I could have got only a general idea which could more readily be obtained in text books.   So in Europe I gave my chief attention to other more immediately interesting things.

For instance, when I saw a hospital, I wanted to know how it was run—who paid the running expenses; when I visited a bank, I wished to learn how the money was deposited and paid out.   By similar first-hand queries, I learned something of the postal system and the military conscription then in force in France but not in England.   A perplexing institution was representative government.

When I asked a gentleman what the "election law" was and what kind of a bureau the Parliament really was, he simply replied with a smile, meaning I suppose that no intelligent person was expected to ask such a question.   But these were the things most difficult of all for me to understand.   In this connection, I learned that there were bands of men called political parties—the Liberals and the Conservatives—who were always fighting against each other in the government.

For some time it was beyond my comprehension to understand what they were fighting for, and what was meant, anyway, by "fighting" in peace time.   "This man and that man are enemies in the House," they would tell me.   But these "enemies" were to be seen at the same table, eating and drinking with each other.   I felt as if I could not make much out of this.   It took me a long time, with some tedious thinking, before I could gather a general notion of these separate mysterious facts.   In some of the more complicated matters, I might achieve an understanding five or ten days after they were explained to me. But all in all, I learned much from this initial tour of Europe.

Negotiations for the Saghalien border line Since some time before we had started on our tour, the anti-foreign movement in Japan had been growing worse, and more and more blunders were being made in our foreign diplomacy. In Russia our envoys attempted to settle the dispute over the border line in Saghalien. I was present at the actual discussion of the dispute, so I know how they ridiculed our protests.

Our envoys thoughtfully spread out their map and pointed out that, according to the diagram in which Japanese territory was printed blue and Russian territory red, the border line would be such-and-such; therefore, Japan would naturally claim all the land within that line. The Russians, thereupon, retorted that if the colors on the map were to decide the extent of national territory, they could easily claim the whole world by painting the entire map *red*; also that Japan could claim she possessed the whole world by painting the map *blue*. This raillery made it impossible for the Japanese envoys to conclude any argument. Finally they were obliged to resign their efforts and suggest that a decision might be postponed until the land had been actually surveyed.[7]

I felt thoroughly discouraged after sitting through this negotiation. What hope for the future of Japan as long as our people showed this foolish pride, keeping aloof from the actual give-and-take of the rest of the world? The more this movement of Expel-the-Foreigners increased, the more would we lose our national power, to say nothing of prestige.

---

[7] Note on p. 353.

I was mortified when I thought over the possible outcome of national exclusiveness.

Cordial hospi-
tality of the
Russians

But if state negotiations ended in disappointments, the entertainment of the envoys and ourselves did not so end. During our visit in St. Petersburg, we were offered the entire use of an official residence. There were four or five on the committee of entertainment who spent all their time in our behalf. They did everything possible for the enjoyment of the embassy. When official duties were disposed of, the committee would conduct us to places of historical interest and natural beauty, and also to factories and places of commercial interest. By and by we became well acquainted with the committeemen, and we had many opportunities of talking with them on very friendly terms.

I had heard the rumor that there was a Japanese in the service of the Russian government. His name was said to be Yamatoff,[8] and they said he was undoubtedly a Japanese. This rumor spread, not through the official committee, of course, but through other sources until it was really an open secret. I was anxious to meet this man, but never had the opportunity. However, I am sure that this was not a groundless rumor. There were unmistakable touches of Japanese in the accommodations of our lodging.

In our rooms there were sword racks such as we used at home; on the beds were pillows with wooden bases; in the bathrooms we found bags of rice bran; even our food was cooked somewhat in our style; and the rice bowls and chopsticks were entirely too Japanese to have been thought of by the Russians. There was no doubt at all in my mind that a fellow-Japanese had attended us somehow. But we

[8] Note on p. 353.

came away without finding out who he was. In my old
diary I find this little verse in Chinese style apropos of this
mysterious person:

> Upon rising I come to the table, eat my fill, and fall asleep
> again.
> So, eating and sleeping, I spend the year that comes and
> goes away.
> If ever I should meet a man you know, I will tell him,
> 'The sky of Europe and the sky of Japan are not at all
> unlike.'

I am urged to stay in Russia One day it happened that I had a
conversation in private with a member
of the reception committee. He drew
me alone into a separate room and
began to talk of my personal affairs.

"I do not know anything about your own future plans,"
he went on—"what you may intend to do on returning to
Japan. But are you a very wealthy person?"

"No," I replied, "I am not at all wealthy, but I have no
present difficulty in living. I am in the government service
which yields a certain compensation."

"Well," the inquisitive friend continued. "I do not know
much about Japan. Possibly I am not qualified to speak.
But from general reasoning I feel that Japan is not a country
for an ambitious youth. It is a small country—little opportunity for doing big things. What would you say to settling
yourself in Russia?"

I replied honestly as I felt, "I am in the service of the
embassy. I cannot withdraw and stay here as you suggest."

"Oh, yes, you can—easily," answered the Russian. "If
you make up your mind to do so, you can. I will hide you
somewhere, and the Japanese would not be able to find you.
The envoys are leaving here soon. As soon as they are

gone, your service with them is at an end. Besides, there are many foreigners in Russia—many Germans and Dutch and English. It wouldn't be at all strange to find a Japanese among them. I could strongly recommend your staying, for there are all sorts of occupations here. Your living is assured; there is the chance of making money, even of becoming rich."

This was spoken in all seriousness in the quiet of a private room. There was no sign of any pretense or playfulness. But since I really felt no necessity, nor curiosity, to seek a career in Russia, I gave an indifferent answer. Then again, two or three times, I was requested to consider the offer. Of course I never considered it and came away.

This incident made its impression on me. I had heard that Russia was different from all the other countries of Europe. Now I understood it. For during my visits in England and France, and also in America the year before, nearly all the people I talked with were eager to come to Japan. In fact, I was often bored by having people ask me about jobs in Japan; some had even wanted me to take them along. But I had not met anyone in those lands who advised me to stay in his country. I could guess from the committeeman's eagerness that it was more than a mere personal idea. Probably it was a political or diplomatic scheme; it might even have been an underhanded venture.

I could not tell this incident to any of my colleagues. For any suggestion of private communication would place suspicion on myself. So I kept it secret even after I returned to Japan. Indeed, it is not improbable that other members of our party had had the same experience and, likewise fearing suspicion, had also kept silent. At any rate, I decided that Russia was a country in which we could not safely unburden our minds.

We returned to France and were about to sail for Portugal

when news of the "Namamugi affair"
An Englishman reached us. (An Englishman named
is killed and Richardson was killed in Namamugi
French hospital- near Yedo by members of the Satsuma
ity cools clan as he rode his horse across the path
of the Satsuma Daimyō's train.) Sud-
denly the entire attitude of Napoleon's government changed.
I do not know what may have been the general opinion of
the people over the affair, but the official attitude was
decidedly cool. When the host assumed that attitude, we,
the guests, felt a peculiar embarrassment which was unpleasant at the least.[9]

As we were about to take the boat, we found a guard of
honor lined all along the road for a distance of almost a mile.
This, we felt certain, was not purely a salute of farewell; it
was a demonstration of the French military power as well.
Naturally we did not expect to be fired at, and there was
nothing to be afraid of, but this insinuation was really too
much to bear. I find the notes in my diary make this mention of the incident:

"Leap-August[10] 13, Bunkyū 2. At 8 o'clock in the morning,
we reached Rochefort, a French naval port, ninety French
*ri** from Paris. An army of soldiers, over one thousand
strong, placed in gorgeous array on both sides of the road,
from the place where we left the steam train down to the
harbor—a distance of about ten *chō*.[11] This, in appearance,
was like paying a salute, but in reality it was showing their
power. We were on the train all night before and could
not sleep well. In spite of fatigue, we were not allowed a
moment's rest and were put on the ship at once. Moreover,
we were not provided with carriages, but obliged to walk
the entire ten *chō* to reach the vessel."

---

* 90 kilometers.
[9] Note on p. 353.   [10] p. 354.   [11] Ibid.

We drew into Lisbon in Portugal where the envoys had some mission to complete. Then we entered the Mediterranean, then the Indian Ocean, and finally we returned safely to our native shores.

VIII

I RETURN TO ANTI-FOREIGN JAPAN

Back in Japan once more, I found the country at the height of the anti-foreign movement. Ii Kamon-no Kami had been assassinated during my journey to America. This time there was an attempt on the life of Andō Tsushima-no Kami by the relentless *rōnin*, though fortunately he escaped with a minor injury. One of these *rōnin* was said to have escaped into the residence of the Lord of Chōshu. When I heard this, I knew that Chōshu had joined the movement. All Japan was now hopelessly swept by the anti-Western feeling and nothing could stop its force from rushing to the ultimate consequence.[1]

Anti-foreign violence extends to us scholars
Until now this anti-foreign movement had only been something existing in society, separate from my personal life. When I was a student in Ōsaka, of course, there was no possibility of personal harm whatever opinion I held. Even after I came to Yedo, I had never thought of having a public enemy, or felt any fear of assassination. But now, since our return from Europe, the situation had changed. The *rōnin* were appearing in the most unexpected places; even some of the merchants engaged in foreign trade suddenly closed up

---

[1] Note on p. 354.

their shops for fear of these lawless warriors. The *rōnin* were behaving then like the present *sōshi*, our political ruffians, and there was no telling what they might do.

The reason the *rōnin* included us in their attack was that they thought we scholars who read foreign books and taught foreign culture were liars misleading the people and opening the way for the Westerners to exploit Japan. So we also became their prey. This was certainly a nice situation. I thought that if I avoided all dramatic utterances and behaved very cautiously, I should escape the ire of the *rōnin*. But that was not to be. If I had given up all study of foreign books and come out advocating an anti-foreign movement, I would surely have earned their praise as a patriot. But I did not want to be a patriot in their sense.

Whenever I seemed to grow a little bolder and to make something of a venture in my own field, then the *rōnin* would seem stronger and more active. One of my colleagues in the government service, Tezuka Ritsuzō, had a really narrow escape. Once when he was visiting the headquarters of the Chōshū clan, he had made some mention of foreign affairs. At that, the young men in service on the estate, taking him to be an outspoken advocate of free intercourse, suddenly fell upon him. Tezuka ran for his life followed by the young men with drawn swords. Unable to outrun them, he saved himself by leaping into the moat near Hibiya, though it was a cold season for swimming.

Another interpreter, Tōjō Reizō, himself a member of the Chōshū clan, actually was taken by surprise—his house broken into by the ruffians. He barely escaped by the rear door. Thus all students and interpreters of Western languages continually risked their lives.

Yet I could not think of giving up my major interest nor my chosen studies. I decided that it would be useless to worry over the predicament. The only thing left was to be moderate in speech and manner, and not to discuss social or political problems too openly, or with anyone I did not know well. So having resolved on this, I lived as discreetly as possible, and spent my time in translating and writing. In this connection, I shall not tell much at this time, for I have given a full account in the introduction to my collected works, Fukuzawa Zenshū,[2] published this year.

Strangely enough, in this age of Expel-the-Foreigners, the number of students in foreign culture seemed to be growing. So I gave my energy to the increased demands of my little school. My maintenance was amply provided for by the salary from the government for my service in translating.

Thus, half in fear, half in the joy of work, I spent my days, months, and years. Once I drew a panicky breath. It is a funny story. I was living in Shinsenza[3] when one day my maid announced that a samurai-gentleman was at the entrance and had asked to see me.

"What kind of a person is he?" I asked.

"He is a tall, one-eyed man, wearing a long sword."

This I felt was a fatal caller.

"What did he say his name was?"

"He would not tell, Sir. He said if you met him, you would know."

Now I was sure! But when I stole a peep at the man, it was my old friend from Ogata School, Harada Suizan from Chikuzen. I broke out cursing before I knew it.

"You damned fool!" I cried. "Why didn't you tell me it was you? I was shivering with fear."

I took him in and, after a good laugh, we spent the afternoon in pleasant talk. The scholars of foreign culture had to expect a good many queer surprises.

---

[2] Note on p. 355. [8] Ibid.

The momentum of the anti-foreign feeling increased; the Shōgun Iemochi himself made a journey to the Emperor in Kyōto, and took part also in the battle with the Chōshu clan.[4] In the midst of such disturbances within our land, England demanded satisfaction for the murder of Richardson.

British warships appear

The British fleet arrived in Yedo in the spring of the third year of Bunkyū (1863) to present their formal demands. It was declared that England had been trying to meet Japan in the most friendly spirit with the most lenient policies; but now that Japanese subjects had done violence to the persons of British subjects, even to the extent of murder, the government of Japan must bear the responsibility. The terms required the payment of one hundred thousand pounds by the central government and twenty-five thousand pounds by the clan of Satsuma, and the execution of the murderer before British representatives. A period of twenty days was fixed for reply.

This indemnity document came on the nineteenth of February. As I was one of the translators in the service, I was sent for at night to the residence of Matsudaira Iwa-mi-no Kami, the minister of foreign affairs, in Akasaka. With my colleagues, Sugita Gentan and Takabatake Gorō, I worked till dawn translating the long letter from the British Minister. All the while we were afraid to think what might be the outcome of our own translation.

Two days later the Shōgun, apparently unconcerned of the imminent crisis, set out from Yedo for Kyōto to visit the Emperor. Soon the period of twenty days had expired. The government pleaded for a postponement of another twenty days. After much argument, it was agreed upon, but again the second twenty days passed quickly. The

---

[4] Note on p. 355

government could not agree, one party agreeing to the payment, another advocating war.

The confusion in Yedo was becoming acute. People were sure there would be war; there were even rumors as to exactly when the shooting would begin. There was another postponement of twenty days; then ten days more of grace. While the government kept putting off an answer, I felt that war was unavoidable after all, and began preparations for escape to a safer position than my house in Shinsenza.

The end of the last postponement drew near, and the British declared there could be no more putting off for even a day. As I was in the bureau of translation, I knew every detail of the situation, and the suspense was truly unbearable.

The blustering French Minister Once I was ordered to translate a letter from the French minister, de Bellecourt. I don't know what his purpose was, but the minister made a downright assertion that France was absolutely on the side of England in the present problem, and in the event of open hostilities, the French fleet would be ordered to bombard Yedo in alliance with the British.

It was very like the present situation in China. Our government was simply worrying over the threats and bullying of the European diplomats, and could not decide what to do. I knew the situation well which made me all the more uncomfortable. As matters became more acute, the senior officers pretended they were ill, and none of them would attend the conferences. Finally, only the minor officers were talking the matters over in a series of confused arguments. No one could tell who was really the responsible authority.

Two days before the absolutely final day of reckoning, I gathered together my furniture and made ready to move

The crisis is now upon us   to Aoyama where a friend, physician Kure Kōseki, lived. He was a relative of Mitsukuri and had consented to shelter my household in case of war. I thought the enemy would not purposely harm the ordinary people, so our Aoyama refuge would be quite safe. I had tied up all our furniture and put cards on it, all ready for carrying out. Even yet there is a chest of drawers in my household with marks of the roping on it. As I passed by the drill grounds on the seashore of Shinsenza, I noticed the cannons turned seaward ready for action. I believed war was really imminent.

The government had proclaimed that an outbreak would be signalled by a rocket fired from Hama-goten, the seashore palace of the Shōgun, nowadays known as Enryōkan.[5] The Yedo tongue is clever in making puns and jokes. A humorous verse got circulated then in reference to this signal:

> *Hyōtan no*
> *Hirake hajime wa*
> *Hiya de yaru*

Since the first line may signify either *gourd* or *warfare*, the second has the idea of *the beginning*, and the last may equally be taken for *cold* or *rocket*, the whole verse may be read in two ways:

1. The first drink from the gourd, we take it cold.
2. The first shot of the war, we do it with the rocket.

Another funny incident came about in connection with this anticipated warfare. I thought I would have to lay in a stock of food, so I ordered thirty bales of rice from our regular dealer and asked him to keep them for me; also I bought a barrel of *miso*, or bean paste, and placed it in our barn. But as time passed, and as the situation grew more

---

[5] Note on p. 356.

tense, I began to realize that rice and
With this rice bean paste were the most useless of all
and bean paste supplies, for, fleeing in a time of attack,
we are ready for how could we carry the heavy bales
the war and barrels along? I had always heard
that if we had rice and bean paste, we
would be well provided for any kind of warfare. But now I
was discovering that these were the things most in our
way. If we had to flee, we would go without them. In the
midst of our excitement, this reflection caused a general
outburst of amusement.

At that time I had several students staying in my household, and had on hand a sum of a hundred or a hundred and
fifty *ryō* in gold two-*bu* coins. As we might all be separated
in the rush of a fleeing crowd, I thought it better to divide
this money rather than to have myself or my wife carry all
of it together. Then each one would have something to
rely upon in a crisis. I divided the money in four or five
parts and put it into bundles to be tied around the waist.
Thus equipped, we were ready for the next day's war.

But an unforeseen event happened.
The miracle man, Among the senior officers in the govern-
Ogasawara Iki- ment was the lord of Karatsu, Ogasa-
no Kami wara Iki-no Kami. Evidently in secret
he had conferred with Asano Bizen-no
Kami, a magistrate of Yokohama, and on the very last day
of the arbitration truce, the tenth of May, as I remember,
Ogasawara suddenly emerged from his seclusion, where, as
he announced, he had been confined by grave illness, and
set out from Yedo in a war vessel.

His vessel was promptly followed by an English gunboat.
It was reported that the English boat intended to fire if the
Japanese vessel steered straight out to sea, because Ogasa-
wara had made it known he was sailing to the "Province of

the West." But unexpectedly the ship veered to Yokohama; the minister landed and went directly to the British minister, St. John Neale.[6] To him Ogasawara handed the hundred thousand pounds indemnity in silver coins on his own responsibility. This was equal at the time to about four hundred thousand Mexican dollars. The crisis between the countries was over for a while.

The next move of the English was toward Kagoshima, the capital of the Satsuma clan to demand a further indemnity of twenty-five thousand pounds for **Indecisive Battle** the family of the deceased and the **of Kagoshima** execution of the man who had killed Richardson. The six vessels of the fleet anchored in the bay of Kagoshima and handed over the official demands to the officers of the Satsuma clan who came immediately on board.

The English officers, Admiral Kuper, Commander-in-Chief Wilmot, and Captain Josling[7] of the flagship, then waited for the reply. When it was long delayed, they decided to commandeer as their temporary security the two ships which the Satsuma had purchased from Europe. They were about to tow these ships out from their moorings near the island of Sakura-jima in the bay when, in sudden retaliation, the clansmen on shore opened fire. The English ships returned salvos, and thus the battle of Kagoshima began. This was in the latter part of May, the third year of Bunkyū (1863).

The British flagship, not expecting an immediate engagement, had not yet weighed anchor. When she saw the necessity of changing her position, she found the wind inconveniently strong and the bay deep, and she was forced to cut her chains to get away. This is how the British

---

[6] Note on p. 356.   [7] Ibid.

anchor fell into the hands of the Satsuma. The gunners on shore were pretty clever. They concentrated their fire on the flagship alone and several shells hit their mark. One of the largest of the round shells exploded on deck and killed the commander-in-chief and the captain besides wounding several others. The English fire, in turn, was quite as destructive, and most of the town near the seashore was demolished. Yet, after all, there was no decisive victory.

Although the Satsuma guns had killed the two British officers, their fire had no further effect on the ships. On the other hand, while the English had been destructive on their side, they were not able to land. The affair resulted in nothing except the losses. About the tenth of June, the British fleet returned to Yokohama. A funny episode is told in connection with this conflict.

After the battle was over, the British officers had much discussion over the fragments of the shell that hit the flagship:

"The Japanese couldn't have manufactured this shell," said one. "Where did they get it?"

"This," said another, "looks to me like a Russian shell."

"Yes," said the third, "Russia must be backing Japan!"

This was but a few years after the Crimean war. The relations between England and Russia were like those between a dog and a monkey. It seems to me that their relations have not improved much since.

Godai and Matsuki went on board the British ship — The two Satsuma ships which the British fleet had taken for security were commanded by Matsuki Kōan (later Terajima Tōzō) and Godai Saisuke (later Godai Tomoatsu). The Japanese sailors had been ordered to land, but the two captains went on board an English vessel. But before they left their ships, they had set timefuses in the magazines which wrecked the vessels entirely. Although they were not prisoners-of-war, they were hardly rated as guests of the British ship. At any rate these men reached Yokohama with the fleet; it was so reported in the Yokohama newspapers[8] of that time, but we heard no more of their movements and lost contact with them completely.

Of these officers, Matsuki had been my companion in the embassy to Europe. He, Mitsukuri and myself had been intimate friends for a long while. So Mitsukuri and I were anxious about our lost friend, and together we often wondered what might have been his fate. There was no way to trace him. If he and Godai had been sent back to Satsuma, they would surely have been set upon and assassinated by the young warriors of the clan. On the other hand, if they had been delivered to the shogunate government, they would have been imprisoned pending a trial for their relations with the English. But we never heard of them either as victims of their clan or as prisoners of state. Then about a year later, Matsuki turned up unexpectedly in Yedo. This is a long story, and there is much that belongs before it in the natural sequence of events.

Peace negotiations between Satsuma and the British

Soon after the English fleet returned to Yokohama, certain Satsuma representatives came to Yedo to negotiate peace. They were Iwashita Sajiemon, Shigeno Kōnojō (later Aneki), and an unofficial advisor, Ōkubo Ichizō (later Ōkubo Toshimichi). These men were desirous of concluding a truce for the time being, but having no one able to handle the negotiations, they were much perplexed. Then

---

[8] Note on p. 357.

fortunately a man offered to mediate between them and the English—Shimizu Usaburō (Mizuhoya Usaburō), a merchant who possessed some knowledge of English and was enthusiastic in foreign affairs.[9] He was certainly an unusual man for his rank in society. He had had an interesting experience.

The British fleet, on sailing for Satsuma, had needed an interpreter. Their own interpreter, Alexander Siebold,[10] could speak Japanese but was not able to read the written characters. So Shimizu was asked to accompany the fleet as assistant to Siebold. Shimizu, who loved adventure, jumped at the opportunity and, receiving his credentials from the custom house in Yokohama, went on board the flagship, and had the unique experience of seeing the battle of Kagoshima from the British side.

So to this Shimizu went the messengers of the Satsuma clan to ask for his mediation with the British. Shimizu called at once at the British Legation in Yokohama to deliver the request for a truce.

The attendant at the door of the legation, hearing his purpose, said that such a weighty business could not be negotiated with a merchant, but "a man of more authority must be sent." Shimizu argued that social rank did not matter in this event, and that so long as he bore the credentials of the clan, he should be regarded as having full powers to speak. His stern argument finally won him admittance, and he immediately presented his message to the minister, St. John Neale.

But no reasonable negotiations could be made. The minister declared in an overbearing threat that a number of additional vessels were already en route from the Indian Ocean, and that a body of several thousand troops was pre-

---

[9] Note on p. 357. [10] Ibid.

paring to embark soon for Japanese shores. "Truce making
at such a juncture is out of the question."

Shimizu had to go back to the Satsuma delegates and
report his failure and the impossibility of proceeding with
the British minister. Then the Satsuma delegates, finding
the situation growing increasingly more difficult, called on
the British minister in person. After long negotiations,
they agreed to pay the required indemnity of twenty-five
thousand pounds, or about seventy thousand *ryō* at current
rates. However, the clan had to procure the sum privately
from the shogunate government, and being unwilling to pay
the money in the name of the head of the clan, paid it under
the name of his near relative, Shimazu Awaji-no Kami. As
Richardson's assassin had escaped, they could only promise
his execution when he was arrested.

Those present at the negotiations were Iwashita and
Shigeno of the Satsuma and Ugai Yaichi and Saitō Kingo
of the shogunate government. Ōkubo Ichizō did not take
any official part in the settlement. It was about the first or
second of November, the third year of Bunkyū, that the
affair was finally closed.

Matsuki and Go-
dai hide out in
Saitama

I may seem to have wandered far
from the story of my friend, Matsuki,
but now I come to him again. When
Matsuki and Godai came on board the
English ship, they met Shimizu. They
were all old acquaintances; Shimizu had often studied
English with Matsuki. Naturally they were surprised to
meet each other in such odd circumstances.

"Why are you here?" "How did you get here?" Their
questions were asked excitedly of each other. So it was not
altogether an unpleasant voyage with the English fleet back
to Yokohama. But to land in Yokohama was another problem. Shimizu, of course, was free to go on shore, but

Matsuki and Godai were "men under a shadow." Then Shimizu, always ready to go through any adventure to help others, took the situation in hand. He first went on shore and requested the help of an American, Van Reed,[11] who agreed to provide a boat for secretly conveying the two men to the shores near Yedo.

Next, permission to leave the ship had to be obtained from the admiral. They went to him with rather anxious minds, but the admiral proved to be very generous and easily granted the permission. So Shimizu and Van Reed, having planned the venture very carefully, took the two fugitives secretly by boat in the darkness of night. They had planned to land on the coast somewhere between Yokohama and Yedo, but at that time there were guard stations every few hundred yards along the highway between the two cities, and all suspicious looking men were stopped and questioned. It would have been impossible to walk with the two samurai swords at their sides. So Matsuki and Godai left their swords, hats, and all identifying property with Van Reed and, attired like boatmen or farmers, they rowed on to the shore at Haneda, landed in the dark, and made their way toward Yedo along unfamiliar roads.

While they were still some distance away, day began to appear. The two fugitives, now scared, hired a litter on the road and, hiding their faces, entered Yedo. It was dangerous to stop in an ordinary inn. Shimizu, who had gone on ahead, was arranging an accommodation in a *funayado** at Horidome where he knew the proprietor personally. There was much worrying and waiting, but Matsuki and Godai arrived safely about noon the next day.

There they stayed for two days, and then moved to Shimizu's native village of Haniu in Saitama. But finding

---

* Shipping agent with accommodation for passengers.
[11] Note on p. 357.

this still insecure, Shimizu took them again to Naramura where a relative of his had a country house. This was a lonely, out-of-the-way location, and the two men felt safe to stay there a long while. Godai went to Nagasaki after several months, but Matsuki remained for nearly a year.

All the while, the Satsuma clansmen were hunting for the two missing officers. Besides the delegates mentioned, Higo Shichizaemon and Nambu Yahachirō and others of the Satsuma estate in Yedo were engaged in the search. After a thorough investigation, these men began to suspect Shimizu, and they questioned him several times about the missing men. Shimizu excused himself by saying he knew nothing, for he was afraid that the two men would face execution if caught. But the Satsuma men were suspicious of him, and soon the officers of the shogunate government began to examine him. It was harder now for him to feign ignorance. Shimizu wished to release Matsuki from his hiding place if he was going to be pardoned, but if he was doomed to be executed, he would keep him there as long as possible.

Finally, reaching the end of his wits, Shimizu went to Kawamoto Kōmin, an old teacher of Matsuki's, to ask his advice. The old scholar thought it best to tell the truth, for probably the Satsuma men would not go so far as to take the life of their helpless victim. Shimizu, then, made a formal address to the clan and told them of Matsuki's hiding place with the request that Matsuki should not be put to death. This was granted, and Matsuki came out from his retreat a free man.

To prevent any future embarrassment, he changed his name to "Terajima Tōzō,"[12] and to this day, through his long career, he has been so known. However, his identity

---

[12] Note on p. 357.

has been kept a strict secret, as Shimizu told me, known
only to seven Satsuma men.   I suppose those seven men are
that group including Iwashita and Ōkubo.

Matsuki sudden-
ly appears
During this entire episode, I knew
nothing of the movements of Matsuki,
alias Terajima.   A long interval elapsed,
and in the fourth year of Bunkyū—I do
not recall the month, but it was not in the cold season—
probably in summer or autumn, Higo Shichizaemon came
to my house one day.

"Matsuki is in town and wishes to see you, but would you
object if he came here himself?" he said suddenly.

"Is he still alive?"   I exclaimed.   "I have talked about
him every time I met Mitsukuri."

"Yes, safe and sound."

"Where is he?"

"Here in Yedo, but would you receive him if he came
here?"

"Of course!"   I said.   "I would like to see him at once."

The next day Matsuki came, and I felt as if I were receiving a man back from the other world.   I then learned about
his life since his disappearance and of his being saved by
Shimizu.   There in my house in Shinsenza we had a hearty
meal together.   He confided to me that he was hiding in
Shirokane-Daimachi, at the home of his wife's father, a
physician named Sō.

I immediately notified Mitsukuri of this, and together
we visited our friend the next day in Sō's residence.
We three sat and talked from noon till late at night.   According to his own account, Matsuki, or Terajima now, was
in good standing with the Satsuma clan, but not being sure
of the attitude of the shogunate government, he had to be
careful.   But as he had committed no particular crime, he
was not in danger of peremptory arrest.   As for his living,

he said, he was doing some translating for his clan.
"I am all through with firearms," Terajima declared,
"absolutely. No more warfare for me. Why, even at the
report of a gun, my head goes dizzy. It makes me shiver
to think of that fighting in Kagoshima."

He went on to tell that it had been a ticklish job to set
the fuse in his own ship, and that he had just escaped with
his life. At that time he had twenty-five *ryō* with which he
landed and made his way to Yedo. He recalled how the
Englishmen of the fleet wanted some fresh fruit during their
wait in Kagoshima Bay; some clansmen contrived to board
the ships on the pretense of bringing fruit, but their plot
did not succeed at all. He continued with event after event,
but I shall cut short his narrative for the account of the
anchor.

It seemed that none of the Japanese knew that the British
flagship had cut her chains when she was so suddenly
fired on in Kagoshima Bay; that is, nobody but Shimizu who
was aboard her. Later he told the fact to the Satsuma
leaders and advised them to salvage the anchor and keep it.
But they paid little attention to the suggestion, and let the
anchor lie until later when some fishermen brought it
ashore. Thus the anchor came into the hands of the clansmen.

They returned the captured anchor without a second thought After they had made peace and paid the twenty-five thousand pounds, the Englishmen casually asked them to return the anchor. The Satsuma offi-cials, without a second thought ev-idently, had delivered the anchor as if
it was so much scrap iron. This, we must admit, was a
stupid move. After all, the outcome of the battle had not
been decisive for either side. The English had cut their
chains; they had suffered the loss of two high officers; and

finally, they were obliged to retreat without making a land-
ing. This would seem to indicate a defeat. But on the
other hand, the Satsuma had suffered a great damage; they
could not follow the retreating enemy, nor could they return
the fire when the English ships renewed bombardment the
next morning. Therefore, it would seem a defeat for them
too—a defeat for both sides.

So there was no necessity that the Japanese should hand
back the anchor without a rebuttal. This simply shows
how little the Japanese knew of international ethics at that
time. From the very beginning it is doubtful whether it
was reasonable at all for England to demand the sum of one
hundred twenty-five thousand pounds for the death of a
single private man. Although it is now an affair of thirty-
odd years ago, we Japanese still feel the injustice of that
demand and settlement.

When the Satsuma men proposed a truce, what enormous
threats and boasts the British minister made, and how
naïvely the Japanese believed, or were afraid to disbelieve!
Indeed, the whole issue was closed before the Japanese
people really knew what they were up against. Such an
outcome would not be possible today. Even the Americans
were saying at the time that they hoped Japan would not
pay the full amount. And when I recall how the minister
from France came out with his most amazing threats,
I begin to doubt the sanity of the men concerned. Yet it
was all settled amicably. I have no further comment to
make.

From the imperial court in Kyōto there was issued an
edict that, beginning on the tenth of May, the third year of
Bunkyū (1863), the expulsion of all foreigners was to be
enforced. In obedience to this order, the Chōshū clan fired
upon a Dutch merchant vessel passing through the straits
of Shimonoseki. Fortunately the vessel was not sunk, but

many complications arose from the incident, and unrest
grew from bad to worse.

A great misfortune befell me in June
Ogata Sensei's of the same year. One day I was sur-
sudden passing; prised by a message from my old teacher,
Murata Zōro- Ogata, who had come to live in Yedo
ku's strange be- some time before. The messenger said
havior that the old master had been suddenly
taken ill and had vomited blood. I had
just visited him a few days before and found him very well
—how could this be? But I lost no time in hurrying to his
house. At that time there was no means of quick transportation—not even the *jinrikisha*.* I ran the whole distance from my house in Shinsenza to Ogata's place in Shitaya. But when I ran breathless into his house, I found him
sunk in death. What could I do now? So sudden and keen
was the blow, I seemed to be living in a dream.

Some of his pupils who lived nearby were already there;
others kept coming in. The small house was soon filled
with forty or fifty men who overflowed from the parlor into
the kitchen and the entrance hall. That night we were to
sit up for the last watch over our old master.

At about midnight, as I was sitting on the steps at the
entrance, Murata Zōroku (later Ōmura Masujirō)[13] came and
sat by me.

"Well, Murata, when did you return from Chōshū?" I
opened the conversation.

"A few days ago."

"What do you think of that firing on the Dutch vessel in
Shimonoseki? Wasn't it a crazy thing for Chōshū to do?"
Suddenly Murata took on an angry look.

---

* A small, two-wheeled carriage pulled by a man. It came into use after the
Imperial Restoration.
[13] Note on p. 357.

"Why so? What is crazy about *that*?" he returned.

"It is rather wild to think of expelling the foreigners in this age, isn't it?"

"You insult the Chōshū leaders! They have adopted a definite policy on foreign relations, and they aren't going to allow any arrogance on the part of the Westerners, especially the Hollanders. With their small country, to dare act as they have! We won't allow that. Even if we have to fight to a finish, we'll keep the foreigners out!"

This vehemence was not like the Murata I used to know. I let the conversation drop as soon as I could and, hurrying over to where Mitsukuri was sitting, told him of my surprise at Murata's fierce change in attitude and what he had said.

We, as his friends, had been anxious about Murata ever since he was called to Chōshū, because at the height of the anti-foreign feeling, when a student of foreign affairs was taken into service at the center of that movement, his personal safety was in jeopardy. We had often talked of this together. And now, when he came back, we found him thus completely changed. I was much puzzled. Was he pretending to hold that attitude for fear of attack from his clansmen? He could not be such a fool as to adopt a belief in their Expel-the-Foreigner idea. But there was no telling; he was acting peculiarly. So Mitsukuri and I decided to let our friends know that Murata was not to be counted as of our group any more; no knowing what might happen if we spoke too freely with him.

I am telling this exactly as it appeared, and I really do not understand to this day our friend's temporary change in attitude—whether he was simply shamming for self-protection, or whether, like one who " would swallow the tray after licking the poison," he had become converted to the anti-foreign side after he had gone to Chōshū. At any rate, we,

Mitsukuri Shūhei, myself and others, were for a while afraid to come near him.

The third year of Bunkyū (1863) was a most troubled year in the development of foreign relations. On our side, all Japan was swept by the anti-foreign movement, and on the side of the Westerners, England pressed her demands after the death of Richardson. It was a trying time. As I was working in the translation bureau of the foreign department, I had opportunity to see most of the official letters. In other words, I had access to the most secret diplomatic transactions. Of course I could not take the documents home, but whenever I translated them at the office or at the residence of the minister of foreign affairs, I memorized the contents of each letter and wrote them out as soon as I reached home. I secured, for instance, the contents of the letters dealing with the Richardson affair:—the first statement from the British minister, the outline of our government's reply, and all subsequent documents.

Naturally, these transcripts were not to be passed around freely. I made them the subject of conversation with my most intimate friends. They were interesting documents. But one day I gathered them and threw them all into the fire. I had an urgent reason for doing so.

Wakiya is sentenced to death   There was in Kanagawa a certain Wakiya Usaburō who served somewhat in the capacity of assistant magistrate. As this was a rank of importance, he had considerable standing. One day, it is told, he wrote a letter to a relative in Chōshū, and the letter was intercepted by a detective. Although it was personal throughout with no reference to a definite matter of state, one passage in it was interpreted as treasonous by the official. The statement was: "I am very anxious about the trend of things at present. I do wish some great spirit or clever minister might appear and direct the country to security." These words implied—so the officials decided—that the writer was making light of the present Shōgun; in other words, he must favor the downfall of the present ruler. Therefore he was a criminal—a traitor.

I was working in the translation bureau and saw the confusion. During the clamor I saw Wakiya pass along the corridor; he was not bound, but was escorted by guards. The next day we learned about his letter and the reason for his arrest. His house was searched at once and he was imprisoned in Temmachō. After the formality of a trial, he was quickly condemned to death in the prison. The inspector to testify at his death was Takamatsu Hikosaburō, an acquaintance of mine. He told me later of his personal regret, but he had to perform the duty.

When I realized Wakiya's sentence, I was frightened. For if he was condemned to die for the simple statement in his letter about a "great spirit and clever minister," what might not my transcripts of the secret dispatches of the government bring upon me? I saw myself in the Temmachō prison and my head being struck off! No sooner did I reach my home, then in Teppōzu, than I collected these papers and burned them.

Thus the telltale documents were out of existence. But I was still anxious, for I remembered giving a copy of a part of the papers to a relative of mine; on another occasion I had lent these to a certain man of the Hosokawa clan. I now thought that the latter might have made a copy of them for himself. I really suffered agonies of suspense. Furthermore, I dared not write a letter to inquire about them, for it would be dangerous to commit myself again in writing.

I continued to worry and hope that nothing might come to light. Then, fortunately, the Imperial Restoration came and I felt relieved of my liability. Now I can talk quite freely about it all, and even have it taken down in shorthand as I am doing now. But in those days, for five or six years prior to the Restoration, I was living under a heavy burden. And the debt I felt I owed, and which might be demanded at any time, was—my head! I could not confide it to any of my friends, not even to my wife; I had to bear it alone.

There is no comparison between the serious extent of my "crime" and that of poor Wakiya's. What a sad contrast, and a cruel one, that he who wrote an innocent letter to a relative should be put to death, and a man who had transcribed the secret transactions of the government should go free. It is hard to know on what the fortune or misfortune of a man may rest. Predestination, some call it.

For this reason, as well as for others, I am indeed grateful for the Imperial Restoration. If I had those transcripts now, I could work out an account of conditions in the third year of Bunkyū; also they would be valuable sources of Japanese diplomatic history. But not caring to exchange them for my head, I did away with them. However, should anyone have a copy of those documents, I would like to look at them again.

Every foreign ship is fired on at Shimonoseki After this, it seemed as if there was nothing but anti-foreign agitation in the country. Chōshū fired on every ship that passed through Shimonoseki Straits. American and English war vessels were fired on after the barrage on the Dutch merchantman. The outcome of the continued attack was that the four countries—England, France, Holland, and America —made a joint protest to the shogunate government, demanding three million *yen*. This was paid after long disputes. Still the anti-foreign wave did not subside. The shogunate was now harrassed on both sides—on one side,

by the agitating clans which clamored at the point ot arms
for the closing of the country, and on the other side by the
united power of the Western nations demanding the "open
door." Trying madly to satisfy both sides, the shogunate
at length invented a term, *sakō* (closing of the ports) to use
in place ot the advocated *sakoku* (closing of the land). A
minister of foreign affairs, Ikeda Harima-no Kami, was sent
to France to negotiate the policy of *sakō*.

The shogunate, as the governing force, had lost all its
prestige. There were almost daily assassinations. The
country had become a fearful place to live in. In this state
of affairs I tried to live as discreetly as possible, for my chief
concern had become how I might escape with life and limb.

Heyday of the old warrior spirit   Militarism ran wild in this period before and after 1863. People in general were concerned with nothing so much as showing off the old warrior spirit. That, however, was not to be
wondered at, for the shogunate itself was encouraging it.
Although, as its outward policy, the government of the
Shōgun professed peaceful relations with the West, that was
simply because it was obliged to do so under the circumstance. If one were to examine the individual officials, one
would have found each one an ardent hater of everything
new and Western. All those who had any influence or
commanded respect were wearing long swords. Many of
the fencing masters of the city had been honored with com-
missions by the government, and they suddenly became the
idols of the people. It was no time for the students of
foreign culture to hold up their heads.

This vogue of militarism spread everywhere. It infested
even the priests of the Shōgun's court who were known
generally as *sadō bōzu*, the "tea-ceremony priests," since
they were employed in serving tea and performing social

offices to the higher feudal nobles around the Shōgun. These priests usually wore short swords and crêpe overgarments, gifts from the lords, and they would walk along with a mincing gait. But now, with the new militaristic trend, some among them actually adopted long swords and were seen tossing their tonsured heads like warriors.

The fashion among the Shōgun's retainers was an overgarment of unbleached hemp with crests in black lacquer. According to tradition, this garment was worn by Ieyasu at the battle of Sekiga-hara (his decisive victory in 1600 which established the Tokugawa supremacy). Also it was told that the old Lord Mitsukuni of Mito had been fond of wearing it. So this overgarment became the fashion of the militarists.

This warlike spirit spread even among the population of Yedo. For the feast of *Tanabata*,[14] it had been customary to tie poem-cards and hang bits of watermelon and paper toys of fans and such things on bamboo sprays. But at this time, the fans and melons gave way to toy helmets and paper swords. It was all beyond me now; the whole spirit was one of war and worship of the ancient warriors.

I sell off all my swords

Having decided that swords were unnecessary objects in my scheme of things, I resolved to dispose of mine. I took all I had—not very many, perhaps five or ten—and sold them to a dealer, Tanaka Jūbei, who lived in Shinmeimae. But as a sign of my position I still had to appear with a pair, so I kept the short sword which my father used to wear with his ceremonial garments. I obtained a sheath for it long enough to give it the appearance of a long sword; I then bought a knife at a hardware store in Shinmeimae and fashioned a short scabbard

---

[14] Note on p. 357.

for it. Thus I wore these two swords for the mere sem-
blance of formality. The rest I sold and, as I recall, they
brought sixty or seventy *ryō*.

I tried to make myself appear as modest and inconspicu-
ous as possible. As a young man I had learned *iai-nuki*, the
art of drawing the long sword in an emergency, and I had
frequently practised it at home and at school in Ōsaka.
But when the military spirit grew strong, I put away my
iai-swords in a closet and pretended I knew nothing of
swordsmanship at all. I pretended that I had never even
drawn a sword in my life and was merely wearing them
for appearance's sake. For thirteen or fourteen years I did
not once venture out of doors at night. Really until the
fifth or sixth year after the Restoration, I lived practically
as a recluse, making writing and translating my chief
concern.

IX

I VISIT AMERICA AGAIN

In the third year of Keiō (1867) I had the opportunity of going again to the United States of America. It was my third voyage to foreign lands.

Some years previously when the shogunate had considered obtaining some warships, they had requested the American minister, Robert H. Pruyn, to negotiate the purchase, and handed him the amount of eight hundred thousand dollars in several payments. In the third or fourth year of the Bunkyū era (1863–1864), one vessel named the Fujiyama had been delivered. The cost of this had been four hundred thousand dollars. Since then various affairs had occupied the government, and the Civil War in the United States had broken up her foreign interests. And so the delivery of the second ship had been much delayed.

So much time having elapsed without any business being concluded, and our government still having the four hundred thousand dollars to its credit, it was decided to send over a mission to conclude the purchase of the second ship, and also to obtain some rifles for the army. The head of the mission was Ono Tomogorō who, as Okanjō Gimmi-yaku (assistant minister of treasury), was a man of rank and much influence in the government. The second commissioner was Matsumoto Judayū. Their appointments had been made the previous year. In my eagerness to visit America once more, I visited Ono at his residence many times and sought his influence. Finally he agreed to include me in his party and we sailed on January the twenty-third. As the task was to purchase a vessel, the party included some men of the navy besides the few interpreters.

The first steamship service across the Pacific In this same year a regular packet service was opened between Japan and America. The first vessel to arrive was the Colorado and we took passage on her return voyage. It was a fast steamer of four thousand tons, veritably palatial in comparison with the small boat on which I had previously crossed. The former had required thirty-seven days; this rapid liner arrived in San Francisco on the twenty-second day. There were as yet no transcontinental railways, so we embarked again for Panama by the Pacific Steamship Company line after a wait of about two weeks. We crossed the isthmus by train, and then again took ship to New York, our voyage ending on March nineteenth. We went directly to Washington and called on the Secretary of State at once to proceed with our deal.

The way this business was done certainly reveals much about our government of those days. It would be supposed that the mission would have had a receipt for the eight hundred thousand dollars that had been duly paid. But in reality there was hardly anything that could be recognized as an official voucher. Our files included some ten pieces of paper with simple notations of "fifty thousand dollars," "one hundred thousand dollars," etc. But there was no statement of how or for what purpose Mr. Pruyn had received the money. Among the papers were several odd-shaped sheets with nothing but the amounts and the name "Pruyn" inscribed. The American parties might easily, if so inclined, have assumed a sceptical air and refused to honor such pieces of paper.

There was much discussion among the members of the mission before the voyage, but they decided finally that this apparent neglect could be made a "proof" of friendship between the two countries. Japan had trusted the American minister—rather, the Japanese government had put its faith in the goodwill of the American government, and no formal agreement was deemed necessary. The word of mouth of a minister should be as reliable as any formal treaty. The papers were simply memoranda to which we would not attach any importance.

With this attitude we opened the negotiations, and we were greeted at once by Mr. Pruyn himself. Without any hesitation or formality he wanted to know if we would take a ship or have the surplus fund returned. The mission felt relieved—we would take a ship. So we were taken on a tour of inspection, and finally decided on an iron-clad named the Stonewall, later called by us Azuma-kan. Then we purchased several hundred, or several thousand, rifles. Still, some seventy or eighty thousand dollars of our fund remained, and this we left in the care of the American government. Then turning over responsibility for the vessel and the arms to our naval officers, the rest of the party set out for home.

It was not until the following year, the first year of the Meiji era (1868) that the ship reached Japan. Our country had already brought about the Restoration, and the warship arrived in command of an American captain made deputy by our naval officers. Long afterwards I happened to hear from Yuri Kimimasa, who was then in charge of the financial bureau of the new Meiji government, that he had great difficulty in finding funds to pay for the ship.

"The new government had so little money at that time," he said. "We had to manage somehow or other to scrape together several hundred thousand dollars for the ship."

I let him know that the former government had paid in full, and that there was a balance still left in Washington. Yuri looked at me in amazement. "Is that so?" he simply said.

It seems that Japan did pay twofold for the vessel, but there is no reason to believe that America or the American officials were guilty of using the money. It must have disappeared somewhere in the deal.

Now that I recall it, there was something irregular in my own conduct during this trip. It is true that I was in the service of the shogunate, but that I had not the least idea of rendering service is also true. By my own reiterated declaration, I was opposed to the closing of the country and to all the old régime of rank and clan. Further, I regarded as my enemy any person who advocated the retention of these ideas. Naturally, in turn, those adherents to the old system would regard me as a heretic. When I considered the general condition of the government, it was entirely of the old régime—the narrow, self-esteeming, illiberal, feudal society—unwilling to permit free intercourse with the outside world.

Abominable official buys "cheap dollars" Here is an instance of their method. The banking agent who usually served the government as well as the officials personally was Mitsui Hachirōemon.[1] The members of the mission to America received allowances in Japanese silver one-*bu* coins which they were to change into American dollars before leaving. Of course the exchange rates were daily fluctuating, and it was very troublesome to know when it was most profitable to exchange them. One of the officials summoned to his hotel in Yokohama a manager of Mitsui's, and after a long

---

[1] Note on p. 358.

consultation about exchange rates, said, "I see that recent rates are not so favorable to us, but I imagine you have quite a stock of dollars exchanged when the rates were better. Will you have my money changed into those cheaper dollars?"

The manager bowed his head to the floor and replied, "I bow myself to your will. I shall make the exchange of your money at that rate." And he brought more American dollars than the current rate required.

I was disgusted at this preposterous notion—as if "cheaper dollars" were marked on the coins! Here was a man defying the law of exchange and showing no faintest signs of shame or embarrassment. Yet, indeed, he was not by any means an unprincipled man; he was a gentleman in all other respects. Not only he but the merchant likewise showed no resentment over the outrageous act. I realized then that this, after all, was not the fault of the individual man; it was due to the deplorable custom of the times. The present régime was thoroughly bad. As a government it could not stand much longer.

In connection with many pressing problems, the government was pursuing a policy of severe retrenchment, and it was declared that even the government of Shōgun, at this time of emergency, must not refrain from making money. Thereupon some officials in charge of "profits for the country" were appointed, and all sorts of suggestions were advanced.

One scheme was that a canal should be dug at a certain point in the city of Yedo so that tolls might be collected. Another idea was that all wine brought into Shinkawa[2] should be taxed. Still another was that a certain area of waste land should be put under cultivation with government super-

---

[2] Note on p. 358.

vision. At another time, some one thought that the collection of all the nightsoil in the city might be brought under government management and disposed of to its own profit.[3]

Our resistance against "profit for the country" Then a certain authority on foreign affairs made a grand speech at a gathering of his fellow scholars: "The government is determined to take over all the profit from the nightsoil disregarding the rights of the brokers. What is this but downright despotism? In history I have read that the citizens of the American colonies resisted their mother country, England, when she imposed a tax on tea. The ladies of America gave up all use of tea and even gave up the pleasures of tea parties. Now, let us follow the example of those Americans and give up the entire production of nightsoil for the express purpose of resisting the despotism of our government. What do you say to this proposal?"

The speaker was given a round of applause.

Under the new policy of economy, it was to be expected that our party going to America should include a man to look after the profits for the country. It seems that he had reasoned that the price of foreign books would rise with the development of foreign studies in Japan, and therefore that the government could profit by importing them. One day he gave me a private order to purchase many books in America. But I did not easily acquiesce in this idea.

"It is a very good undertaking," I replied. "Japan is in need of more foreign books. What a godsend that our government should sponsor this! I shall do my best to gather the most useful ones and to see that they are sold as cheaply as possible to all who need them for their studies. That is your idea, is it not, Sir?"

---

[3] Note on p. 358.

"Oh, no," he answered. "Our purpose is to sell them at a profit for the government."

"Then," I said, "the government is going into business. I did not join the mission in order to promote a money-making scheme abroad. But if the government announces its purpose of money-making, I can become a merchant too, and look out for my own share of the commission. Either way is satisfactory to me. If the government agrees to sell books at their original price, I shall go to any amount of trouble to hunt out good books and make the best terms I can in buying them. Or, if the government decides to make profit on them, I shan't let the government do it alone. I will take a share of it myself. Now, Sir, this is a dividing point between two policies. Which would you prefer, Sir?"

Such was my line of argument, but after a while I lost the goodwill of the higher officials. As I look back on the incident, I feel I was guilty of overstepping propriety whether my argument was sound or not.[4]

Down with the Government

Another episode occurs to me. One of the party, Seki Shimpachi, and myself were accustomed on the voyage to order drinks in our cabin. The cost was not slight, but we did not mind, for all our expenses were being borne by the mission. We ordered all the drinks and food we wanted, and spent the time talking to our hearts' content on all manner of subjects.

"The government has to go," I was saying once. "There is no use in holding on to it. Look at the rottenness it is getting by with. Here the officials are always using the phrase *goyō* (by the lord's order) in their proceedings. Even in buying wine and fish, they pay for them at a low rate. under the high sounding privilege of *goyō*. When a fish boat

---

[4] Note on p. 358.

comes in from Kazusa or Bōshū, these officials must step in first and have the pick of the catch almost for nothing. It would be endurable if Shōgun Sama himself were to enjoy the fish, but his cooks are really selling them for their own profit. We might guess other things from this. This government is absolutely gone—rotten!

"But now, putting that aside, look at this foolish anti-foreign policy. The government makes a pretense of advocating free intercourse with all the Western nations. It has to do so, being in a responsible position. But the truth is, our government is really an exponent of expel-the-foreigner. Think of those good-for-nothing fortresses looking like sea-slugs that have been built at Shinagawa. The crowd is not yet satisfied and they want to build more of them. Then, what is the idea of Katsu Rintarō's going to Hyōgo and building that round white fortress like a fire brazier? Aren't these all preparations for the expel-the-foreigner policy? Any government that has a policy of this kind ought to be smashed at once. Don't you think so? I certainly do!"

Seki thoughtfully considered. "That may be sound reasoning," he said. "But is it quite right for us to be making this argument? We are enabled to come on this trip to America because the government is paying for it. What you eat and drink and wear are paid for by the government. I feel some scruples in talking about smashing the government."

"Oh, no, that is all right," I went on. "We are hired by the government simply for our usefulness as interpreters. They don't respect our personalities in any way. The situation is like that of the *eta* employed in curing leather. The great lords of the government cannot do such lowly work. Then luckily they find a man, an outcast, who will do what others disdain. So they

Let the outcast do the dirty work

hire him to mend the soles of their sandals. Our situation is like that—an *eta* taking work in the household of a lord. Why show any scruples then? Go ahead and strike at the government! But the difficulty is—who will go first? I don't want to be the ring-leader in the movement.

"The only ones who are making a noise about overturning the régime are irresponsible bullies, the *rōnin* from the Chōshū and Satsuma clans. If those men should ever take hold of the government and begin controlling affairs, that would be the last straw, the finishing touch to the anti-foreign policy! Perhaps the present régime is a shade better than what those desperadoes might make of it. Yet it must go, sooner or later. But, for the present, I can only look on, having no way to effect the revolution. Isn't it a sad situation?"

I am ordered to be penitent Thus we talked while we drank as if there were nobody in the world who might take exception to our remarks. Though we were in our own stateroom, we were careless about keeping the door closed, and talked loudly. I am sure that parts of our conversation were reported to the higher officials, for when we returned to Japan and I resumed my work in the foreign office, I was reprimanded by the minister. He said that I had committed some offensive acts during my service abroad—so I was to confine myself at home and be penitent.

This punishment of confinement was quite easy to bear, for it only meant that I should not report to the office for work though free to go anywhere else. Indeed, I was rather grateful for this enforced leisure. I obediently confined myself at home and began writing a book which I called "A Guide to Travel in the Western World" (Seiyō Tabi Annai).[5]

---

[5] Note on p. 358.

"**Fukuzawa's brother has joined the Satsuma Clan**" It was the end of June of the same year when we returned to Japan. The situation there had grown more difficult; the unrest and distemper almost came to the surface. I made no attempt to take part in affairs, but stayed at home and devoted myself to teaching, writing, and translating. Even then people were circulating strange rumors about me. One of these implied that my brother was in Kagoshima having joined the Satsuma clan; therefore, I too was to be regarded as suspect. Probably this rumor originated in my denunciation of the present government. But there was no reason to put my brother, who had left this life more than ten years before, in Kagoshima. I offered no explanation or defense against these worthless rumors. Nor did I make any public utterances on political matters though many "patriots" were constantly offering new ideas and policies for reform. I was watching as from afar these activities of busy men.

One day Nakajima Saburōsuke came and asked me why I was keeping so closely at home. I told him of the penance I had been ordered to keep ever since returning from America.

"How absurd!" exclaimed Nakajima. "In this busy time a man like you should not live like a hermit."

"But," I said, "how can I go to the office when I am not wanted there?"

"Well, I'll see to that."

Nakajima went to Inaba Mino-no Kami, a *rōchū*, and advised him to get me out of my confinement and back into service again. This official had formerly been the head of the Yodo clan, and is the same old gentleman who now lives in retirement in Tōnosawa in the Hakone Mountains. Nakajima Saburōsuke himself was police commissioner of the

old town of Uraga.   He was a fine example of a samurai;
he and his son were killed in the battle of Hakodate (the
last struggle between the shogunate and the forces of the
imperial government at the time of the Restoration).   A
monument to their memory now stands in the park at
Uraga.

**I was disrespect-
ful to my superi-
ors**

If I have given the impression that I
blame the official for my punishment
after the American journey, I do not
intend it to appear so. I think I deserved
it. It was my obligation to respect every
order of Ono Tomogorō, because he had included me in the
party out of his own goodwill after I had many times begged
him to do so.   Yet I had been doing everything in my own
way, and sometimes had actually opposed him.   For instance, while we were still in America, it became clear that
Ono had grown indignant towards me.   He said, "You may
consider your work now finished.   You may leave the party
and return to Japan ahead of us."

But I refused to be cowed by such a command.   "You have
brought me out here far from home, used me all these days,
and now that the work is done, you want to send me back
alone.   But you don't have such authority.   When I left
Japan, I took my leave from the higher officials of the
government, and that means I am here under the official
order of the ministry, and not under yours.   Therefore, I
don't intend to return to Japan by your order alone."   I may
have won in this argument, but I know I was far from being
discreet.

One day, while we were at the dinner table and talking
freely on many subjects, I remarked, "I think our government is doing wild things.   This crazy idea of expelling the
foreigners and closing the ports!   Think of such an infantile
notion as erecting forts at Shinagawa to enforce that policy!

And I see that there are several men right here at this table who took part in the building of those forts. Do they think, I wonder, that Japan can be preserved by such a policy? Be cautious! Japan is a very precious country!"

As I look back now, I feel I must have been mad to make such remarks in such a place at that time. Ono was a pretty headstrong man, but I should not hold any grudge against him. It was certainly logical and natural for him to regard me as he did, considering my behavior and particularly my free utterances.

X

A NON-PARTISAN IN THE RESTORATION; THE GROWTH OF A PRIVATE SCHOOL

As the third year of Keiō (1867) drew to its close, the general spirit of unrest waxed stronger. It was natural that it should affect my students; some went back to their native provinces, others strayed off, and less and less of them sought instruction in my school.

At about this time the property of the Nakatsu clan in Teppōzu, where I was living, was taken over by the government to be made a foreign compound, and we were ordered to vacate. So I purchased ground in Shinsenza which had formerly belonged to the Arima clan, and near the end of December moved there. The Nakatsu property was at once turned over to the foreigners.

Then with the new year,* in early January, came the battle of Fushimi, the defeat of the Shōgun's army, and the retreat back to Yedo of Shōgun Yoshinobu himself.[1] Again great confusion swept the country. And this marked the beginning of the Imperial Restoration. As for myself, I took no part whatsoever in any political move. But since the Restoration is really the beginning of all present politics, I think I must go back to my childhood—to the growth of my earliest ideas—to explain why I did not take part in

---

* The fourth year of Keiō which was also the first year of Meiji (1868).
[1] Note on p. 359.

political activities, though I realize this will suspend for a while my narrative of the rest of my life.

My behavior at the time of the Restoration
Back in those childhood days, I lived under the iron-bound feudal system. Everywhere people clung to the ancient custom by which the rank of every member of a clan was inalterably fixed by his birth. So from father to son and grandson the samurai of high rank would retain their rank. In the same way those of lower rank would forever remain in their low position. Neither intelligence nor ability could prevent the scorn of their superiors.

I resented the custom not the men
Born as I was in a family of low rank, I recall being always discontent with the things I had to endure. But later, whenever I felt myself insulted, I resented the fact of the insult but did not hold it against the person who committed it. I was rather sorry for such men, for I regarded them as coarse fools who did not know the wherefore of sensible behavior.

Had I been an accomplished scholar or Buddhist philosopher then, I might have conceived the theory of the equality of mankind or some doctrine of love for all men. But I was still a boy in my teens; it was rather unlikely that I would hit upon such profound ideas. It seemed to me very simply that it was despicable for a man to be a bully. So I could never take out my feelings in illtreatment of my inferiors to avenge myself for the abuse I had received—I was of low rank, but there were many men lower than myself. This was what people used to call "taking revenge on Yedo in Nagasaki." But that was against my nature. I was all the more respectful toward men below myself.

This respect for people of lower rank was not original with me. It had been handed down from both my parents.

It is inherited from my parents My father, being of the same rank as myself, had no doubt been subjected to many unpleasant experiences by his contemporaries. But there was no instance of his showing any disrespect to others in return. To cite an instance: My father made a great deal of a scholar, Nakamura Ritsuen, who lived in Minakuchi of the Ōmi province, and treated him as kindly as if he were his own brother. Nakamura was an able scholar, but he was the son of a dyer who had lived in Nakatsu. Therefore nobody in our clan would befriend this "mere merchant's son." My father, however, admired his personality and, disregarding all social precedents, took him into our house in Ōsaka and, having introduced him to many people, brought it about finally that Nakamura was made a household scholar in the Minakuchi clan. So the relation between the two men became no less than that of real brothers. Even after my father's death, Nakamura Sensei continued to regard our house as his second home, and his cordial relations with us lasted all through his life.

So I believe my feeling of respect for all people was bred in me by the custom of my parents. In Nakatsu I never made a show of my rank in my mingling with any persons, even with the merchants of the town or the farmers outside. Of course there was no use in trying to resist the proud aristocrats even if I had wanted to. I resolved, therefore, to keep away from them—neither seeking their favor nor giving them a chance to abuse me. With my mind thus set, I lost all desire to make a name in the clan.

I had no desire for a career in my clan There is an old saying: "Become a great man and return to your native province wearing brocades." Such was not my ambition. Rather, I would have been embarrassed by brocade. My general thought was that I would break with the clan whenever the situation became too unpleasant. And so, though I kept it to myself, I had decided to leave the clan out of my thoughts in planning my career.

In the course of my education, I went to Nagasaki and to Ōsaka. Then I was called to Yedo to teach the young men of my clan. All this time I remained unconcerned as to politics in the clan. It was very usual for scholars to submit memorials for reformation, recommending, for instance, that the study of foreign languages be promoted, or that the military organization be improved. But, unlike the majority, I never made any such effort. Nor have I once addressed the chancellors, openly or in private, regarding my ability or my wishes, or what post I would like to have, or what salary increase I desired.

After coming to Yedo I was to see some experiments in my clan. They once adopted a foreign system of drilling. At another time they decided on the Kōshū system, and began blowing the conch shell at the drill. Again, they attempted to encourage studies in Chinese and made plans for improving the schools. All such movements I silently watched without any signs of praise or disapproval.

There was an old retired chancellor in the clan who was fond of discussing politics. One day I visited him, and the old gentleman began to speak of the unhappy relations between the imperial court and the Shōgun, and how Konoe Sama was doing things not expected of him, and certain chancellors were not managing things ably, and so on, lamenting over the benighted conditions of the times. It might have been expected that the listener would join in. But I did not do so at all. I simply said that there were things in the times that were unpleasant to some, but from the point of view of the men at the post, it would be impossible to do everything in a way to please everybody. Probably as things were, they were about as well as could be. I said to the old chancellor that it was rather useless to criticize the conduct of other people.   Thus I refused to take sides with the old gentleman.

Having taken such an attitude, I could hardly enter the politics of the clan, nor seek a career in it.   Consequently I lost all thoughts of depending on the favors of other men. Indeed, I attached little value on any man or clan.   I simply lived in the quarters provided for me in the clan estate and did not ask for anything more.   My life was a very quiet and ingenuous one.

I sell off the Lord's gift on the very day   One day I was told to report to *o-ko-nando* (bureau of supplies) in the main headquarters.   When I did so, the official gave me a silk overgarment (*haori*) bearing the crest of our lord, which he described as a special gift from him.   This, in other words, was the "honorable granting of the crested dress."   I was not particularly touched by the honor, nor did I complain of the quality of the stuff.   I accepted the gift with plain thanks.   On my way home, when I called on Suganuma Magoemon, an old friend of my late brother's, who had just come up from our native province, I found him engaged with a tailor, apparently planning a new overgarment.   I spoke up:

"Magoemon San, are you ordering a new *haori*?"

"Yes."

"Well, there is a nice silk *haori* for sale.   Would you take it?"

"Why, good!   But what about the crest?"

"It has the crest of our lord.   Anybody of our clan could wear it."

"All right.   I would like to look at it."

"If you really wish to, I have it right here."   **And I**

took out the silk cloak I had just received from our lord.
"Why, this would just suit me," said my friend, much
impressed. "But what about the price?"

"We will let the tailor put a price upon it."

So we talked the matter over with the merchant, and he
decided it was worth one *ryō* and three *bu* as it was a garment without inner lining. I sold him the garment, took
the money, and returned home to Teppōzu.

According to the custom of the clan, this honor of receiving the crest-bearing cloak would have been recorded in the
family history, dated and described, as an event in the
family. But I rather preferred to have the money, for with
that one *ryō* and three *bu* I could buy the foreign book I had
found the day before. Or, if I did not buy the book, I could
have the pleasure of a drinking bout. It does seem that my
mind was rather childlike, perfectly innocent of all worldly
ambitions.

**There must be
logic even be-
tween lord and
vassal**

This lack of attachment to the clan
may seem quite creditable now, but in
the eyes of my fellow-clansmen it was
taken as a lack of loyalty and human
sympathy. It was in pressing this point
that they sometimes challenged me to
argument at parties where drink had loosened tongues. I
always replied in this way: "You must not call me disloyal
or unfeeling, for I have done nothing against the clan and I
have always followed orders strictly. If you still call me
disloyal, I don't know where my omissions lie. Not only
that, but I have never made any request of them to have my
rank changed or my salary increased. You may inquire of
the upper officials and chancellors. It is not in my nature
to exert myself with the expectation of reward. If this is
disagreeable to them, let them dismiss me. I shall obey the
order and get out.

"All the intercourse of life is governed by the rule of give and take. If the clan says, 'You should be grateful for the patronage given your family for many generations,' I shall have a word to say in reply: 'There is no occasion for you to demand gratitude, for my family has rendered honest service for a long time.' On the other hand, if the clan extends some appreciation to us, saying, 'We are glad to acknowledge the good service of a family like yours,' then I should feel like saying in return, 'I am deeply grateful for your constant employment. During our family's history, there have been some good-for-nothing men, also some weaklings. In spite of these, you have been good enough to give us our fixed salaries and enabled us to live comfortably. The benevolence of our clan is as exalted as the mountains and as deep as the sea.' So would I humble myself and return thanks. This is what I consider the law of give and take. I don't want to have gratitude demanded of me, or to be called disloyal without reason." In this way I dealt with the charge of my "disloyalty" to the clan.

I ignore the Clan's call to arms   A few years before the Restoration, the Chōshū clan was declared guilty of treason and the government had announced that the Shōgun himself would lead the combined forces of several clans against it. Accordingly, our Nakatsu clan sent orders recalling the students in my school for service. I think Obata Tokujirō and others were among them—about ten in all. But I said that it was too dangerous for the young men to go to war; they might be killed by stray bullets however carefully they went about in the battlefield. For this kind of absurd war, if they wanted figureheads in their ranks, they could as well hire farmers from the provinces. My students were too precious; even if they were not to be hit by the bullets, they might hurt their feet on thorns. So I had them answer that they were all too ill to carry arms. If we were to be punished, the worst would be dismissal from the clan. I did not consider the right or wrong of the conflict; I simply said it was not the kind of activity that students should take part in.

So I kept the young men at their studies, but the clan was weak and did not force the recall of the young men. It did, however, place the responsibility on the parents, declaring that the present disobedience of the youths in Yedo was due to poor training by their parents. Under this contention, the old folks in Nakatsu suffered the penalty of fifty or sixty days of "closed gates."

Such was my way of life. It was as if my mind were washed clean of what people call the "yearning for honor."

The Shogunate is no better After I had been employed by the shogunate for some time, I was ordered to become a regular retainer of the Shōgun himself.* I became then *hatamoto* with a prescribed salary of one hundred and fifty bales of rice though actually it amounted to only one hundred. It was the general custom for *hatamoto* to let his servants address him as *Tono Sama* (Great Master), while men of lesser rank would have themselves addressed as *Danna Sama* (Master). Unconcerned as I was with my rank or career in this new post, it never occurred to me to have the higher form of address used in my house.

Then a friend of mine, a native retainer of the Shōgun, came to call one day. I think it was Fukuchi Genichirō.[2] He inquired at the entrance:

"Is *Tono Sama* within?"

"No, Sir," replied my maid "There is no such personage here, Sir."

---

* Fukuzawa's relation with the Nakatsu clan remained unchanged.
[2] Note on p. 359.

"Is he not at home then?   Is *Tono Sama* out?"

"No, Sir.   This is not the residence of such a gentleman, Sir."

Thus the maid and my guest were arguing when I heard it from my room in our small dwelling, and went out to welcome the guest.   I realized then that it was natural for my maid not to understand *Tono Sama*, for it was a word never used in my household.

A revealing conversation aboard the ship   Though I did not engage in politics, I was not entirely ignorant of the political world.   On the voyage to Europe, I used to talk over the problems of the time with the other interpreters, Matsuki and Mitsukuri.

"What do you think of it?"   I said one day.   "The shogunate cannot hold the country together much longer.   It seems to me that all the clans might get together and form a federation like Germany.   What do you say to this idea?"

Matsuki and Mitsukuri agreed with me that this would be the most peaceful solution of the crisis.

Then going on to talk of our own careers, I said, "If I am to say what I'd like to do if I could, it would be to become tutor to the big chief (the Shōgun) with a salary of two hundred bales of rice a year and the chance of teaching him all the new ideas of civilization and bringing about a great reformation in the country."

Matsuki clapped his hands and exclaimed that that was just what he too would love to do.   A salary of two hundred rice-bales and post of tutor to the Shōgun was the level of ambition for Matsuki at that time.   This represented the average thoughts of all the foreign culture students of the age.

Later Matsuki, under his new name of Terajima, took high offices in the new imperial régime, even becoming a minister of foreign affairs. That seems to me a pretty wide departure from his early ambition, and rather a sad departure, knowing, as I do, his true personality.

But to return to the contemporary situation in the country, I noticed that all the ambitious adventurers and so-called patriots had collected in Kyōto around the imperial cause. The shogunate in Yedo, on the other hand, was trying to keep its own as the central government against this rising power. These two political forces had come to be called *Kinnō*, the supporters of the Emperor, and *Sabaku*, the supporters of the Shōgun. If I may sum up my position between those two sides:—

> 1. I disliked the bureaucratic, oppressive, conservative, anti-foreign policy of the shogunate, and I would not side with it.
>
> 2. Yet the followers of the imperial cause were still more anti-foreign and more violent in their action, so I had even less sympathy with them.
>
> 3. After all, troubled times are best for doing big things. An ambitious man might cast his lot with one or the other of the parties to win a place for himself. But there was no such desire in me.

To tell how I came to feel this way—ever since my first arrival in Yedo, I had not been impressed by the men in the Shōgun's government. At the first meeting they would appear to be genteel, well-mannered, and smooth in speech— so much finer than men in the provinces. But that was only superficial. Really they had no brains to think with, nor did they seem to have much physical vigor either. They were direct retainers of the Shōgun, however, and I was merely a retainer of a provincial clan. To them I had to bow most ceremoniously and use "sama" in mentioning their names whether the man was present or not. I was simply being officious to them as one would to *kuge*, the courtiers of Kyōto, but inwardly I was thinking very little of them.

The pompous arrogance of the Tokugawa men However, the pompous arrogance of these Shōgun's men was beyond what people nowadays can conceive. A trivial instance perhaps, but on the highway, it was a calamity for us to meet any of these men or retainers of the Shōgun's near relatives who had the privilege of wearing the hollyhock crest of the Tokugawa family.

We might leave our inn on a cold winter morning to take a ferry. After waiting for an hour on the windy river bank, we would see the boat coming. Then just as we were about to step in, should some men wearing the hollyhock crest arrive, we would have to wait another hour for the next ferry. Again, at some wayside station, when the litter-bearers were scarce, we would look everywhere for vacant litters. Once we had found some ready and were about to stow ourselves in, up would stalk a wearer of the hollyhock crest, and we would have to stand aside. After a few instances of this kind, even a good-natured man would begin to rage. Such are only a few examples of the arrogance of the shogunate. I was still a young man; in an outburst after one of my own experiences on the highway, I decided from the bottom of my heart that here was the worst government in the world.

It may be that my hatred of the government had started from my naïve dislike of oppression, but there were other causes which provoked me to stand against it. I had been reading foreign books since my youth; also I had traveled in America and in Europe, and had come to see what policy Japan must take to preserve herself among the powers of the world. But now I found the government doing things hopelessly against my idea.

It is often thought that the Tokugawa government

The Shogunate itself was the chief opponent was inclined toward foreign intercourse while the country at large opposed it; some historians of late have declared that the chief chancellor, Ii Kamon-no Kami, was an advocate of open intercourse, and a book has been written to support this. But the idea is the grossest of errors. In reality, I should say, Tokugawa government, if closely examined, was the leading opponent of foreign intercourse in Japan.

Lord Ii was indeed the purest and finest of old-time samurai. I heard that during the burning of the great castle of Yedo, he led the boy Shōgun to the Maple Hill within the grounds. There, finding the grass grown deep, and fearing it might make a hiding place for assassins, he drew his own sword and cut aside the tall grass. Then, holding the young lord in his arms, he stood guard the entire night until the tumult had died and the fire burned out. Such is a true picture of the brave chancellor. While it is also true that he once had some anti-foreign agitators in Kyōto arrested and executed, he was only punishing them for defying the government.

Thus I can see that Chancellor Ii was both brave and loyal as a retainer in the old clan of Tokugawa. But as to international relations, I must say that he was the foremost in anti-foreign sentiment. The only reason that he and the Tokugawa government allowed foreign intercourse was that they were in direct contact with the foreign powers and were obliged to carry on such intercourse. If the curtain had been drawn aside from the back stage politics of the shogunate, I know what a shocking nest of anti-foreign broodings would have been discovered. I cannot therefore be blamed for my position in regard to this government. Another instance of the stubborn conservatism of an official may be pertinent here.

I was reading Chambers's book on economics.[3]   When I spoke of the book to a certain high official in the treasury bureau one day, he became much interested and wanted me to show him a translation.   He said that if translating the entire book was too much, he would like to see the table of contents.   I began translating it (it comprised some twenty chapters) when I came upon the word "competition" for which there was no equivalent in Japanese, and I was obliged to use an invention of my own, *kyōsō*, literally, "race-fight."

When the official saw my translation, he appeared much impressed.   Then he said suddenly, "Here is the word 'fight.' What does it mean?   It is such an unpeaceful word."

"That is nothing new," I replied.   "That is exactly what all Japanese merchants are doing.   For instance, if one merchant begins to sell things cheap, his neighbor will try to sell them even cheaper.   Or if one merchant improves his merchandise to attract more buyers, another will try to take the trade from him by offering goods of still better quality.   Thus all merchants 'race and fight' and this is the way money values are fixed.   This process is termed *kyōsō* in the science of economics."

"I understand.   But don't you think there is too much effort in Western affairs?"

"It isn't too much effort.   It is the fundamentals of the world of commerce."

"Yes, perhaps," went on the official.   "I understand the idea, but that word 'fight' is not conducive to peace.   I could not take the paper with that word to the chancellor."

I suppose he would rather have seen some such phrase as "men being kind to each other" in a book on economics, or a man's loyalty to his lord, open generosity from a merchant in times of national stress, etc.   But I said to him, "If you

---

[3] Note on p. 359.

do not agree to the word 'fight,' I am afraid I shall have to erase it entirely. There is no other term that is faithful to the original."

I did delete the offending term in black ink and let him take the papers. From this little incident one may gather the character of the other officials whom he represented in the government.

At the time of the expedition against Chōshū, many foreigners in the country showed much interest in the affair. One of them, an American or an Englishman, wrote a letter to the government, asking for the reasons of the expedition and the crimes the Chōshū clan had committed. The elder statesmen must have held a special session to frame a reply, for they returned a long letter. Anyone might have expected some reference to the Chōshū clan's antagonism to foreigners, or their firing on foreign vessels at a time when Japan was formally concluding treaties with the peoples of the world.

But the letter showed no such reasoning at all. It said that the Chōshū clan had "disturbed the peace in Kyōto, disregarded their Emperor's wish, disobeyed the orders of the Shōgun, and that their crimes were more numerous than the bamboos on Nanzan . . ."—all this presented in the most involved Chinese classic style. When I read this letter, I came to the conclusion that the government was fundamentally desirous of clinging to old traditions and of keeping its gates closed. Whatever sympathy I may have had was lost then.

Again, to consider the other party, the *Kinnō*, who were supporting the Emperor against the Shōgun, their antagonism to foreign intercourse was even more keen than that of their opponents. After all, both parties were alike in their anti-foreign prejudice, the only difference being their method of striving for the same goal. But since they were quarreling fiercely over this difference, it was likely they would come to the point of shooting guns at each other.

At that time the defenders of the imperial policy were a shade worse; they were actually murdering people, setting houses on fire, and declaring that even if the whole land were to be reduced to ashes, Japan must be kept from foreign influences. The mass of the people echoed this cry, adding to the confusion. I was sure that these ignorant rogues were the ones to ruin our country if they once came to hold some power. I could almost see the disaster in my mind's eye, for these men seemed to be gaining power. When I had this feeling, how could I have any sympathy with the *Kinnō* party?

About this time the widow of my former teacher Ogata sent for Mitsukuri and myself. She was now living in Yedo, and she had always seemed like a mother to me.

"You are both serving under the Shōgun," she said to us, "but such work is without much hope. Give it up, and go to Kyōto. You will find all sorts of interesting work there."

It seemed that recently she had had visits with Murata Zōroku and Sano Eiju and other politicians who were active supporters of the imperial cause. It was natural for the good old lady to remember us and give us this news.

I gave answer to her kind advice: "Thank you, Madam; I am sure there would be great possibilities in Kyōto, but I cannot side with the movement to drive out the foreigners even if I have my head wrenched off for refusing. Don't you agree with me, Mitsukuri?" We both declined the kind lady's advice.

Here is another thing to explain. As I had left home so early without having been in any local office of my clan, I did not learn the taste for an official life. Even now in the central government of Yedo, I was only a translator and I regarded myself as a sort of hired man. The discomfort I had come through as a man of low rank had penetrated to the marrow of my bones, and it was impossible for me to seek an official career which necessitated the bending of my knees before other men. Nor did I ever entertain the idea of rising high above all men, for I did not care to hold my head above others any more than to bow down before my superiors.

I have always used the honorific form of address in my speech generally—not of course to the lowly workmen or grooms or petty merchants in the really casual order of life, but to all other persons including the young students and the children in my household. At the same time, I never felt undue awe toward men whom people single out as great in the political world.

Of course, to elderly men with white hair, I paid due respect, but if the person seemed to exact homage because of his title and office, I lost interest in conversing with him. I do not know whether this comes from inborn nature or from the habits of my student life, but I am the same to this day. At any rate I am inclined to believe that I was born under a star which led me away from the political world and kept me apart from all the activities of the Restoration. But now let me continue with the course of events from which I have so long digressed.

Shōgun Yoshinobu had returned to Yedo defeated and a dreadful time was to follow. The entire city seemed to boil and throb with discussion as if the whole populace had gone mad with the suspense. Not only samurai but doctors and priests with tonsured heads and scholars, called by the people "lazy long-sleeves," were arguing about what the government should do. Whenever a man met another man, the same topic was made the center of their loud conversation.

In the castle of the Shōgun all order was gone, and in this

time of stress the usual etiquette was overlooked. The great waiting rooms, such as the one with the decorative paintings of geese, called the "Room of the Geese," and another, called the "Room of the Willow," had formerly been the most exclusive chambers of the feudal lords calling on the Shōgun. But now in these days of hectic unrest, the rooms had become the haunts of rough and ready men. They were sprawling in these rooms pitching into arguments at the top of their voices. Some were seen to pull out brandy flasks from their sleeves and take long gulps.

In such times naturally the work of translating was suspended, but wishing to follow the trend of affairs, I was usually at the castle every day.

One day I found two men in formal dress sitting in the office of our bureau. One of them was Katō Hiroyuki[4] whom I knew; the other I do not recall. I spoke to my acquaintance:

"Good day, Katō. What does your formal dress mean? Has anything important happened?"

"Do you not know," replied Katō in a serious tone, "the grave situation? We are waiting for an audience with his lordship."

His lordship, the Shōgun, had just then returned to the castle from the disastrous expedition, and there was much fear of the enemy's pursuit to Yedo. Many of the patriots, experts on tactics, and general politicians were there ready to propound to the "Great General" all sorts of schemes for defense. Some said that the first defense line should be laid at the river Fuji; others disagreed and said the natural barrier of the Hakone mountains should be used, and then the enemy could be annihilated at the foot of the Futago peaks. All agreed that the three centuries of great work

---

4 Note on p. 360.

begun by the deified ancestor of the Tokugawa must not be lost in a day. Even if the enemy bore the brocade banner of the Emperor, we, as retainers of Tokugawa, could not desert our master; let us rather fall with the Shōgun. That was the way of the faithful warrior.

So there was an endless train of men, waiting for their turn to present their views to the grand chief. Katō was undoubtedly one of them. I went on to ask him: "How about it—do you think Yedo may be stormed? Or do you think we are safe here? You ought to know. Do tell me."

"What would you do, if I told you?" said Katō.

"If we are to have war," I said, "I must hurry and get my things together to run. If there is no risk of a fight here, I shall stay peacefully at home. The chance of war has a grave consequence with me."

"This is not the time to indulge in humor, you fool!" returned Katō with glaring eyes.

"I am not joking," I replied. "It is really a matter of life and death. If the war is going to be, I must run to save my life. It is your privilege to fight, if you want to. But I am for saving my life."

I still recall how indignant he looked. Another time I was approached by an official of the bureau of foreign affairs who asked how many followers I had.

"Why, Sir, do you inquire about my followers?"

"Because," he said, "in case of a siege, all the retainers of the Shōgun are to assemble here with all their men. His lordship has ordered us to have ready in advance a supply of food for all. Therefore I must know the number of your men."

"Thank you, Sir," I answered. "I am much obliged for your kind precaution, but I shall ask you to leave my household out of your rations. I have no followers, nor have I a master. Besides, when the war begins, I won't be quite so

languid as to come to the castle for my meals. I shall be far
away in some safer quarters." And I took another sip of the
tea I was drinking.

If there had been any of the old fighting spirit left among
the men under Tokugawa, my head would not have stayed
on my shoulders very long after that. But such was the
spirit among these men in the last period of the shogunate
that my reckless words passed unchallenged. Therefore, it
was not surprising that no war followed.

A short while before this, on the return of Shōgun Yoshinobu from his unsuccessful campaign in the west, his government, with the idea perhaps of making some reforms,
had created many new offices and appointed men to hold
them. It was ridiculous to see so many offices that were
merely empty titles. There was even a magistrate of Hyōgo which was the town from which the Shōgun's forces had
just been driven. Certainly this magistrate was appointed,
but I doubt he actually went to take office there. Many
persons were made *ometsuke* and *otsukai ban* (official cen-
sors). I believe that both Katō Hiroyuki and Tsuda Shinichirō[5] were appointed to one or other of these offices. I was
likewise honored. A ceremonial messenger arrived one
night to present me with the official order. But I turned it
down with a cordial apology that I was "ill" and unfit for
the office.

By and by the Emperor's army came pushing into Yedo
and established a temporary headquarters called Chinshō-fu.
Shōgun Yoshinobu retired to Mito to prevent open hostilities. All this was happening in the spring of 1868 (the
fourth year of Keiō which was also the first year of Meiji).
At that time I was just moving into a new place at Shinsenza in Shiba.[6] I had bought about four hundred *tsubo* of

---

[5] Note on p. 360.   [6] Ibid.

ground (about fourteen thousand square feet), and as there were only a storage house and a long tenements, I was building a new dormitory for the students and a private house for my family.

When I started to build, there was not another person in the whole city of "Eight Hundred and Eight Streets" who was contemplating such a venture. Rather, everyone was making bundles of his belongings, ready for escape to the country. Some had even taken off the metal parts of their stoves and were using mud ovens for cooking. This was a lucky circumstance for me as all the carpenters and masons were delighted to get work then. And so many workmen came together, all eager to work for as much as would buy them food, that my houses were done very cheaply and quickly. Moreover, I was not building a new house; I had obtained an old house belonging to the clan, and was using the material from it. So, although I built pretty extensively —about 5400 square feet all together—the cost was not more than four hundred *ryō*. I think it was April when the construction was finished.

Occasionally friends would come and try to discourage me in this undertaking. "Who else in the world would think of building a house now when everybody is getting ready to move out? What is your idea?"

My answer to them usually was: "Perhaps it does seem strange that I should be building nowadays. But suppose I had built it last year? How would it be? I couldn't very well carry the house with me in case I were obliged to escape to other quarters. And it may be burned down in the fighting. Or it may not. Even if it should burn down, I would not regret it, thinking I had lost a house that I built last year."

So I went ahead and had it finished and the house was not destroyed. It was like succeeding in some risky speculation. I found out later that because of my going on with the building, there was much less evacuation of families in and about Shinsenza. People seemed to think that if someone was building a new house, perhaps things were not going to be so bad after all. Yet I really was worried, for there was no telling whether a war might not break out or some great fire start near us. I decided I had better have some safer place to escape to when it did come. I once thought of digging a big hole in the yard for a hiding place. But no; that would be uncomfortable when it rained. I then thought of hiding under the floor of the storage house, but even that would not be proof against cannon balls.

Then I remembered the estate of the Kishū clan nearby—which has since been made the detached imperial palace of Shiba.* As I had been teaching several of the young men of the clan, I asked them to let me see the grounds of the estate. I found in the large garden a spot where two thick mud walls met at an angle, and this seemed the best place to hide in. But it would be dangerous to enter through the main gate. So I hired a boat and kept it tied on the shore not far from our house. With it we could row over to the Kishū estate and make our way to the place between the walls. My family then consisted of my wife and two children—Ichitarō, the eldest son, and Sutejirō, the second son.

When the invading army did come, however, it proved to be very well disciplined, and no unreasonable violence was ever done. Only one day when Ichitarō, then about five years old, had gone to visit my mother-in-law (that old woman in the other room)† who was living on the estate of our clan in Shiodome, we had the scare of a skirmish. There were thought to be some suspicious men hiding in the Masuyama estate near by, and the soldiers of Chōshū (now of

---

* The present Shiba-rikyū Park.   † These words in the parenthesis were addressed to the shorthand writer.

the imperial faction) had surrounded the property and begun an assault. That meant real combat. There were various rumors about. Once I heard that the men were caught, and again I heard that they were killed. Then someone told us that a man was seen cut down in the big ditch around the estate, and again that he was run through by a spear.

We were anxious about the chance of their setting fire to the estate and of the risk to the boy and the grandmother. Of course we wanted to send for them, but that was impossible. During all our excitement, evening came on and all grew quiet again. Even in this skirmish, it seems the soldiers were very mild. They did not attempt to molest any civilians or harm other men not engaged in the fight. Some of the officers actually went around announcing that the populace need not be alarmed, as there was strict regulation and perfect control of the troops. So, contrary to what most people expected, there was really nothing to fear.

My school prospers With peace and a stable government established, in April of that year my school house was finished. At the turn of the year, I had seen my students mostly dispersed; there were only eighteen left. But in April many returned and the school increased considerably. There was a good reason for its rapid growth.

On my second journey to America, I had received a much larger allowance than on the previous one. With all my expenses being paid by the government, I was able to purchase a good number of books. I bought many dictionaries of different kinds, texts in geography, history, law, economics, mathematics, and every sort I could secure.[7] They were for the most part the first copies to be brought to Japan, and now with this large library I was able to let

---

[7] Note on p. 360.

each of my students use the originals for study. This was certainly an unheard-of convenience—that all students could have the actual books instead of manuscript copies for their use.

This use of American text books in my school was the cause of the adoption all over the country of American books for the following ten years or more. Naturally when students from my school in turn became teachers, they used the texts they themselves had studied. And so it was natural that those I had selected became the favored text books throughout the country.

Absolutely neutral between the Imperialists and the Shogunate As I have described, the army of the Emperor was unexpectedly mild and without the violence that we had feared. But we had to be careful to avoid any suspicion, for the military was quite sensitive on political affairs. So I opened my house and school to everybody and made it plain that there were no arms concealed, and that they were welcome to search. It being clear that I was perfectly neutral, the soldiers of both sides came and, seeing that I treated them alike, both became friendly.

After the imperial forces had entered Yedo, but before the serious resistance against them by the Shōgun's men at Ueno,[8] there was a little skirmish near Ichikawa. A certain young man of the shogunate had taken part in the fight in the evening, but on the morning following he came to my dormitory saying that he was tired and sleepy.

" Why are you taking part," I said to him, " when it would be just as wise to quit? This is dangerous business." That was about the extent of my interest in the engagement.

Here is the case of Furukawa Setsuzō.[9] At that time he

---

[8] Note on p. 361. [9] Ibid.

**Furukawa's
guerrilla warfare**
was captain of one of the Shōgun's vessels, the Nagasaki-maru. He came one day to tell me of his plan to start a guerrilla warfare with his ship. As he was the man I had brought from Ōsaka when I first came to Yedo, and since he had been like a brother to me, I tried to stop him.

" It would be wiser for you to give up that idea," I said, " because you will surely be beaten. I shall not argue which side is right now, but since the majority of the country has been won over to the other side, you have no chance at all. Better give it up."

But Setsuzō was in high spirits. " Oh no," he said, " I'll show you about that. I'll take my ship out and gather up recruits all over the country, and then strike from behind while they are occupied in laying siege on Yedo. Then we will sail away to Ōsaka and make a surprise raid there. That will make the imperialists know something or other."

Since the man would listen to no reason of mine, I finally said, "All right. Go on if you insist. Win or lose, it will make no difference to me. But I do feel sorry for O-Masa San (his wife); I shall see that she lives in comfort. But if you must, go on anywhere and satisfy yourself." We thereupon parted.

**An insane student returns
from America**
Let me tell another episode of the times. There was a student from the Sendai clan, named Ichijō, who had been to America to study after having spent some time in my school. Unfortunately he lost his mind while in America, and his friend Yagimoto Naotarō, also a former student of mine, brought him back, taking care of him all the way on the voyage. By the way, Yagimoto, I learn, was until recently a clerk in Aichi prefecture, and is now mayor of a city there.

Well, he had brought his demented friend on shore at Yokohama when he found that the Sendai clan had been declared an enemy of the imperial régime. Police were arresting all Sendai men found in or near Yedo. As Ichijō was a Sendai man, the police came at once. But they could do nothing with a man so plainly mad as he was. He was left free, but the poor fellow became subject to a complex of fear and persecution. He refused food as he believed he was being poisoned, and so was starving himself for a week. Yagimoto feared the victim might die unless something could be done to make him eat.

Suddenly the poor fellow remembered "Fukuzawa Sensei" and said he would like to see me. Yagimoto went to the magistrate's office in Yokohama to request a permit for removing the patient. The magistrate was then Terajima, my old friend, and he granted the permit, saying there could be no objection if he was going to be with Fukuzawa. So the poor fellow came to my house in Shinsenza and some amusing things happened.

I greeted him in the ordinary way and offered him tea. Then I asked him to have lunch with me. I would say, "Now take this, for I am eating it too. If you don't like that, share this rice ball with me. See, like this, you take the other half. Isn't that good?"

The patient began to eat, and once started, he did not mind eating anything. He seemed to feel safer in my house and he was improving, but of course we had to have him watched day and night.

Among the temporary guests with us were men from Satsuma and Tosa, both allies of the Imperial court. They took their turn in nursing the patient who represented the enemy clan. Then sometimes various members of the Sendai group came secretly to visit the demented fellow. So it happened that under the same roof were the two rival factions taking care of a sick man. There was no sign of discord, no antagonism of any sort; and that must have been one of the reasons my school was left undisturbed during those difficult years.

I treated everyone impartially, absolutely without distinction as to political affiliations. Some of my students ran off and joined the insurgents while some imperial army men came to study in my school. Such a situation cannot be created by purpose or by pretense. I never admired the old régime of the Shōgun and I was not by any means endorsing the new administration. I was letting both sides have their will to fight it out, if they would. This being my doctrine, both my school and I were able to come through the Restoration safely.

I am called by the new government At length complete reinstallation of the imperial power was effected, and temporary offices of the new government were opened in Ōsaka. Soon there came orders for many men in Yedo to report to Ōsaka to fill new offices. Kanda Kōhei, Yanagawa Shunzō and myself were among the first to receive orders. Yanagawa did not want to move to Ōsaka, so he requested that he be employed in Yedo. Kanda agreed to go to Ōsaka. I refused it flatly and sent the conventional excuse of being "ill."

After a while the government was moved to Yedo and I was again ordered to take a post in it. The offer was repeated several times, but I refused each time. One day Kanda called to urge me particularly to enter the service.

"Don't you think," I said to him, "a man should determine his own conduct? You have entered the government service because you wanted to do so, and I admire you for it. I am staying out because I don't like the service. The principle is the same. You should praise me for what I am doing

204 A Non-Partisan in the Restoration

rather than come and urge me to take office. You are not
acting like a friend."

Reward the bean-
curd man first
Kanda was an old friend, so I spoke
my mind to him without fear of being
misunderstood. Yet several times after
this, I was called to take office. Once
Hosokawa Junjirō came to propose to me that I take charge
of the government schools—this was before the Mombushō
(the Ministry of Education) was established.

"You have already done special service for the country,"
he went on. "The government has recognized it. So it
offers you a signal position of honor."

I replied again in my unfailing attitude: "What is
remarkable about a man's carrying out his own work? The
cartman pulls his cart; the bean-curd maker produces bean-
curd; the student reads his books. Each one follows what
is his obligation. If the government wants to recognize the
ordinary work of its subjects, let it begin with my neighbor,
the bean-curd maker. Give up any such ideas about my
special work."

It may seem that I was unreasonably stubborn, but the
whole reason of my stand was that I believed the new government to be carrying the ancient policy of exclusiveness
and antagonism against Western culture, and I feared that
the change from shogunate to imperial régime would bring
no good to the country.

I was much mistaken in this, fortunately, and the government gradually turned to liberalism, bringing on the fine
development we see today. I am most grateful that my
fears were not realized. But in those days I could not see
that the future would bring better times to us. I was judg-
ing only from what I actually saw, and had decided that
biased and foolhardy men from various clans were getting
together to make a worthless government which might even

bring disaster to the country. So I was standing apart, determined to do something in my own way for Japan. To show
that my belief was not groundless, I can cite an instance.

"Purification of an English Prince" Soon after the Restoration—in either
the first or second year of the Meiji era
—an English prince arrived to pay a
formal visit at the Tōkyō castle. It
seems there was much discussion as to
the ethics of conducting a foreign visitor into the imperial
presence. It was decided that some ritual of purification of
the English prince would be proper before he crossed the
bridge (Nijūbashi) over the moat to the castle. And this
became the basis of a ridiculous incident.

At that time the acting minister from the United States
was Mr. Portman.[10] It seemed that the President of the
United States was not in the habit of personally reading the
reports of the ministers in foreign lands unless they contained very pertinent or unusual matters. Now, when Mr.
Portman heard of this purification of the English prince, he
realized it would be a good episode to base his message on
and thus have it reach the President. So he headed his
report with the remarkable title, "The Purification of the
Duke of Edinburgh." It continued something like this:

"Japan is a small secluded country, very self-respecting and
very self-important. It is customary, therefore, for its inhab-
itants to regard foreigners as belonging to the lower order of
animals. Actually, when the English prince arrived to be
received by the Emperor, they held a ceremony of purification
over the person of the prince at the entrance to the castle.
This ritual of purification traces its history to ancient times
when water was used in cleansing the bodies of persons entering sacred precincts. In the middle ages when paper was

---

[10] Note on p. 361.

invented, they simplified the ceremony by substituting paper
for water. In this reformed rite, they use a streamer of paper
at the end of a staff called *gohei*. The body of the subject is
swept by this staff and so is cleansed of all impurities and pol-
lution. Such being the ancient rite in the land, they employed
this method on the person of the Duke of Edinburgh, because
in the eyes of the Japanese, all foreigners, whether of noble
lineage or common, are alike impure as animals."

So ran the clever report of the American minister. I
heard about it from Seki Shimpachi, then serving as interpreter at the American embassy. Seki told me minutely of
this incident, repeating as closely as he remembered the
words of the original message. He laughed over it, thinking it a good joke on our government. But I did not laugh;
I felt like crying over this revelation of our national shame.

**An American
statesman's ob-
servation on
Japan**
About that time the former American
Secretary of State, Mr. Seward, arrived
with his daughter on a tour through
Japan. He was a noted statesman in
America, having been Secretary under
Abraham Lincoln, and at the time of the
assassination he had also been attacked. Mr. Seward had
never been congenial with the English, but had always
shown friendship for Japan. But now on his tour in the
country itself, he declared that after seeing the condition
of things, he could not say much more in commendation
of Japan. He was sorry, he said, but Japan with her inflex-
ible nature could hardly be expected to keep her independence.

In truth I could see that the officials of the government
knew nothing better than the dregs of the Confucian philosophy with which to guide their actions. They were
simply lording it over the people with arrogance and pretense, and there was little that pointed to the establishment

of the new culture.   Now that I had the corroboration of the
foreign statesman, I was truly discouraged.

Yet I was Japanese and I could not sit still.   If I could do
nothing toward improving the condition of politics, I could
at least attempt something by teaching what I had learned
of Western culture to the young men of my land, and by
.translating Western books and writing my own.   Then
perhaps through good fortune I might be able to lead my
countrymen out of their present obscurity.   So, helpless but
resolute, I took my stand alone.

I have never told anyone of the dire, helpless state of my
mind at that time. But I am going to confess it now.   Watching the unfortunate condition of the country, I feared in reality that we might not be able to hold our own against foreign
aggressiveness.   Yet there was no one in all the land with
whom I could talk over my anxiety—no one anywhere, east,
west, north or south, as I searched.   I seemed alone in my
anxiety and I knew I did not have the power to save my
country.

**What will
become of my
children?**
If in the future there should come
signs of foreign aggression and we were
to be subjected to insult from foreigners,
I would probably find some way to
extricate myself.   But when I thought
of my children who had longer lives to live, again I was
afraid.   They must never be made slaves of the foreigners;
I would save them with my own life first.   At one time I
thought even of having my sons enter the Christian priesthood.   If in that calling they could be independent of others
in their living, and if they could be accepted as Christian
priests, I thought, my sons would be spared.   So, in my
anxiety, though I was not a believer in that religion, I once
contemplated making priests of my boys.

As I look back today—over thirty years later—it all seems

a dream.   How advanced and secure the country is now!   I can do nothing but bless with a full heart this glorious enlightenment of Japan today.

It was during the first year of Meiji, or the fourth year of Keiō (1868), that I moved my school from Teppōzu to Shinsenza in Shiba.   Now that it had taken on somewhat the status of a regular school, I gave it the name Keiō-gijuku[11] after the name of the era, this being a few months before the announcement of the change.   Students who had scattered during the unsettled times were now returning, and the school again prospered.   As the number of students increased, a more systematic supervision became necessary.   So I drew up a book of regulations and, finding it impractical to have every student make a copy of it, I had the manual printed and distributed.

Our innovation —collecting tuition Among other items, it included one on the collection of monthly fees which was an innovation in Keiō-gijuku.   Until then in all the schools of Japan, probably in imitation of the Chinese custom, the students gave some gift of money on entering as a private formality.   After this they revered the master as Sensei, and about twice a year, at the Bon festival in summer and at the end of the year, they brought presents to him.   These gifts were sometimes money, sometimes articles, always presented in the old convention of wrappings and *noshi* (ceremonial seals).   They represented tuitions, in quantity or value, according to the financial status of the students' families.

It seemed to us that no teacher would really give his best under such a system.   For teaching is a man's work, too. Why then should not a man accept money for his work?   We

---

[11] Note on p. 361.

would openly charge a fixed amount for our instruction no matter what other people might say about it. We composed a new word *jugyōryō* for tuition and ordered each student to bring two *bu* every month. These collected fees were divided among my older pupils who had been appointed to do the teaching. At that time a teacher boarding in the school could live on four *ryō* a month; so if we had this amount for each from the tuition collected every month, we would have sufficient to keep ourselves alive. Any amount over and above that was to be used for the maintenance of the buildings.

Of course by now there is nothing unusual in this business of collecting tuition; every school follows it. But when we first announced it, such an innovation startled everybody.

We threw off all the dignity of the old master and simply told the students to bring the two *bu*—"Don't bring the money wrapped up or with the ceremonial labels on it. And if you don't have the exact amount, we will make the change for you." Yet some would, at first, hand in the tuition wrapped in paper, tied in *mizuhiki* (ceremonial cords). Then we would tell them the wrapping was inconvenient in examining the money, and we would purposely open it there and hand back the wrapping. Such were our rude ways, and no wonder they startled the good people around us. But now it is amusing to see that our "rude" manners have become the custom of the country and nobody gives a second thought to them.

In anything, large or small, it is difficult to be the pioneer. It requires an unusual recklessness. But on the other hand, when the innovation becomes generally accepted, its originator gets the utmost pleasure as if it were the attainment of his inner desires.

It was our fortune that the school in Shinsenza was not burned in the combat of the Restoration. By and by our

A pitched battle within our sight classrooms and the details of administration were somewhat organized, but affairs in society around us were far from peaceful. In May of the first year of Meiji (1868), there occurred the fierce battle of Ueno.[12] A few days before and after this event, all theaters and restaurants and places of amusement were closed, and everything was in such a topsy-turvy condition that the whole city of "Eight Hundred and Eight Streets" seemed in utter desolation. But the work of my school went right on.

On the very day of the battle, I was giving lectures on economics, using an English text book.[13] Ueno was over five miles away, and no matter how hot the fighting grew, there was no danger of stray bullets reaching us. Once in a while, when the noise of the streets grew louder, my pupils would amuse themselves by bringing out a ladder and climbing up on the roof to gaze at the smoke overhanging the attack. I recall that it was a long battle, lasting from about noon until after dark. But with no connection between us and the scene of action, we had no fear at all.

Thus we remained calm, and found that in the world, large as it was, there were other men than those engaged in warfare, for even during the Ueno siege and during the subsequent campaigns in the northern provinces, students steadily increased in Keiō-gijuku.

Our school is the one remaining link in Japan's civilization At that time all the schools formerly supported by the government of the Shōgun had been broken up and all their teachers scattered. The new régime had no time yet to concern itself with education. The only school in the whole country where any real teaching was being done was

---

[12] Note on p. 361. [13] Ibid.

Keiō-gijuku. Once I had an occasion to address the school:

"In former times during the Napoleonic wars, the history of Holland was brought to a sad climax. Not only her homeland but even her provinces in the East Indies were in jeopardy, and there was no territory over which she could hoist her flag. But there remained one spot on the face of the earth where Holland was still mistress. That was Dejima in Nagasaki, for that was Holland's concession in Japan. The sieges of Europe did not extend their influence this far, and there from the top of a high pole, Holland's national flag was proudly fluttering in the breeze from Nagasaki Bay. Holland was never completely erased from the face of the earth. Thus the Dutch often boast of their country.

"As I see it, our own Keiō-gijuku stands for Western studies in Japan as much as Dejima did for Dutch nationalism. Whatever happens in the country, whatever warfare harasses our land, we have never relinquished our hold on Western learning. As long as this school of ours stands, Japan remains a civilized nation of the world. Let us put our best efforts into our work, for there is no need of concerning ourselves with the wayward trend of the society."

Such was my manner of encouraging the young pioneers. As to the administration of the school itself, there were many difficult problems I had to solve. After the wars, as I have said, the number of new entrants increased considerably, but the students who came were most difficult to manage.

New students are difficult to manage; scribbling is prohibited
Many of them had come directly from the battlefields. Some had been fighting since the previous year, and now that the wars had ceased, came to our school to seek a new career instead of going back home. Among them was a certain young warrior from the Tosa clan who wore a pair of swords in red lacquered sheaths. Even though he did

not carry a gun, he was a typical soldier with all the fiery spirit ready to draw at the least provocation. This fellow was once seen wearing a woman's pink dress. When I asked him where he got it, he declared proudly that he had taken it as booty in the battle of Aizu. I was puzzled at first how to deal with him.

In my simple list of regulations drawn up soon after we moved to Shinsenza, I ordered that there was to be no borrowing or lending of money among the students; the hours of retiring and rising were to be fixed; all meals were to be taken at regular times in the refectory. Then all scribblings, not only on the walls and paper doors, but on the desks and lamp shades, were to be strictly prohibited. Such were the simple rules, but I had to see them enforced after they were issued.

Whenever I found a scribbling on a paper-lined door, I would cut out that portion of the paper with a knife and order the men of that room to repaste the hole with new paper. When I found scribbling on the shade of an oil lamp, I summoned the owner of the lamp. Sometimes a student would protest: "I didn't do it; somebody made those marks on my lamp." But I would say, "You are a fool to let others tamper with your own lamp. For the penalty of playing the fool, you must repair the lamp, for I am not going to allow any lamps with scribbling on them in this dormitory."

I never hesitated in enforcing the least detail of the rules. Once I found that one of the students—I don't remember the name—had a pillow, on the wooden base of which there were some indecent phrases scribbled.

"You know very well," I said to him, "that even on private belongings no scribbling is allowed. I suppose you won't deny this. I could shave off the surface of your pillow, but I won't do that. I intend to break the whole thing up. You will have to get a new one."

I smashed the pillow under my foot and stood there stern and defiant as if ready to meet any attack he would make. But the student did not move. I am rather large in stature, but I know nothing of *jūjitsu*—in fact, I am one who has never struck a person in all my life. On this occasion I put up a show of ferocity, a piece of bluffing based on my size, and the fellow was utterly cowed.

After this, all the other hard-boiled young men grew less rampageous and the dormitory became more orderly. Gradually the really studious ones began to take the lead. They worked hard and helped to improve our general atmosphere. And we stayed in Shinsenza until the fourth year of Meiji (1871).

Already the wars had ceased and the country was turning toward peace and progress, but the new government was still busy organizing itself, and for five or six years education was left alone. And ours remained **The Ministry** the only center in the country where **of Education is** Western learning was being taught. **established** Indeed, I think it was until after the completion of *haihanchiken* (the abolition of the clan system and the organization of the prefectural government)[14] that Keiō-gijuku remained the only school in European studies. After that, the Ministry of Education was established and the government began to give more attention to the public education. Our own school went on in the same way, the number of students being always between two and three hundred.

The chief subject of instruction in my school was English. Chinese, which was the basis of all previous education in Japan, was pushed to the second place. While elsewhere the boys had to know Chinese before taking up English, we

---

[14] Note on p. 362.

were teaching English first and Chinese later. So it happened that there were many students who could not read Chinese at all though they were reading English with ease.

There was Hatano Shōgorō,[15] for instance, who at first had difficulty in reading even his letters from home. But he was gifted and had a spirit keen for literature. He went on and quickly mastered the Chinese classics and became, as everyone knows today, an accomplished scholar.

The final purpose of all my work was to create in Japan a civilized nation as well equipped in the arts of war and peace as those of the Western world. I acted as if I had become the sole functioning agent for the introduction of Western learning. It was natural that I should be disliked by the older type of Japanese as if I were working for the benefit of foreigners.

My fundamental principle in education In my interpretation of education, I try to be guided by the laws of nature and I try to co-ordinate all the physical actions of human beings by the very simple laws of "number and reason."[16] In spiritual or moral training, I regard the human being as the most sacred and responsible of all orders, unable in reason to do anything base. Therefore, in self-respect, a man cannot change his sense of humanity, his justice, his loyalty or anything belonging to his manhood even when driven by circumstances to do so. In short, my creed is that a man should find his faith in independence and self-respect.

From my own observations in both Occidental and Oriental civilizations, I find that each has certain strong points and weak points bound up in its moral teachings and scientific theories. But when I compare the two in a general way

---

[15] Note on p. 362.   [16] Ibid.

as to wealth, armament, and the greatest happiness for the greatest number, I have to put the Orient below the Occident. Granted that a nation's destiny depends upon the education of its people, there must be some fundamental differences in the education of Western and Eastern peoples.

In the education of the East, so often saturated with Confucian teaching, I find two things lacking; that is to say, a lack of studies in number and reason in material culture, and a lack of the idea of independence in spiritual culture. But in the West I think I see why their statesmen are successful in managing their national affairs, and the businessmen in theirs, and the people generally ardent in their patriotism and happy in their family circles.

I regret that in our country I have to acknowledge that people are not formed on these two principles, though I believe no one can escape the laws of number and reason, nor can anyone depend on anything but the doctrine of independence as long as nations are to exist and mankind is to thrive. Japan could not assert herself among the great nations of the world without full recognition and practice of these two principles. And I reasoned that Chinese philosophy as the root of education was responsible for our obvious shortcomings.

With this as the fundamental theory of education, I began and, though it was impossible to institute specialized courses because of lack of funds, I did what I could in organizing the instructions on the principles of number and reason. And I took every opportunity in public speech, in writing, and in casual conversations, to advocate my doctrine of independence. Also I tried in many ways to demonstrate the theory in my actual life. During my endeavor I came to believe less than ever in the old Chinese teachings.

So, today, when many of the former students of Keiō-gijuku have gone out into the world, if I hear that they are practising the sciences of number and reason in whatever business they may follow, if I hear that they are upright in character, sharing in the principle of independence—that is the chief pleasure I find enlivening my old age.

It is not only that I hold little regard for the Chinese teaching, but I have even been endeavoring to drive its degenerate influences from my country. It is not unusual for scholars in Western learning and for interpreters of languages to make this denunciation. But too often they lack the knowledge of Chinese to make their attacks effective. But I know a good deal of Chinese, for I have given real effort to its study under a strict teacher. And I am familiar with most of the references made to histories, ethics, and poetry. Even the peculiarly subtle philosophy of Lao-tzu and Chuang-tzu I have studied and heard my teacher lecture on them. All of this experience I owe to the great scholar of Nakatsu, Shiraishi. So, while I frequently pretend that I do not know much, I sometimes take advantage of the more delicate points for attack both in my writings and in my speeches. I realize I am a pretty disagreeable opponent of the Chinese scholars—"a worm in the lion's body."

The true reason of my opposing the Chinese teaching with such vigor is my belief that in this age of transition, if this retrogressive doctrine remains at all in our young men's minds, the new civilization cannot give its full benefit to this country. In my determination to save our coming generation, I was prepared even to face single-handed the Chinese scholars of the country as a whole.

Gradually the new education was showing its results among the younger generation; yet men of middle age or past, who held responsible positions, were for the most part uninformed as to the true spirit of Western culture, and whenever they had to make decisions, they turned invariably

to their Chinese sources for guidance. And so, again and
again I had to rise up and denounce the all-important Chinese influence before this weighty opposition. It was not
altogether a safe road for my reckless spirit to follow.

**My publications
are all at my
own risk**
The years around the Restoration
period were most active ones in my
writing and translating. But as I have
already written minutely of these in the
preface to my collected works (Fukuza-
wa Zenshū),[17] I need not now repeat. All of my books were
done entirely on my own initiative without orders from or
consultation with others. I never showed the manuscripts
to any of my friends, to say nothing of asking prominent
scholars for prefaces and inscriptions. They might be
devoid of grace and form—I perhaps should have sought an
old scholar for a graceful foreword—but I preferred, then, to
have my books stand on their own merits. Naturally they
remained unapproved by men of the old school, whether true
or false. Still all my books proved very successful with the
great tide of new culture sweeping the whole country.

**The school is
moved to Mita**
In the fourth year of Meiji (1871) Keiō-
gijuku was moved from Shinsenza to
Mita, the present site of the school. This
is an important event in our history and
merits some special record.

In May of the previous year, I had suffered a severe attack
of fever, and this probably made me sensitive to natural
surroundings. I began to notice the air in Shinsenza as it
was a very low and damp location. I decided to move my
residence, and was about to buy a house in Iigura when the
members of the school began to suggest that if Fukuzawa
were to move away, why, the school should go with him.

---

[17] Note on p. 362.

We then remembered that there were many unoccupied estates of feudal clans[18] in the city which would be suitable for a school site as well as for my residence. So every day some members of the school walked around looking for a vacant property that would be suitable for our use.

After a long search, they decided that the estate of the Shimabara clan in Mita, Shiba, was the best. It was on a hill overlooking the great bay of Tōkyō with good air and a fine view. We were unanimous in the selection, but of course the property still belonged to the Shimabara clan. The only way to get it was to request the prefectural government to confiscate it from the clan, and then to lease it to us in turn.

We accordingly sought the governor, also asked Sano Tsunetami and several other officials of our acquaintance for their aid. One day I called on Prince Iwakura though it was very unconventional to ask a nobleman for an impromptu interview. Yet he saw me and I was able to tell him about the condition of the school, and I confided to him my hope of leasing the estate of the Shimabara clan. Prince Iwakura gladly acceded to my request. While things were thus going along well, it happened that the prefectural government of Tōkyō had a problem which they were obliged to ask me to solve.

The city of Tōkyō was still using a system of military patrol and soldiers of various clans marched along the streets with guns on their shoulders. The practice was very unsightly—it made Tōkyō seem to be continually in a battle area. The government was planning to adopt a Western police system, but being unable to secure exact information on its organization, one of the officials called on me one day to ask me privately to make a study. His attitude seemed to imply some favor in return.

---

[18] Note on p. 362.

I saw the opportunity and said, "That will be no trouble at all. I shall set about it with all haste, but there is a request I should like to make of the government. I have already told the governor privately that I wish to lease the Shimabara estate in Mita. Will you remember this when I complete the study?"

Thus I put into action a little scheme for the transaction of the property. The official understood.

I collected several English books on civic government and translated the portions dealing with police systems, making a book out of it which I presented to the prefectural office.[19] Very soon, upon the basis of my translations with due changes for the existing conditions, a modern police, known as *junra*, was created. This was later renamed *junsa*, and the new system fitted quite adequately the conditions of the city in peace time. Thus the prefecture came to owe me some obligation.

Our request concerning the estate was soon acted upon. The clan was ordered to offer up the property, and I in turn received an order to take over the use of the land. About ten acres of the ground was leased to us, but I purchased the buildings on the ground at one *yen* a *tsubo* (six feet square), or in all about six hundred *yen*. It was in the spring of the fourth year of Meiji that we moved our school to the new location.

We used the former palace for class rooms, and the former ladies' apartments for a dormitory. The ground was so extensive and we felt so free that there was nothing we could say against our new home. Later on when we needed more room, I took at low cost the unoccupied houses of several clans in the neighborhood, and turned them into an annex for the dormitory. Thus our school became very

---

[19] Note on p. 362.

suddenly a huge institution and the number of students increased accordingly. This removal and reorganization marked a new phase in our history. Let me tell an interesting episode.

The ground had suddenly become thirty times larger and the grandeur of the palace was truly incomparable with our former school house. The hallways of the class building—that is, the old palace —were nine feet wide. There I used to walk continually on my tours of inspection. Especially on Sundays, which was our day for general house-cleaning, I would look into every nook and corner of the dormitory. Naturally I would meet students a countless number of times as I came and went. Every time I met them, they paused and bowed low. This was a nuisance, for each time they bowed—and new students were particularly active—I had to return the salute. I asked the members of the staff one day whether or not they were also annoyed by this bowing. They unanimously agreed that it was a nuisance, and the only one since moving from our old quarters.

Salutation is prohibited

"Very well," I said. "I'll put up an announcement to stop it." So the following bulletin was posted on the wall:

> "In this school roughness and disregard of others, toward older persons or among fellow-students, are prohibited. It is, however, a useless practice for students to bow to teachers and their seniors in the hallways or other busy places in the school precincts. A nod will be sufficient. It is not in accord with the morals of the scholar to waste time in useless etiquette. This announcement is made for the benefit of every member of the school."

This may sound as if we were encouraging unmannerliness among the young men. But it was not so by any means. The Japanese people had lived under oppressive social restrictions for centuries and had acquired the habit of passive obedience. In directing these people into a more active life, the injunction against bowing was one step. I am sure the effect was noticeable.

The custom still holds in Keiō-gijuku. We are very strict in keeping to our regulations, and not hesitant in punishing students for the least breach in their behavior. We would not be dismayed if any of them complained and left us. Thus we have perfect control over the body of youths, but we never require a proof of it by the salute and ceremony of the old bow. And our students are not by any means ill-mannered. Indeed, I believe they have become finer and more manly as a result of the abolition of the meaningless etiquette.

Tortuous ma-noeuver to pur-chase the ground
As I have described, the land in Mita had been loaned to me. With no rent or tax to be paid, it was as if the ground was my own property. But as long as it was loaned land, we were in danger of being ordered to vacate it at any moment. Also I could see that there were many other landholders in Tōkyō who were in the same predicament as myself. So I was constantly looking for some way to make the property my own.

There was a certain council, called Sain, in the government of that time. As I knew a member of this council, I remarked to him about the impractical nature of this loaning of the land. My argument was that as long as the government allowed private use of the land, it should legally be made private property so that each holder could plan for its permanent disposal. I urged him to make this suggestion to the council. I also argued the same cause with any member of the government I met.

Whether my advocacy took effect or not, one day in the latter part of the fourth year of Meiji, I heard a rumor that the government was planning to make sales of its loaned lands to the persons then holding them, or to those having some connection with the former feudal owners. I was overjoyed and, knowing that a certain official, Fukuda by name, was in charge of all matters of property, I visited him in his own home and persuaded him to let me know as soon as the new proclamation was made. After a few days Mr. Fukuda sent me a message saying that the proclamation of the sale of land was to be made that very day.

Without losing a minute, I got the money together and the very next morning sent a man to the prefectural office to close the deal for the property. The official was surprised saying that the announcement had just been made the day before and that no one else had applied. The book and the receipt form had not been prepared as yet.

But we insisted on paying the money then and there even if we had to wait for the formal closing of the deal. So that very day the property became mine unofficially, and very soon afterwards we received the formal title deed. Thus Mita became the permanent location of Keiō-gijuku. In addition to the main part of the estate, I obtained a little more ground facing the street, the whole extent amounting to over thirteen thousand *tsubo*. The rate of purchase was fifteen *yen* for a thousand *tsubo* of the main estate and a little higher for the ground facing the street. The entire cost of the thirteen thousand *tsubo*, or about eleven acres of land, was therefore a little over five hundred *yen*, which means that we obtained the property practically free of charge.

I had come to like the place more and more as I lived there, and everybody in the school agreed with me that we had the most desirable situation in the city of Tōkyō. That made me all the more anxious to secure the property. And I had a kind of premonition that something untoward might happen if I did not act immediately. I was right in this, for when the government's announcement to sell the former feudal estates became generally known, a member of the Shimabara clan came to me and requested that I return the estate to the ex-lord of Shimabara. The property, he said, was very much involved in the lord's family history.

I replied that I knew nothing about it; I did not even know who the former owner was; I had simply purchased the property which the government had announced for general sale. If they had any complaint to make about it, they should present it to the government offices. This representative of Shimabara was very tenacious and came to me many times. Finally he suggested that I divide the estate with the ex-lord half and half. And still I refused. I insisted that it was not a matter to be talked over between us, but that he should go to the prefectural offices. At length he gave up and all question of the property was dropped.

I consider myself very fortunate that the ground remained in my possession. Its large extent—actually close to fourteen thousand *tsubo*—its high location, level site, the magnificent view of the sea, and the fine air make it without rival in the whole city of Tōkyō. The site is Keiō-gijuku's one premier asset. Were we to offer it for sale now, we would find that the value has leaped a hundredfold, or even a thousandfold, from the original five hundred *yen*. Some greedy members of the school are eagerly waiting for the time when they can so easily make money on it!

Teachers' monthly fight over the money Though we had no endowment, we were able to manage the teachers' income by distributing the monthly tuition. All the teachers were former students of the school and they gladly accepted whatever was forthcoming in salary. I myself took not a cent, but rather gave what I could for the needs of the school. The teachers had the same attitude. Though they could have earned large salaries elsewhere, they remained in Keiō to work for the upbuilding of the school. It was as if they too donated their private income. So this school without foundation continued to thrive.

In reality, at the end of every month, there was a merry dispute among these men over the proper division of the fees.

"No, I shouldn't take this much," one would say.

"But your share is too small," another would exclaim.

"No, I don't need this much. Yours is too small."

"No, mine is too much!"

Their voices would rise as the quarrel waxed stronger. I would be watching from the side and would break in: "Now, there you are again. There isn't enough here to fight over. Don't be too particular in dividing it."

It seems to me that the success of Keiō-gijuku was due largely to the services of those teachers who worked for it as if the school were their individual concern. The founding of a school could never have been one man's work. All human affairs proceed best, I think, when they are not meddled with too much but entrusted to the discretion of those concerned.

Since times have changed, we have collected a maintenance fund; also another fund for the establishment of college departments;[20] and recently we have started a newer drive for more income. But nowadays I usually stay out and leave most activities to the younger men.

---

[20] Note on p. 363.

XI

THE RISK OF ASSASSINATION

I think I have made it clear that I never intended to make enemies. But in an age when anti-foreign sentiment was running high, it was unavoidable that in my position as an advocate of open intercourse and free adoption of Western culture, I should make some adversaries.

It is not too much to have enemies who attack by means of words and epithets. But to have enemies who would resort to violent means is a different matter. Nothing can be worse, more unsettling, more generally fearful, than this shadow of assassination. No one without the actual experience can really imagine it. It is something indescribable by word or by any artifice of the writing brush. When there is some physical ailment or some definite soreness in the body, one can describe it to his wife or friend, but in regard to assassination, one cannot ask for sympathy even from those nearest him, for when told, they would worry about it even more than the one in immediate danger, and their anxiety would not relieve the situation in any way. I was not guilty of any crime, and it was no shame to be singled out by the ruffians, but feeling that there was no use in communicating an unpleasant possibility, I bore the anxiety by myself.

Many a fearful moment have I come through, often frightened by the lonely "sound of the wind" or the sudden "cry of the crane." It was somewhat like the present scare of the epidemic of hydrophobia when people are frightened by all good dogs because there are some mad dogs running loose. I suspected nearly every man on the street.

A secret escape hole in the floor The house which used to be my residence in the early years of Meiji still stands on the right hand side of the gateway to our grounds.[1] When I was having it built, I ordered the carpenter to make the floor a little higher than usual and to lay a trap door in one of the closets. This was to be my secret means of escape in case I should be suddenly visited by the ruffians. I think the trap door is there yet, and so far as I know, no one knows of it, for I did not tell the carpenters what it was for and I did not explain such an unpleasant contraption to my family. It was an unnecessary worry I had to bear alone.

History of assassination in recent years To recount the history of assassination since the beginning of our foreign intercourse—in the beginning, people simply hated the foreigners because all foreigners were "impure" men who should not be permitted to tread the sacred soil of Japan. Among these haters of foreigners, the samurai were the most daring and having their two swords conveniently at their sides, some of the younger and less restrained of these would spring on the "red-haired outlanders" in the dark. Still there was no reason for them to turn on the subjects of Japan, and so the students of foreign culture were yet safe from attack. While studying in Ōsaka, and even after coming to Yedo to teach, I had no feeling of danger for several years. For instance, when I heard of an attack on a Russian in Yokohama soon after the opening of the port,

---

[1] Note on p. 363.

I was merely surprised by the cruel incident, but I felt no personal concern about it.

Very quickly, however, the hatred of foreigners went through a tremendous development. It became more systematized, the objectives came to include many more persons, and the methods of slaughter became more refined. Moreover, political design was added to it and since the assassination of Chancellor Ii in 1860, the world seemed to become tense with bloody premonitions in the air.

Tezuka Ritsuzō and Tōjō Reizō were attacked by the Chōshū clansmen for the simple reason that they were scholars of foreign affairs. Hanawa Jirō, a scholar of national literature, had his head cut off by an unknown man because of his sympathy for foreign culture. And the stores dealing in foreign goods were attacked for no other reason than that they sold foreign commodities which "caused loss" to the country.

Here then was the beginning of the national movement, "Honor the Emperor and Expel the Foreigners." It was claimed that the Shōgun was not prompt enough in carrying out the desires of the imperial court which had decreed the expulsion of all foreigners without exception. From this, it was argued that the Shōgun was disobedient, was disrespecting the great doctrine of the land, and moreover was catering to foreign aggressiveness. Following this train of argument, it was but a step to calling all scholars of foreign culture traitors. And now we had to be careful. Especially when I heard of the attack on my friends and colleagues, Tōjō and Tezuka, I knew that the hands of the assassins were not far from my door. Actually I was to go through some very narrow escapes.

The period from the Bunkyū era to the sixth or seventh year of Meiji—some twelve or thirteen years—was for me the most dangerous. I never ventured out of my house in

the evenings during that period.   When
How I envied   obliged to travel, I went under an as-
the pilgrims!   sumed name, not daring to put my real
name even on my baggage.   I seemed
continually like a man eloping under cover or a thief escap-
ing detection.

One day I met a couple of pilgrims on their round of
temples.   On their hats their names and the village, county,
and province whence they came were clearly written.   I
sighed with envy.   "If I could only be as free as that!"   I
thought of my own situation and the present state of affairs
in society.   Growing sentimental, I spoke to the pilgrims,
gave them some money, and talked to them for a while,
asking them whether they were man and wife, whether they
had children at home, or parents, and many other things.
The incident lingers in my memory.

Here is an anecdote of a trip which I made to Nakatsu in
the first year of Ganji (1864).   I was leaving my native town
with Obata Tokujirō and a group of seven or eight young
men of the clan whom I was bringing to Yedo to study in
my school.   The weather became uncertain as we set sail
from Nakatsu and the ship began to make irregular stops
for shelter.   Really there was no telling
Frightened in a   where the ship might take us.   One day
barbershop   to my consternation the boat made for
the port of Murotsu in Chōshū which
was the center of the anti-foreign movement.   I was traveling under the name of Miwa Mitsugorō, the actual name of
one of the students I was taking to Yedo.   This young man,
by the way, is now with the brewery company in Meguro.
Under that name I landed and ventured out to a barber shop.

While shaving me the barber began to talk politics.
"Let's smash the Shōgun's government!——Drive out all
the red-haired outlanders—!"   Then he began to sing a

popular song. I don't remember the words exactly, but it was something to the effect of "Nagato soon will be the Yedo of all Japan." Out in the street, soldiers with guns on their shoulders, in various costumes, were swaggering about. I knew that the moment my identity was revealed, I would be the target of those guns. But I kept my composure, praying secretly for a good wind so that we might be sailing out of the harbor very soon. It was like being a cripple surrounded by a pack of wolves.

Again in Hakone Finally we reached Ōsaka. We landed from the wayward boat and took to the road. In the Hakone mountains we stopped at an inn, called Hafuya, near the pass. I found that there was a man staying there by the name of Toda who had come from the direction of Yedo. He was the commissioner of imperial graves with an office in Kyōto. There was no question of his being an ardent anti-foreign sympathizer, and he seemed to have many followers with him. I did not sleep much that night, and made an early start on my journey before daybreak—without much commotion.

I could not call on Nakamura Sensei During this journey I passed by the residence of Nakamura Ritsuen of Minakuchi in Ōmi and did not enter to make a call on him. I still regret this because, as I have told before, he had an uncommon relation with my family. Sometime before this, on my first coming to Yedo, I had stopped to visit him on my journey. The old sensei was very pleased and told me many memories of the past.

"When your father died," he said, "I went to Ōsaka at once to look after your mother and her children. And when you were ready to take the boat for Nakatsu, I carried you in my arms to the vessel which was tied at the mouth of the river Aji and said good-by to you all there. I hardly expect you to remember that, for you were then only three years old."

It made me feel as if I had met my own father. He wished me to stay overnight, and I did so. Such having been the relation between us, I should have paid him another visit, of course. But I had heard recently that he was giving special attention to Sun-tzu* in his lectures and he had even ornamented the entrance to his house with ancient armor. There was no question of his being an anti-foreign advocate. Certainly Ritsuen Sensei would never think of harming me, but he had many young pupils of fiery spirit. I could never have returned safely once I had entered his threshold. So, unwillingly, I let myself pass his house without turning in. After that I never had another chance to see him; he is now dead. To this day I cannot help being sorry about going past that house and not entering.

So far I have been recalling experiences before the Restoration. In that era there was really no instance of pressing danger to me, and my anxiety was more or less due to my own nervousness. But after the Restoration I ran into some highly provoking situations.

In the third year of Meiji (1870) I went again to Nakatsu to bring my old mother and my young niece[2] to Tōkyō. At the time I was entirely ignorant of any attempt made upon my life, but I have since learned of what was a very close call for me. I felt no particular fear in Nakatsu and it seems strange now to realize what I had come through.

A relative sneaks on me in the dark Back in Nakatsu was a second cousin of mine, Masuda Sōtarō, a rather unusual sort of person, who later came to be known as one of the insurgents in the insurrection around Saigō.[3] He died in the battle of Shiro-

---

* A Chinese classical authority on military tactics (6th century, B.C.)
[2] Note on p. 363.   [3] Ibid.

yama. I had known him ever since childhood and our homes being close together, we used to visit each other frequently. He was thirteen or fourteen years younger than me and, knowing him since childhood, I still felt that he must be a child. But he was indeed no longer one.

Sōtarō's mother was the sister of a Shinto priest, and this priest had a son—that is, Sōtarō's cousin—who was a well-known scholar of the school of Mito.[4] Sōtarō had studied with this scholar and had become a confirmed convert to that philosophy. Moreover, the family was of distinguished lineage, one to be proud of as representative of feudal society. I remember his father, as he was my mother's cousin—a very fine samurai. Brought up by this strict father and educated by the scholar of the Mito school, Sōtarō was naturally a pronounced advocate of "Honor the Emperor and Expel the Foreigners."

During my stay in Nakatsu I never suspected anything of so young and so affable a neighbor who visited me again with a smiling countenance. But all the while this smiling countenance was calmly looking over the situation with a view to putting me beyond any more argument. His purpose in calling was nothing less than to learn more about our way of living.

One evening—perhaps he felt his scheme was now ripe—Sōtarō came and hid himself in our yard. In a country town like Nakatsu, people never think of erecting strong walls around their houses or of locking the doors against thieves. I happened to be entertaining a guest that evening. It was my senior friend, Hattori Gorobei, and a very hearty sort of man he is. He and I were sitting together in the living room, drinking and talking. We went on and the hour grew late. All the while, outside in the dark, Sōtarō was

---

4 Note on p. 364.

waiting, watching our every move. At midnight we were still talking and drinking; an hour later we still showed no indication of breaking up. Finally Sōtarō was worn out and gave up his cherished plan. This seems to be an instance where my habit of drinking really saved my life.

When all was ready for our removal, the house closed and our belongings packed, we were to go by boat to Kōbe—the vessel being a rice transport. From there I had planned to continue to Tōkyō by a foreign steamer. Then we learned that the boat was tied at Unoshima, two or three miles to the west, because the bay of Nakatsu was too shallow for it. We decided to go to Unoshima the night before and be there ready to go on board in the early morning. That would permit us to rest more leisurely as I was still weak from an illness I had recently suffered; besides, it would be better for the elder companion and the children with us. We were blissfully ignorant of anything that was about to happen. *The unknowing person is as calm as Buddha.* I found out later that on that night occurred really the narrowest escape of my life.

The young proprietor of the inn, where **A narrow escape** we took our accommodation, was one of those important persons whom people call "patriots." After seeing us lodged in his own house, he sent off a secret message to some accomplices in Nakatsu that tonight would be a good chance to finish their plot on Fukuzawa's life. So the patriots—or rather the murderers—got together at a place called Kanaya and held a conference. They came to a unanimous agreement that they should make a raid on Unoshima and kill me. Their immediate pretext for the act was that Fukuzawa was now enticing the young lord of the Nakatsu clan to make a voyage to America. There was not one in the group who protested against taking the life of a man who held such an idea.

The crucial moment of my fate was about to arrive. My party consisted of my old mother, the young niece, the wife of a near-relative, Imaizumi, and her little six-year-old son, Hidetarō. So there was only myself who could have furnished any resistance to an onslaught. And I was still weak from my recent illness. There would have been no escape for me if a group of spirited young rascals had rushed into our quarters at the inn.

Then one of those strange things happened—should I call it a merciful act of Heaven? There arose a dispute among the "patriots." This act promised to be one of full success with no risk of failure, and every one of them wanted to have the honor and sure fame.

"We will go in first this time," said one group.

"No, you won't," cried another group. "We want to show off our skill tonight."

So the argument went on and on into the night. The voices grew louder till finally a man in the next house was aroused. He was one Nakanishi Yodayū, a much older man. He got up and went over to see what the disturbance was about. When he found out, he said, "Whatever is your reason, to kill a man is not a good thing. You should certainly give up all idea of going on with this killing."

The young ruffians now turned upon the old man in a body and began to argue whether they should stop or go ahead. In the full surge of the argument, they did not realize that time was passing. Before morning, of course, my party had gotten up and gone on shipboard without knowing anything of the hectic proceedings near by. After a peaceful voyage we reached Kōbe.

My mother had not been in Ōsaka since leaving at the time of my father's death, thirty years before. I had long wished that she might enjoy to her heart's content a sight-seeing in the old city, and in Kyōto too. But when we

Mother's wish of sightseeing is dashed

arrived in Kōbe and went to an inn, I found a letter from Tōkyō awaiting me there. It was from Obata Tokujirō with the information—"Ōsaka and Kyōto are not safe these days. I have also heard of some other things concerning yourself. I wish, therefore, to warn you to take the mail boat as soon as possible without making known your identity to anyone."

I was sorry to receive such disheartening news, but thinking I should not worry my old mother, I made up some trivial excuses, and we took an early steamer to Tōkyō without the much anticipated sightseeing.

Caution proves uncalled for

Quite contrary to the episode at Unoshima is another one which seems very ridiculous. A few years later—I think it was in the fifth year of Meiji—I made another journey to Nakatsu to inspect some schools. While there, I advised the lord of Nakatsu to remove his residence to Tōkyō. Of course it was not a light thing for a feudal lord to leave the territory of his former fief. That I well knew. But in the changing era when the fief was really no more, if he stayed there and tried to live in the old way, he would soon reduce himself and his dependents to poverty. I advised him to make a drastic decision and go to Tōkyō. My lord agreed with such a spontaneous decision that it was like the proverbial thunder clap, too sudden for anyone to cover his ears. We made preparations before anyone had time to make protests, and within six or seven days every member of the household, including the old retired lord and the young lady-daughter, were taken on board a ship sailing from the bay of Nakatsu to Shimonoseki where we were to take a steamer.

We had embarked all right, but the wind died down in the evening and our little craft was drifting near Mizuoki with-

out making any headway. The precarious situation aroused
my thoughts: "Now, this is a nice fix. The young ruffians
of the clan will surely make a raid on the boat if we do not
move out to a safer distance. And if those fellows do come
on board, I know who will be the object of their attack. I
had better do something while there is a chance."

I got up and went on land long before dawn though it was
the summer season of short nights, and ran along the coast
to Kokura, the next port where the boat was to pick me up.
In this way I thought I had cleverly outwitted the attack of
the angry clansmen, but truly it turned out to be a heroic
labor lost, for I heard later that during the night all was quiet
in Nakatsu; not a single warrior raised even a proposal for
the attack. So it seems that whenever I did make use of my
ingenuity to forestall an attack, there was no real danger.
The very real escapes always came when I was off guard.
Such was the dilemma.

**Frightened cow-
ards run for their
lives**
Here is an amusing tale of a dramatic
encounter of a much earlier period, coming in the third or fourth year of Bunkyū (1863–1864). There was a *hatamoto** named Fujisawa Shima-no Kami who
lived in Rokkembori of Fukagawa. He was a general in the
army of the Shōgun and a great enthusiast for foreign ways.
One day he held a party at his residence and invited several
of the scholars of foreign culture, including Koide Harima-
no Kami and Narushima Ryūhoku and other doctors of
Dutch medicine. I was also there among the seven or eight
guests.

This was in the dangerous period when I did not venture
out at all in the evenings. And I was taking particular care
to keep my swords well polished. The party was very

---

* A retainer of the Shōgun.

pleasant, and we kept on talking in spite of ourselves until it was nearly twelve at night. Then suddenly all the guests began to wonder about going home. Not that we had any guilty consciences, but in those days the scholars of foreign culture were all out of favor with the society at large.

Our host rose to the emergency and hired a covered boat for us on the neighboring river. In this craft we were to be carried to various parts of the city along the rivers and canals. Those who lived near by got off first, and one by one as the boat came to the vicinity of a home, someone landed. Finally an old doctor named Totsuka and myself were landed at Shimbashi. Totsuka went in the direction of Azabu and I was to walk to my place in Shinsenza.

It was a walk of a little less than a mile. The time had already turned an hour past midnight—a cold and clear winter night with the moon shining brightly overhead. Its silent, white beams made me feel unusually chilly for no good reason. I walked along the broad, vacant street—no one in sight, absolutely still. Yet I remembered that strolling ruffians had been appearing every night, cutting down unfortunate victims at dark corners. I tucked up the wide ends of my divided skirts in order to be ready to run at any signal and kept up a fast pace.

As I was passing Gensuke-chō, or thereabouts, I saw a man coming toward me. He looked gigantic in the moonlight though now I would not swear to his stature at all. On came the giant. Nowadays there are policemen to depend upon, or we can run into someone's house for protection, but at that time no such help was to be expected. People would only bar their doors more heavily and would never think of coming out to assist a stranger calling for help.

"Now, here is a pretty pass," I thought. "I cannot run back, for the rascal would only take advantage of my weakness and chase me more surely. Perhaps I had better go

ahead. And if I go ahead, I must pretend not to be afraid.
I must even threaten him."

I moved out diagonally to the middle of the street from
the left side where I had been walking. Then the other
fellow moved out too. This gave me a shock, but now there
was no retreating an inch. If he were to draw, I must draw
too. As I had practised the art of *iai*, I knew how to handle
my sword.

"How shall I kill him? Well, I shall give a thrust from
below."

I was perfectly determined that I was going to fight and
felt ready if he showed the slightest challenge. He drew
nearer.

I really hated the idea of injuring a man—I could not stand
seeing a man hurt, much less doing the injury myself. But
now there seemed no alternative. If the stranger were to
show any offense, I must kill him. At that time there was
no such thing as police or criminal court. If I were to kill
an unknown man, I would simply run home, and that would
be the end of it. We were about to meet.

Every step brought us nearer, and finally we were at a
striking distance. He did not draw. Of course I did not
draw either. And we passed each other. With this as a cue,
I ran. I don't remember how fast I ran. After going a
little distance, I turned to look back as I flew. The other
man was running too, in his direction. I drew a breath of
relief and saw the funny side of the whole incident. A
coward had met a coward as in a farce. Neither had the
least idea of killing the other; each had put up a show of boldness in fear of the other. And both ran at the same moment. To be killed in such a juncture would really have
been a "dog's death." He must have been frightened; I
certainly was.

I wonder where this man is today. Though the incident

occurred thirty odd years ago, he might easily be living still, for he looked quite young. I should like to meet him and talk over that night when two frightened men came so boldly up to each other on the moonlit road in the first hour of morning.

XII

FURTHER STEPS TOWARD A
LIBERAL AGE

Assassins turn to statesmen As I have said before, I felt my life in greatest danger during the twelve or thirteen years around the period of the Restoration. But the way of society is always amusing. When the new government had become fully established and certain officials assumed particular power, the attention of the people began to concentrate on these men. Every grievance, whether public or private, was charged to their responsibility. Furthermore, by reason of jealousy and private envy, these few men in high offices were made the sole object of attack. We scholars of foreign affairs, on the other hand, began to feel relieved.

Beginning with the attack on Prince Iwakura at Kui-chigai, all the untoward incidents had their origin in the political difficulties of the time, and after the assassination of the Minister of Interior, Ōkubo, in the eleventh year of Meiji (1878), we scholars were entirely forgotten. We could extend our sympathy to these gentlemen in office, but were rather grateful for our own safety at last, for the public could find nothing to envy in our present posts.

In the last chapter I said that I was determined to kill a man at Gensuke-chō and I said I knew how to do it. Perhaps that gave the impression that I was a warrior and a lover of swords. But the truth is quite the opposite. My one cherished hope was to see the abolishment of the swords of the samurai altogether. Truly I was wearing a pair of fine swords at that time, my long blade being of the sword-smith Kongōbyōe Moritaka and my short one of Bizen Suke-sada. But not long after that I sold them both with all the other weapons in my household, and went around with a pair of improvised swords just for the appearance.

I've discarded the sword but I can wield it   One day I was visiting my intimate friend, Takabatake Gorō, at his house in Hongō. While talking with him I noticed a very long sword in the alcove (*tokonoma*). I asked him what he was doing with that tremendous weapon that looked like a practice sword for *iai*.

"Well," he answered, "I got it because swordsmanship is becoming so popular these days and everybody seems to be taking a new interest in swords. I am a scholar of foreign culture, but I don't intend to be left behind."

I looked at him and said, "So you think you are going to scare the ruffians away with that long weapon? But don't be fooled by that. That isn't going to scare anybody. Look at me. I have sold all the swords in my possession except these two. And this long sword is really a short one made to appear like a long sword; the other is only a kitchen knife set in a sheath. It isn't like you to be meddling with that showy contraption while I am trying to prove that all such display is useless after all. Give it up. I ask you to. And now for a final proof—can you really draw that sword? I am sure you cannot."

"I can't," he replied. "It is too long for me."

"There you are! I have none of the craze for swords, but I know how to handle them. Let me show you how to draw that long sword."

I took up the heavy weapon and stepping out into the

garden, showed my skill in *iai* by swinging the blade, which was fully four feet long, from its sheath at my girdle. After showing two or three different forms of the art, I turned to my friend with the full strength of my argument.

"Now, take in the facts. I, who know something about the use of swords, have given up mine, and you, who don't know anything about them, want to exhibit them in the *tokonoma*. Don't you think something is wrong? I do not intend to stop with our group of Western scholars, but I look forward to the time when all men will give up the swords entirely. So you should put away this kind of thing right now. If you still have to wear a pair for appearance, why penknives or anything in a sheath will do just as well."

A dagger out of a fan At about the same time, while I was in the translation bureau of the old government, I heard one of the men saying one day: "An interesting fan has appeared. We have known the iron fan since old times, but how much it is improved by the new invention! This new thing looks exactly like a fan on the outside, but when you pull it, a dagger appears."

I stepped in to break up his enthusiasm.

"What is so interesting about a dagger coming out of a fan?" I said. "It ought to be the other way. It should look like a dagger on the outside and when you pull it, a fan ought to appear. If you show me such an invention, I'll call it good. What fool would want to invent such a barbarous thing!"

When the old government of the Shōgun fell, I at once renounced my rank as samurai and gave up wearing the two swords. Also several of the men in my school followed my example. It might seem to anyone today that people would be glad to give up the instruments of such deadly use, but the ways of the people were different then.

When I first called at the residence of my lord Okudaira in Shiodome without those "things on my waist," the officials insisted that I was disrespectful to his lordship to enter the estate thus incompletely dressed. Once some of our members, Obata Jinzaburō and others, had an uncomfortable experience when they were accosted by some bullies on the street for not carrying swords.

But I had determined upon the abolition of these things and I used to make this sarcastic remark: "It is only the fool who in this enlightened age would carry around the instruments of murder at his side. And he who carries the longer sword is so much the bigger fool. Therefore the sword of the samurai should better be called the 'measuring scale of stupidity.'"

Wada dares the ruffians

Many of my colleagues shared this idea. One of them, Wada Yoshirō, who later became the head of the junior department of the school (Yōchisha), once carried off a very daring joke on these interfering ruffians. Wada was a very gentle, kindly person who looked after the little boys in his charge as if they were all his own children. And the boys came to love him and his wife with the regard of sons for their parents. He was genuinely tender-hearted, but he was also a fighter. Having been born in the Wakayama clan, he was expert from an early age in all the military arts, had a wonderful physique, and was especially skilled in the art of *jūjitsu*.

One evening—I think it was after we moved to Mita—he with a few friends had gone for a walk without the swords as usual. While they were walking along Matsumoto-chō in Shiba, they came face to face with a group of the bullies swaggering along—a considerable number this time—with their long swords sticking out from their sides as if the road were too narrow to hold them.

Thereupon Wada, deliberately striding along the middle of the road, began to void urine as he came. It was a ticklish situation, whether the ruffians would move apart to the sides of the road or set upon Wada for a fight. But Wada was prepared for any emergency; he could have handled five or even ten of them in an encounter. His boldness must have got the better of them; the bullies turned aside and passed by without a word. This may seem a very drastic measure, hardly thinkable in these modern times, but it was not so unusual in that age of turmoil. It rather helped our school in holding its own against the numerous enemies who were ready to fall upon us.

I force a farmer to go on horseback It was not only among the samurai and ruffians but even among the plain farmers and townsmen that I had to oppose the old tradition. Once when I was taking my children to Kamakura and Enoshima for a holiday, we met a farmer coming on horseback as we were passing along the seashore. As soon as he saw us, he jumped off the horse.[1]

I caught hold of his bridle and said, "What do you mean by this?"

The farmer bowed as if in great fear and began to apologize in his voluble way.

"No, no," I said. "Don't be a fool! This is your horse, isn't it?"

"Yes, your honor."

"Then why not ride on your own horse? Now, get back on it and ride on."

The poor fellow was afraid to mount before me.

"Now, get back on your horse," I repeated. "If you don't, I'll beat you. According to the laws of the present govern-

---

[1] Note on p. 364.

ment, any person, farmer or merchant, can ride freely on horseback without regard to whom he meets on the road. You are simply afraid of everybody without knowing why. That's what's the matter with you."

I forced him to get back on the horse and drove him off.

This made me reflect what fearful weight the old customs had with the people. Here was this poor farmer still living in fear of all persons, never realizing that the new law of the land had liberated him. What could be done with this country of ours when there were so many people as ignorant as this! I keenly felt an anxiety that was perhaps uncalled for.

They are like a rubber doll I had another interesting and convincing experience in that period. It was in the fifth year of Meiji (1872) when I was invited to visit Lord Kuki, whom I had known intimately for some time, of the clan of Sanda in Settsu. I was glad to accept the invitation, for recovering as I was from illness, I had wanted to go to the hot springs of Arima which happened to be in that district.

I first went to Ōsaka and from there I was to travel some thirty-seven miles over to Sanda with a night's stopover in Nashio on the way. In Ōsaka I always called at my old master's home, for even though Ogata Sensei had passed away, I was always received by the affectionate old widow. So this time again I went to see her, and told her of my holiday trip to Sanda, and of my visit to the hot springs of Arima. The good lady insisted on lending me a litter as she feared to let me walk in my weak condition.

However, once started on the road, I found I was able to walk much more easily than the lady had expected. Besides, it was in the beautiful season of spring. I told the litter-bearers to go on ahead, and began to walk by myself. After a while I began to feel the lack of someone to talk with, so

I stopped a man who looked like a farmer and asked him the way. Probably there was something of the samurai manner in my speech and, without realizing it, I may have sounded commanding. The farmer replied very politely and left me with a respectful bow.

"Well, this is interesting," I thought. I looked at myself and saw that I was not carrying anything but an umbrella; I was very plainly dressed too. I thought I would try again, and when another wayfarer came up, I stopped him with an awful, commanding voice:

"I say, there! What is the name of that hamlet I see yonder? How many houses are there? Whose is the large residence with the tiled roof? Is the owner a farmer or a merchant? And what is his name?"

Thus with the undisguised manner of the samurai, I put all sorts of nonsensical questions on the stranger. The poor fellow shivered at the roadside and haltingly answered, "In great awe I shall endeavor to speak to your honor . . ."

It was so amusing, I tried again when another passerby came along, this time taking the opposite attitude.

"*Moshi, moshi,*" I began. "But may I ask you something, please? . . ."

I used the style of an Ōsaka merchant, and began the same nonsensical questions. I knew all the dialects of Ōsaka, having been born there and lived there as a student. Probably the man thought I was a merchant on the way to collect money; he eyed me haughtily and walked on his way without giving me much of an answer.

So I proceeded, accosting everyone who came along. Without any allowance for their appearance, I spoke alternately, now in samurai fashion, now merchantlike. In every instance, for about seven miles on my way, I saw that people would respond according to the manner in which they were addressed—with awe or with indifference.

Finally I became disgusted. I would not have cared if they were polite or arrogant so long as they behaved consistently. But here it showed that they were merely following the lead of the person speaking to them. It was quite natural that the petty officials of the provinces should grow domineering. The government had been called oppressive and despotic, but it was not the fault of the government. People themselves invited oppression. What should I do about it? I certainly could not leave them as they were. Could I teach them? That could not be done easily or quickly. Even though the situation was the result of the unfortunate government of hundreds of years in our history, yet these poor farmers knew nothing else but to bow and make apologies to the persons accosting them. Not only that but they would grow arrogant the instant one talked to them modestly. They were exactly like a rubber doll. What hope for their future?

Still the times do change. At present the onetime "rubber dolls" have developed into fine enterprising citizens. Many of them have learned sciences and are practising modern business and industry. And when they are drafted for military duty, they willingly go through "fire and water" for the cause of their country. Nowadays there would not be a single one in the land who could be cowed by this Fukuzawa however much he wielded his umbrella or used the most pretentious diction of the old samurai. That, to me, is the greatest blessing of modern civilization.

I would make myself an example

After all, the purpose of my entire work has not only been to gather young men together and give them the benefit of foreign books but to open this "closed" country of ours and bring it wholly into the light of Western civilization. For only thus may Japan become strong in the arts of both war and peace and take a place in the forefront of the progress of the world.

I was not satisfied merely to advocate it by word of mouth. I felt that I must practise it in my actual life, and that there would be no excuse if there was the least disagreement between my words and my conduct. Hence my self-discipline and my household economy so as never to be dependent on other men. At the same time I did not hesitate if I saw anything that was necessary in advancing the cause of civilization whether it met with the general approval or not.

Some of these radical innovations I have described, such as collecting tuition, discarding the swords, and using public speaking as an entirely new form of communication.[2]

Also, in my writing I broke with old-time scholarly style and adopted the simplest and easiest of styles. This was indeed distasteful to the scholars of the time. But fortunately both my own works and my translation were accepted eagerly by the public—like "water to the thirsty" or "a shower after a drought." The number of copies sold was really surprising.[3]

I know that no scholar or writer, no matter how great he may be, could either write or translate a book that would sell as mine did if he had not happened to hit the right time and occasion. After all, my success was not due to my ability, but it was by reason of the time that I came to serve. I am not sure whether other scholars of the age were unskilled in writing, or whether they were so absorbed in the prospect of gaining high posts in the government that they overlooked their own business. Whatever the situation may have been, I seemed to be alone in the field of writing for popular causes, and it became the sole basis of my livelihood and later of my reputation.

---

[2] Note on p. 364.   [3] Ibid.

Therefore on opening my school I was not obliged to draw on its small income for a personal salary, and was able to use all the tuition for the teachers. Moreover, I was often able to contribute to the school from my own income.

Whether because I am simply free from care or lacking in personal ambition, I have not an overwhelming regard for the school. Though I am always worrying over every detail of it and trying my best to improve it, I always recall that I am not dependent on it and that I have no real obligation to preserve it for the future. With this determination I have little to fear in the world and I can try anything new in the school by simply consulting my colleagues. Hence the air of independence and the practice of things not generally acceptable to the world in our institution.

Then again, while I have always remained a private citizen, avoiding all political connections, I have often expressed my own ideas on political matters both in speech and in writing, and they were sometimes in opposition to the government. But I really do not have any dissatisfaction with the present government. Even though there are officials who were reckless anti-foreign advocates at one time or who have tried to bring discomfort to me, now that society has been reorganized I should never think of bringing up old memories. I am willing to let them proceed in full favor so long as they carry out the new liberal policy.

Yet I have been provoked by certain officials who made a broad distinction between the government and the people, and tried to discriminate against private schools even to the point of placing obstacles in our way.

This kind of petty politics was a nuisance. But I do not intend to dwell upon my grievances here, because that would be too long a story, and also would make me use some disagreeable language. Since the opening of the National Diet, there has been less of this petty spirit among the officials, and I think we shall have more and more accord between government and people in the future.

In that troubled age I had some ex- **My temper** periences through seeking to prolong **would not let in-** the lives of certain condemned men. **justice pass un-** This was done only for my own pleas- **challenged** ure and no political motives were involved in it. Perhaps I might call it an extreme hobby of mine, or I might say I was urged on by my benevolence or by my temper which had been touched to the quick. Anyway, I gave fully of my time and endeavor toward saving some lives.

A certain chancellor in charge of the Yedo headquarters of the Sendai clan was named Ōwara Shindayū. He had been an intimate acquaintance of mine since the period before the Restoration. Though not himself a scholar, he was fond of giving assistance to the young students of Western learning.

He was indeed a gentleman of exceptional character, for unlike most of the men in high official positions, he did not spend his time in gay amusement with the *geisha* or patronizing wrestlers and the like. He probably had a comfortable income from his office as chancellor of a great clan, but he was never known to dissipate it in temporary whims. His chief pleasure was in being generous to the students of his clan. I should be safe in saying that there was hardly one among them who had not shared his table or partaken of his resources. One of these beneficiaries was Tomita Tetsunosuke.

At the outbreak of the Restoration, the Sendai clan had taken sides with the old government of the Shōgun, but they were soon defeated and the leader of the movement, Tadaki Tosa, a chancellor, had taken his own life. Some time afterwards, the country at peace again, a certain faction in the

Sendai clan brought before the Tōkyō government a strange and most uncalled-for accusation—that two men, Ōwara Shindayū and Matsukura Ryōsuke, were the instigators behind the leader of the rebellious movement. Although the government was making no further effort to impose punishment on the former reactionaries, yet with the accusation coming from the clan itself, it was obliged to send a mission to Sendai to arrest the accused.

So Koga Dainagon was sent to Sendai. I heard that it was a clever ruse on the part of the government, for Koga was a relative of the house of Sendai and would be less severe in his judgment.

But this generous policy was not at all appreciated in Sendai. The visiting official was greeted on his arrival with the sight of seven heads of newly executed men. The faction in power was overjoyed at the coming of the mission and had dared this cruel procedure on their own responsibility.

Ōwara and Matsukura were in Sendai at the time, listed among those to be executed, but having some friends to give them warning, they had escaped by running out of their houses through rear doors. And now they were staying secretly in Tōkyō.

These factious members of the Sendai clansmen were going after their own clansmen in Tōkyō. One evening a certain Atsumi Teiji ran into my house, saying that he was being pursued by his own people. Under these dangerous conditions, Ōwara and Matsukura managed to hide themselves in Tōkyō.

As I knew them intimately, I knew where they were and sometimes they came to my house. They were not afraid of meeting the government officials, because the central power had no demands upon them. Their fear was of their own clansmen who were trying their best to catch them and bring them before the central officials.

Then, of course, the government would be obliged to act.

I determined to save them no doubt from sympathy with the poor men but even more from my indignation against the inhuman clansmen. These jellyfish warriors seemed to know nothing better than to sting men out of power. I talked over the matter with Ōwara and decided that I should go to the lord of Sendai directly. So, though it was entirely a labor of my own initiative, I called at the Sendai estate in Hibiya and requested an audience with the lord. Fortunately there was a reason which made it possible for me to talk with him freely.

The lord of the clan at that time had really come from the house of Uwajima, and I was somewhat responsible for his being adopted by the house of Sendai. When the Sendai family was looking for a fitting heir, Ōwara had been given full charge of the selection, because as a resident officer in Yedo, he would have many acquaintances and opportunities to know the most desirable youths in the feudal families. One day Ōwara asked me to investigate the personality of one of the Uwajima sons, because the lord of my own clan had also been adopted from Uwajima.

I made inquiry at once, and the report being satisfactory, I was asked again to inquire whether Uwajima was willing to give up one of its sons to the house of Sendai. So I met one of the chancellors of the Uwajima household, then in Azabu Ryūdo-machi, and obtained a private agreement. It was Ōwara and myself who made all the arrangements, and when all was settled, the formal adoption was carried out between the two houses.

So I did not hesitate to carry my petition to the young lord. After describing the true situation, I put this question to him:

"Do you intend to have these men put to death if they are arrested? Or do you agree to their being released?

Would you do me the favor of answering this question?"

"No," he answered, "I do not intend to take their lives."

"Then," I continued, "would you not go further and try to save the men? Whether you realize it or not, you have a great obligation to Ōwara . . ."

And I related to the young lord the whole circumstance of his election to the present position. Then again I asked him seriously what his determination might be concerning Ōwara.

"I have no personal wish to impose any punishment on him," he answered. "But all such matters are in the hands of my chancellor. If the chancellor agrees, I am certainly willing to have the men freed."

He was still a boy and it could easily be seen that the power of the clan was with his chancellor.

"Are you quite sure that you will not change your mind on this?"

"Yes."

"Then I shall see the chancellor."

I went directly to the quarters and repeated my argument before the important officer.

"Now that I have the sanction of your lord, the life and death of the men depends entirely on your decision. What do you intend to do? Even if you search for them, you will not find them. I know where they are, and I intend to do my best to keep them hidden. Doesn't it seem unreasonable now to persecute men like this? . ."

As I took care to make my approach from several sides, the chancellor could not find any reason to contradict me. He soon agreed to let the men go free. But like a very weak and unreliable man, he said that the situation would be made easier if some powerful clan, like Satsuma, would intervene.

"All right," I said, and off I went to the Satsuma estate to implore aid. The Satsuma appeared a little annoyed as they were asked only on account of their great influence. They agreed, however, to go to the Household Department of the Imperial Government and see what best could be done about it.

In a short while the officers of the Satsuma clan sent me a private report that the government had decided to fix an imprisonment of eighty days on the two men; therefore the accused should submit themselves to the Sendai officers to receive the punishment under their surveillance. I went again to the chancellor of the Sendai clan to assure myself of his integrity.

"The government is going to order an eighty days' imprisonment," I said, "but can I be sure that you will not add anything to this order? You are not going to change the term from *eighty days* to *eight years* by your own authority? Until I feel sure of that, I cannot bring the men to you."

Finally I threatened to take revenge if he should in any way break his promise. Thus having taken the fullest precautions, I accompanied the men to the estate on the following day. It seemed that every official there had formerly been a subordinate of the two "criminals." The two men felt it natural to speak to their former subordinates in their old commanding manner. It seemed a very ticklish business as I looked on.

The two men were ordered to remain in one of the second-story rooms of the Sendai officers' quarters in Udagawa-cho for eighty days. After that they became entirely free—"fit to walk in the clear daylight." Ever since then we have kept up our intimate friendship and I am sure it will continue throughout our lives.

My only reason for occupying myself so deeply in this affair was that I was thoroughly indignant at the weakness and cruelty of the Sendai clansmen, and of course regretful at seeing the two good men in such unnecessary trouble. I had to make the trip back and forth in the city many times, and on foot, for it was before the use of *jinrikisha*.* Although this tiring foot-travel does not enter into my narrative, it was a considerable part of my exertion at the time.

I shall next tell the episodes of the two navy men, Enomoto and Furukawa.

I could almost say that Furukawa had started on his adventure from my own house, for he had dashed off against my advice to support the feeble claims of the shogunate.⁴ Later I heard that he made even a quicker getaway than did his colleague, Enomoto.

From Yedo bay, in his ship Nagasaki-maru, Furukawa sailed down to the coast of Bōshū where he gathered the insurgents hiding in the Nokogiri Mountains and carried them to Hakone Mountains. So the insurrection of Hakone was really Furukawa's doing. After this he sailed north to Hakodate to join other rebel vessels. Then the combined fleet came charging back southward in an attempt to capture the Azuma-kan which was then with the imperial navy. This, by the way, is the vessel we had brought over from America.

Then a calamitous engagement followed in the port of Miyako. Furukawa was beaten, taken prisoner, and brought back to Tōkyō. Next I heard that he was being held by *kyūmonjo* with another naval officer named Ogasawara Kenzō who was among our party on the mission to America. At the time there were no fixed laws or courts for military prisoners and civil offenders; this *kyūmonjo* handled all criminals together.

Though I had once called Furukawa a fool and had told him I would never help him again, when I heard that he was a prisoner, I felt sorry for him. Fortunately I knew a certain doctor in the Geishū clan in whose ward the two

---

* A small two-wheeled carriage drawn by a man.
⁴ Note on p. 365.

men were being held. So I asked the doctor to use his influence for my admittance. It seemed that there was no
particular officer in charge of the prisoners. When I got
into the long tenement (*nagaya*), I saw them sitting together
in a dingy room. I called out to Furukawa:

"Look at yourself now! What a fool you have been!
Didn't I stop you before you ran off? But it's no use to talk
about it now. You are probably hungry for some decent
food. And how about clothes? Have you enough to be
comfortable?"

I returned home and brought back some boiled beef and
some blankets, and made the two captives tell me all about
the wars and their discomforts. In this way I came to learn
a good deal about the *kyūmonjo*.

As to Enomoto Kamajirō (later Takeaki), he was also
captured and brought to Tōkyō a little after Furukawa. I
did not know much about his case at first as he was no
particular friend of mine though perhaps I had exchanged
greetings with him on the street, and I did not pay much
attention to his capture and his confinement.

There was a slight connection between our families as
Enomoto's mother was a daughter of Hayashi Daijirō, a
riding-master in the household of Hitotsu-bashi who was
considered the chief expert on horsemanship in the country.
His daughter was married to one Enomoto Embei, a police
official under the Shōgun. The prisoner was her second son.
My wife's family was distantly related to Hayashi's; she had
been to Enomoto's home with her mother when a little girl
and Enomoto's wife had visited her sometimes.

One day I received a letter from Enomoto's brother-in-law
(his younger sister's husband), Ezure Kaga-no Kami, now
living in Shizuoka. He had once been minister of foreign
affairs and I had worked under him as an interpreter. The
letter stated that the old mother of Enomoto, his elder sister,

and his wife were all in Shizuoka and very anxious to learn about him as they had heard nothing for a long while.

The letter went on to state: "We have heard the rumor 'on the wind' that Kamajirō was brought back to Yedo, but there is no way of ascertaining it. We have written to our relatives and friends in Yedo to inquire, but they are probably fearful of being under suspicion by the government. None of them has replied. So we are writing to you, hoping you will be good enough to let us have some information."

It was a long letter. When I read it, I grew indignant most of all at these unfeeling, selfish relatives of the family. What cowards to treat them so; after all, the old retainers of the shogunate were all like this! Well, I would see what I could do for the poor family if nobody else would.

As I knew the situation in *kyūmonjo* pretty well after my experience with Furukawa, I wrote back to Ezure at once that Enomoto was safe and well although he was in prison pending the government's decision.

Then again I received a letter from the family, asking if it would be advisable for the old mother and elder sister of the man to come to Yedo in hope of being near him. I answered that it would be very well; since I was not afraid of suspicion, they could come publicly. So the mother and sister came and began to send things to their unhappy son and brother in prison.

After a while the old lady began to wish to see her son. But there being no fixed law or regulation, I hardly knew where to submit her petition or what to do. I thought up a way of attracting the sympathy of the prison keepers and made up a letter of "pity-request" for her which read like this:

"I am overwhelmed with sorrow that my son has committed such a crime. But he is really not a wicked man. While his father was living, he was a very faithful son, and especially in his father's illness, he nursed him kindly. I know this myself. So it cannot be that a faithful son like mine would commit any crime against our lord. This son, of all men, cannot be wicked. Please be benevolent and grant him his life. Or, if some punishment must be done, please allow me to suffer it, for I am old and have not much longer to live...."

So I went on, imitating the illogical sentiments of an old woman. I had her daughter copy the letter, and then let the old woman take it to the *kyūmonjo* herself, leaning on her heavy staff. The sight of the old mother and the appealing letter must have moved the officials, for after a while the mother and son were permitted to meet in the prison though of course this kind of plea could not earn a pardon for the prisoner.

By and by I came upon a very fortunate circumstance. It seemed that Enomoto had made some very valuable notes on navigation when he had studied in Holland.[5] At the time of his surrender after the battle of Hakodate, he sent these notes to the commander of the imperial army, Kuroda Ryōsuke (later Kiyotaka), as he thought they would be of use to the country whatever happened to him. One day this notebook was brought to me for translation, because it was written in Dutch. The messenger said they did not know what it contained, but the government wished to have it translated.

As soon as I looked at it, I knew it was Enomoto's notebook of which I had already heard. I could easily have translated it all, but I had a different plan. I sent it back, making a clear translation of the first few pages only. Then I added that it seemed to be a very important study on navi-

---

[5] Note on p. 365,

gation as was evident from the first few pages, but the completion of the whole would be difficult without the help of the one who had made the notes. I could do the translating if it were a printed book, but since it contained the notes made at certain lectures, only the man who had taken them down could do the job properly. Thus I made the government official feel uneasy. I thought this would help in freeing the prisoner.

I knew Kuroda quite intimately; he and I had often paid visits to each other. I do not recall when, but I once gave him a photograph of a certain American general or president or some big man in the Southern Confederacy who, in the crisis of the Civil War, had escaped in a woman's dress after the defeat of his army. I had brought it back with me from America on my previous journey. I told Kuroda the story connected with it and said, "I do not think this American was afraid of death, but he chose to flee for wiser reasons. Life is a precious thing. It is certainly natural for a man to attempt to save his life even if he must escape by wearing woman's clothes. Now, there is Enomoto who has caused a big disturbance in our country. I think he should have his life even if he must undergo some punishment for his part. And think of it, even if you regret it afterwards, you cannot return a man's life to him after you have had him executed. Anyhow, please take this picture as a memento of my ideas and consider it if you will."

Some time later I learned that Enomoto was not to be executed. Of course it was not my manœuvres alone that saved him. I heard that it was the Chōshū faction within the government who were bent on executing him, and they might have seen it done if the Satsuma faction had not intervened. I believe that the great Saigō and others of the Satsuma made all sorts of efforts and finally saved his life.

The exertion in the cause of Enomoto was much harder

for me than my effort to save Ōwara. I had a spell of illness and was confined for a long time. Enomoto stayed in prison until I was recovering, so it must have been in the third year of Meiji that he was released. Unfortunately his old mother died before seeing her son come home.

As I have said, I was not particularly acquainted with Enomoto and there was no reason why I should be so deeply concerned in his affairs. I was led on simply by my feeling against the cowardly inhumanity of his friends just as I was prompted to indignation by the Sendai clansmen, and I grew determined to save him in spite of the others.

I recall talking with my wife at the time and saying, "Here I am working like this, but it is only to save the life of a man—no other purpose at all. I don't know Enomoto very well, but I am sure he is an able man and will be useful in the future to the country. But then, he is, after all, a man of the old government service. Even though he is in prison now, once he is released, he may get a government post. Then it is quite likely he will put on the airs of an important official and lord it again.

"In that case we must not blame him. If we are going to expect gratitude or humility from the man, that will mean that we are selfish and vile in our motive. We must be very sure on this point, for if there is any chance at all that we may feel some ill will toward him in the future, I shall give up my effort at saving him right now. How do you feel about it?"

My wife agreed with me and said that she would be ashamed to hold any such false expectations. We made a firm promise between us then to put the case out of our minds as soon as Enomoto was released.

Years afterwards, just as I had predicted, the gentleman rose high in the government service, becoming in turn a minister to a foreign land, and later a minister of state, the perfect exemplar of the high official. It seems I was not áltogether a poor fortune teller. But in my family my wife and I are the only ones who know anything of the true relations between Enomoto and myself. She and I having made our promise, no one has heard anything of this affair.

I suppose my children will learn of these relations for the first time when they read these notes.

XIII

MY PERSONAL AND HOUSEHOLD ECONOMY

Of all things in the world, there is nothing more fearful to me than a debt unless, perhaps, it be the shadow of assassination. Ever since early childhood, my brother and sisters and I had known all the hardships of poverty. And none of us could ever forget what struggles our mother had been obliged to make in the meager household. Despite this constant hardship there were many instances of the quiet influence that mother's sincere spirit had upon us.

I was told to return the money When I was thirteen or fourteen, I was sent on an errand to pay back what my mother considered a debt of long standing. It had come about like this. When we moved back to Nakatsu after my father's death, my mother needed some money to have repairs made on the family house, and she was obliged to take the advice of a friend to make use of what was known as *tanomoshikō*. This is a kind of collective loan fund in which a number of persons agree to deposit a small sum of two *shu* each for the immediate use of one of the group. Then several times a year they get together and repeat the same process for the benefit of other members who are chosen by lottery until the round has been made. Frequently, however, some of the well-to-do depositors would find it bothersome to keep their interest in the loan fund for such a small sum, and would simply withdraw their claims.

When my mother had availed herself of the *tanomoshikō*, one of the depositors was Ōsakaya Gorobei, a shipping agent, who withdrew without claiming his return. At that time I was only three or four years old and did not know what was going on. But ten years later my mother called me one day and told me of the circumstances:

"This means, you see, that the household of Fukuzawa has been the subject of charity from Ōsakaya. And I have been ashamed of it, for a samurai should not have money obligations to a merchant and allow them to go unpaid. I have been trying to save it, but only this year could I manage it. Here it is; please take it to Ōsakaya and return it with my grateful greetings."

She handed me the money wrapped in paper. When I called at Ōsakaya's and delivered it, the proprietor was much surprised.

"Why, that is very good of you," he said, "but we are embarrassed to receive it, for it was many years ago. You should not trouble yourself to bring up a thing of such long standing."

He wanted to give the money back to me, but I insisted on leaving it, because I remembered what my mother had told me. After some arguing, which was almost like quarreling, I forced the money on the merchant and came home. This happened some fifty-two or three years ago. But I still remember clearly the speech I was told to make at the store and what they answered. I do not recall the date, but it was in the morning, and the house was at the southwest corner of a street called Shimo Shōji. I remember also that the head of the house was not at home and that I met his brother, Genshichi.

The imprint of this early memory has stayed with me ever since. I have never been able to act boldly or selfishly in matters of money. When I became **I would wait till** older, I did all sorts of work from **money came in** actual labor in the fields to pounding and preparing rice as well as continuing my studies in the Chinese classics. At twenty-one I went to Nagasaki and, having no means of paying for my expenses, I first served as a kind of caretaker of a temple and later became a dependent in the household of a gunnery specialist.

When I went to Ōsaka and became a student at Ogata school, I was still afraid of money. I never borrowed any amount there. If I had borrowed, I should have had to pay it back some time—that was clear. If I knew I was going to have enough in the future to pay back the loan, why not wait until the money came? So, not even to the extent of one hundred *mon* did I ever allow myself to borrow. I also got along without once pawning my belongings. My mother used to send me, both in summer and in winter, the cotton clothes which she made herself. I resisted the temptation of putting any of these in a pawn shop for the same reason that I resisted borrowing from a friend.

But when I was really hard up and had to have some money at once—or when I had a drinking spree which I could not resist—I would sell the clothes outright. While I could get only two *shu* by pawning a garment, if I sold it I could make an additional two hundred *mon*. That seemed economy to me.

Nor did I ever try to earn money by copying foreign books. In my position as a student, I felt it illogical to spend any of my time in business. A moment was worth gold, a thousandfold, while the weighty work of learning was not complete. I was simply determined not to spend if I did not have. So from Ōsaka on into my life in Yedo, I continued with this idea. A debt might be easily contracted, but what a nightmare it would be when the lender came and found me empty!

Among my friends I often hear of someone who, in order to pay back one debt, would have to go elsewhere to get a new loan, thus starting another chain of borrowing and repaying. What a feverish life that must be! I do not see how a man can be happy in it even for a day. I may be a coward in the matter of money, but having a debt and being unable to meet it seems to me like being chased around at the point of gleaming sword.

Rather buy an umbrella than hire a litter To cite an instance of my cautious habits against spending—a short time after I came to Yedo, I was visiting a friend in Ōtsuki Shunsai's school in Neribei, Shitaya. I was returning home that night and had already reached the Izumi Bridge when it began to rain. My home in Teppōzu was yet a good distance away. I saw some litter-bearers waiting at the side of the bridge and I inquired the price. They said it would be three *shu*. That seemed too much for getting home when I had a perfectly good pair of legs. So I went into a wooden clog shop nearby and bought a pair of high clogs and an umbrella. These did not cost much more than two *shu*. I put my sandals in my bosom and walked home on my clogs under my umbrella. I nodded to myself as I went along thinking I would have my rain-protection for other rainy days as well.

Such being my careful habit, my pocket money of several *bu* often stayed in my purse for a long time. Of course I have acknowledged my love of drinking and of an occasional carouse with friends. Then I needed some money, but I never went to a restaurant or a bar alone to satisfy a wanton desire. As I was thus careful of my own, I was considerate of the money of others. I must admit, however, that I was not always so conscientious with the money belonging to my clan. With it I could play a craftier part. But that is another story. My general determination was to be independent, to earn my own way and not to beg, borrow or covet other men's property.

I paid the promised money on the very day of the battle   In the third year of Keiō, just before the Restoration, I purchased about four hundred *tsubo*[1] of ground belonging to the Arima clan in Shinsenza. By the laws of the Tokugawa government, the purchase or sale of property had not been permitted among the samurai class although an exchange of property had been countenanced. But near the end of that régime, many basic reforms were effected and even the sale of feudal estates was being permitted. When I heard that one of the Arima estates was offered for sale, I went at once to Kimura Settsu-no Kami's residence near the property and asked his steward, Ōhashi Eiji, to intercede for me.

It was duly arranged; the price was fixed at three hundred and fifty-five *ryō*.[2] As it was a deal between samurai, we did not stop to exchange a contract or to make a deposit. I simply made the oral promise of purchase and agreed to hand over the money on December the twenty-fifth. I gathered together the money, tied it up in a "carrying cloth" (*furoshiki*) and went to Lord Kimura's residence on the promised day.

When I came to his gate, I found it closed—even the small side door was locked. I called out to the gatekeeper to open it for me. He replied, "I cannot do that, Sir."

"But why? This is Fukuzawa."

Then he opened the side door, for he knew that since I had gone to America with Lord Kimura, who was then the cap-

---

[1] Note on p. 365.   [2] Ibid.

tain of the ship, I had been coming here often and was
almost like a member of the household. As I went in, I
felt that something was wrong. Men were running about;
there was excitement in the air. Then I noticed black
smoke rising from somewhere toward the south.

I met Ōhashi on entering the house and asked him the
cause of the turmoil. He lowered his voice and said, "Don't
you know? There is war on now. The men of Sakai are
attacking the Satsuma estate in Mita. You see, it is on fire.
This is no small matter."

"Um, yes," I said. "That is awful. I knew nothing about
it. But that is one matter, and I have another to transact
now. I have brought this money for the purchase of the
estate. Please take it and send it to Arima."

"That's nonsense," answered Ōhashi. "This is no time
to think of buying property. Now, don't you see, all the
estates in Yedo have no value at all, not even a *sen*. Give up
all such ideas."

"No, I will not," I returned. "I must deliver this money,
because I have agreed to do so."

Ōhashi turned his head to one side and said, "Well, I
know you made this promise, but if the times change you
don't need to keep it. And suppose you suggest that they
sell it for half the price, I am sure they will be glad of it, or
even for one hundred *ryō*. Anyhow, stop talking about pro-
mises and all that."

I had to resort to argument to bring him around: "I cannot think of that. You must listen. When we made the
agreement the other day, what was the promise? That I
should deliver the payment on the twenty-fifth of the
Twelfth month. And that was all, wasn't it? We made no
stipulation of changing the agreement on account of some
happenings in society. Or did we say anything about cutting the amount for any reason? Even if we have no

written contract, the words of men ought to be more reliable than paper. As long as there is the promise, I must not break it."

"Then there is another side to it," I continued. "Suppose I did propose to take the property at half the figure, or at one hundred *ryō*, the clan of Arima might very likely agree to it for the time being. But you cannot tell what might come in the future. Now we see the Sakai men laying siege to the Satsuma estate, but it may be only a passing disturbance and the time of peace and plenty may come back again. Suppose afterwards, in peaceful times, I am living on that property. When the men of Arima happen to pass by, they will recall how I got it—'The promised amount was three hundred and fifty-five *ryō*, but only because of a fight in Mita on the day of payment, Fukuzawa got it for one hundred. He made two hundred and fifty-five *ryō* and our house lost two hundred and fifty-five *ryō*.' So they would stare at my place each time they passed. I should not care to live in a house with such unpleasant associations.

"So I don't care what you say. You must deliver the money to Arima for me. It doesn't matter if I lose by it. A bigger war might come along and I might have to desert the place and flee. But I am not too much concerned with future possibilities, for everything in life is uncertain. Even people we depend upon may suddenly die. Then why rely on property? I intend to pay the money now."

At length I forced Ōhashi to take my money to the Arima clan. This scrupulous idea on money matters may come from my old samurai spirit which considers it base to change one's mind for the sake of money.

There is another instance much like the one I have just told. In the early years of Meiji there was a wealthy merchant in Yokohama who had founded a school and was employing some of my young pupils to teach in it. He had

I decline money for my children's education been vaguely hinting that he wanted me to come and take charge. At that time I had two sons, seven and five years old, and a little daughter. I had been hoping to send both boys abroad for their education. But I was not sure of ever earning enough to give them this privilege.

When I looked around to see what other men were doing, I found that most of them, scholars and officials, were trying in every way to have their sons appointed as government students to be sent to foreign countries. When, after all their negotiations and private manœuvres, they succeeded in obtaining an appointment, they were overjoyed as if they had caught some big game on a hunting trip. Of course one might naturally wish a good education for a son, but to go around pleading like a beggar to have him educated—that seemed disgusting to me. If one is poor, or has not the ability to earn, one simply cannot consider the luxury of a higher education for his children.

I had a secret contempt of these men. But when I thought of my own two boys and of the expense of foreign training, the way seemed indeed dubious, for after all the first necessity was money, and I was doubtful of earning enough in the ten years before they would be ready to go. I was anxious and did not hesitate to tell my friends how much I wanted to have money.

The wealthy merchant of Yokohama must have been told of this, for one day he called on me and openly asked me to take charge of his school. He added: "For the work I am asking you to do, I hesitate to offer you any salary, because that would not seem fitting. So, here is my proposal. I shall establish a fund so that you can count on sending your sons to foreign schools. I might make it—say, ten thousand *yen*. You may deposit it in a bank, for you will not need it now.

Then the sum would draw interest and by the time your sons are ready to go abroad, the money will have accumulated to an amount sufficient for all expenses. What do you think of this proposal?"

This was like a gift from Heaven when I was so longing for money. I should have said "yes" on the spot, but I stopped and thought: "This problem is not so simple. To be honest with myself, I have been disregarding his hints about taking charge of his school because I had distinct reasons. If I accept this proposal at this time, it would mean that I was wrong to have been refusing his offer. Or, it is wrong for me to receive this money, for if I submit to this temptation now, by and by I would be doing anything for money.

"Then, too, why do I wish the money now? For my children. I want to make scholars and useful men out of them. But is it a father's duty to make scholars of his sons? I must think of that, too. Of course, a father is responsible for his sons, but is there any reason why a father *must*, by any means, good or bad, give the best known education? Certainly he should provide, according to his means, the best possible education as well as food and shelter. But that should be enough. A father should not break his principles for the sake of his son. The father should be father, and the son son.

"I do not intend to stoop to serve my sons. I shall do my best, but that will be all. If they should miss a higher education through lack of money, that will be their fate."

Thus determined, I declined the offer of the merchant with genuine thanks, for he had made his proposal in the kindest spirit. It was not easy to come to this decision. Watching my children before my eyes, picturing their future in my mind, and gauging my ability to provide for them, I was truly torn between two wishes throughout the conversation.

After this I went on with my usual careful economy and gave continual efforts to my writing and translating. Then fortunately my income increased to an extent greater than I had hoped for. Before my sons came of age, the money was ready. So I sent my nephew, Nakamigawa Hikojirō to England. He is my only nephew and I am his only uncle; we regard each other almost as father and son. While he was in England for three or four years, his expenses naturally amounted to a considerable sum; yet I was able to set aside enough to send my own sons to the United States for six years.[3]

I feel very happy that I declined the offer of the merchant. If I had accepted it, it would have become a bitter regret all through my life. Even now I sometimes recall the incident and feel as if I had preserved a precious jewel from the least flaw.

Pay according to the rule　These are major instances, but in smaller matters I felt the same strain on my principles. In the ninth year of Meiji (1876) I went on a sightseeing journey to Kansai with my two sons. The elder boy was a little over twelve, and the younger ten. We were just three without any servant. First we landed at Kōbe by the mail boat of the Mitsubishi Company, paying the regular ten or fifteen *yen* for the first class passage from Tōkyō. From Kōbe we had a long tour through Ōsaka, Kyōto and Nara. On our return we stayed at an inn in Kōbe where I was acquainted with the propietor, Komba Koheiji. I had asked his head steward to purchase our tickets for the voyage home—two for adults and one half-ticket.

But when we were about to go on board, I found there was only one full-ticket, and two half-tickets. I called the

---

[3] Note on p. 365.

steward to have him exchange one of the half-tickets for a full one, but contrary to my belief that he had made a mistake, he answered assuringly, "That is all right, Sir. You were good enough to tell me the exact age and birthday of the young master—just a few months over twelve. Of course the regulation of the company says something about the age limit being twelve, but nobody pays the full fare unless the child is over thirteen or fourteen."

I broke in: "The rule is a rule; whether my boy is two or three months or two or three days past the age limit does not make any difference. I am paying according to the company's regulation."

The stubborn steward objected to what he thought was a foolish whim of mine, and said he could not think of wasting my money in that way. Finally I ordered him outright to pay the additional fare. "I am paying with my own money no matter what your argument is. Your business is to act as my agent. Do as I tell you."

The ticket was changed during the rush of getting on board. This seems to me quite as clear an obligation as paying the regular price for merchandise. But it seems that some men like to steal a luxury as long as they are not found out. I chanced, just the other day, to see a man come into a first class car of the train I was traveling in. He was obviously hiding in his hand a blue (second class) ticket. Such a thing is always detestable to me.

In the narrative so far I may appear to be a highly upright person in matters of money. But I must admit here that I was not always so. I was quite otherwise when it came to money belonging to my clan. How I came to change completely within a few years' time, and under what conditions, I shall describe now. And it is a pretty long story.

At the time of the Restoration, the shogunate gave its

retainers freedom to choose from the following three conditions for their future:

1. To become subject to the Emperor renouncing the Shōgun;
2. To remain as retainer of the Shōgun and follow him to Shizuoka, his place of retirement; or
3. To abandon their class of samurai and become ordinary citizens.

Without hesitation I chose the last condition and from that day gave up the wearing of swords. At that time I was a retainer of the shogunate, but I was still a member of my own Nakatsu clan and received my stipend of rice from it.

I decline my stipend from my own clan Then, as I renounced my samurai position and relinquished my salary from the shogunate, I reasoned that I should also give up the stipend from my own clan. I had no very big income then, but I was making something from the sale of my books. So with my small needs and modest way of living, I was quite sure that, with continued health and activity, I could take care of my family. Therefore, like a gentleman, I declined to accept any more feudal salary.

Curiously the officials of the clan were not pleased. They insisted that I should receive the stipend of rice as before. Strange it is that when we want something, it is difficult to make people give, but when we refuse an offer, they try to force it on us. The argument almost became a quarrel. Finally the men in the clan office began to say that I was being disloyal to the lord in refusing the allotment, his "generous gift."

"Well then, Sir, if you insist," I said, growing heated on my side, "I shall accept the salary-rice. But I am going to require that you have it polished beforehand; and every

month.   No, not every month but every day, and I want it
cooked, too.   All such expenses may be taken from the
salary.   Under this condition I shall respectfully receive my
salary, for I have no mind to risk the name of disloyalty.

"And when I receive my salary-rice in the form of cooked
food, my plan is to send out an announcement among the
beggars of Shinsenza that there will be free dinners for all
needy persons in the street.   And I shall let the beggars
enjoy my lord's generous gift in front of my house every
morning."

This argument seemed to dumbfound the officials.   My
salary was given up, and all official relations between the
clan and myself were broken off as I had proposed.[4]

I could also be crafty with my clan   This may seem dramatically generous and highminded on my part, but I can recall many incidents a few years before this when I played tricks on the clan to my own advantage that will make this
latter episode sound like a joke.   Whenever I received some
present from our lord, I always took it as a "worshipful
gift" and never thought of paying back my obligation.
After attending a feast as guest of the lord, I used to bow
with a simple "thank you" and never thought of the expense attending his hospitality.   I never recognized the
relation between us as man and man, and so I was never
embarrassed to accept his gift.   I was not alone in this attitude.   All the clan was like this; I dare say every retainer
of every clan in the country had the same attitude.

As long as I had this feeling about gifts from the lord, it
was natural that I should be greedy about money matters
with the clan.   I was happy if I could squeeze even one more
ryō out of the clan, like a successful hunter bagging his game.

---

4 Note on p. 366.

I would "borrow" money as "honorable borrowing," but once the money was in my hands, it was mine. I never thought of paying it back. No honor or shame influenced me; nor would I shrink from a lie or from flattery if they served my turn.

When Obata and others were in Yedo and I was taking care of them, the clan of course would not give me enough to cover their living expenses. I was using my own ingenuity to meet their needs. For instance, I used to make translations from the English weekly paper in Yokohama and sell them to the chancellors of Saga, Sendai and other clans. I also sold some of the less useful books brought back from foreign countries. I had to do something, for the number of students was large and they had constant needs.

I hustle off with 150 *ryō*

On hearing one day that there was some money in the clan's treasury in Yedo, I made up a plausible story and went to the chancellor with it. Having bowed many times, I told him I expected to receive a sum of one hundred and fifty *ryō* on a certain day not far off. Then I requested quite innocently the loan of this sum for the short time intervening. The chancellor, then Hemmi Shima, a very honest and good-natured man, replied, "I suppose there is no objection to giving you the order for an 'honorable loan' if it is to be for a short while."

I hurried to the director of the treasury with this vague and rather non-committal reply, and asked for the money at once. The director was puzzled and said that he had not received any order from the chancellor.

"That will be all right," I assured him. "All is understood. The only thing remaing is the actual transaction."

"Well, if the chancellor knows about it, there is no particular objection on my part," said the composed officer.

This again was a vague reply, but I took it as permission

and went to the next officer who had actual charge of the treasury. I told him that I had gotten all the necessary permissions in succession from chancellor to director, that whatever happened, he would not be responsible, for in three months I was returning the whole loan. So, like a sudden thunderbolt, before there could be any consultation among the officers, I had carried off one hundred and fifty *ryō*. I felt as if I had stolen the jewels from the dragon's palace under the sea. And I had no idea of ever returning the jewels! Deceitful? Well, we lived pretty comfortably for a year on that sum, my students and I!

With a foreign book for pretext, I extract more money

Again, I went one time with a foreign book to another chancellor, Okudaira Iki, to ask him to buy it from me. This gentleman happened to be well versed in the value and cost of foreign books.

He looked at my volume and said it was a rare book and would be very valuable. He went on praising the book more and more, but I knew my business. I felt sure that if I said the usual things, emphasized the value of the book, and said I would be willing to sell it cheap, he would tell me to take it to other quarters. I used different tactics.

"Yes, I know this is an unusual book," I said. "But the true reason that I am asking you to buy it is that I wish to have the money from you, for after you have bought the book, I am going to borrow it for my own use. In short, this is my little scheme to get the money for nothing. I am telling you the plain truth. So please let me have the money in the guise of payment for the book. I am really a beggar in a genteel disguise."

The chancellor himself had once taken advantage of the clan by selling them one of his own books for some twenty *ryō*. I knew the circumstances. If he had refused, I could easily have reminded him of his own little graft. My bargain was almost blackmail. Anyhow, with the former episode in mind, the chancellor felt obliged to give me twenty *ryō*.

I sent fifteen *ryō* of this amount to my mother in our native town and saved my family from its financial straits for the moment. Back in those earlier days of struggle, I often carried out some pretty raw tricks which I rather blush for today. Yet at that time I felt not the least scruple of conscience. Rather, I thought it foolish not to take the money when I could. And as in a hunt, I was proud to catch a "goose" rather than a "sparrow."

Man is a parasite feeding on society
It is difficult now to account for my shameless attitude toward my clan. I had come from a good family and had been reared by the best of mothers. I had indeed made up my mind never to be covetous of the worldly goods of others. Yet why should I have been without shame in using craft against my clan?

I am wondering now if I was not like the "worm" in society—a kind of parasite feeding on the customs of the time—which had grown fat in the continued good season. This worm had always worshipped the lord of the clan, and had regarded him as a kind of superman. To this worm the lord's possessions were like the resources of nature—to be exploited and made use of by all men. I suppose a revolution in society was necessary to rouse me from this illusion. The fall of the Tokugawa régime of three hundred years' standing gave me the cue, and for the first time I realized that my lord was as human as I, and that it was shameful to treat him as I had. I was not the least surprised to see myself undergoing the transition, refusing even the stipend that the clan had willingly offered me. I did not stop to reason this out at the time, but I am convinced now that the fall of the feudal government was what saved me from my slavish attitude.

Impossible to expect China to advance

Applying this personal experience to a greater problem, I might say a few words about present-day China. I am sure that it is impossible to lead her people to civilization so long as the old government is left to stand as it is. However great statesmen may appear—even a hundred Li Hung-changs—we cannot expect any marked improvement.

But if they break up the present administration and rebuild the whole nation from the foundation up, probably the minds of the people themselves would change, and these new minds may acquire the initiative to direct their way toward a new civilization. I cannot guarantee that this will work out as well for China as our Restoration did for us, but for the purpose of insuring a nation's independence, they should not hesitate to destroy a government even if it is only for an experiment. Even the Chinese should know whether the government exists for the people or the people exist for the government.

Untold reasons for the peace in our clan

Turning aside now from the wandering account of my financial experiences, I would like to tell a few things about my clan of Nakatsu, for I have some very pleasant memories. In other clans argument often grew into actual conflict over the question as to whether the members should swear allegiance to the Emperor or preserve their faith in the old government. After the Restoration there were instances of the winning faction forcing the leaders of the defeated side to take their own lives, or shedding blood over the question of how the clan should be reorganized. This was the case in many clans—perhaps eight or nine out of ten.

In our Nakatsu clan there would have been disturbances indeed if I had shown political ambition and advocated any

policy at all.   But I kept my discretion even to the extent of
stopping my friends from discussing politics.   I feel that our
clan's coming through quietly with no bloodshed was due
partly to my influence.   There was not even a dismissal of
an official.

**I advocate
a weak-kneed
policy**

In the third year of Meiji (1870) I went
back to bring my mother to the capital.
Many changes had already come about
by that time.   The officials were willing
to seek my opinions and I was called to
the chancellor's residence.   It seemed that they expected a
very radical speech from me.   Every official of any rank
whatsoever had assembled there.

When I took my place, one of the high officers asked me
with an anxious voice for a suggestion as to future policies
of the clan, saying that he was so puzzled that he felt like a
man in a thick mist.   In reply I said that there was nothing
new that I could suggest doing; in other clans there seemed
to be much dispute over the movement to equalize the
salaries of all retainers, but my opinion was that the old
system should be kept, letting everyone receive the same
amount as before, and so avoiding any conflict.

I noticed a look of surprise on all my listeners.   At the
same time they seemed to be much pleased with my conservative remark.   Then continuing with

**I advocate sell-
ing off the
weapons**

other branches of the subject, I said, "I
am for keeping the old order as far as
salary and rank are concerned, but I
have a suggestion to make on the ques-
tion of armament.   We are holding many rifles and cannon.
That is, we are presumably ready to defend our dignity by
force of arms.   But I would like to ask if it is really possible
to oppose our neighbors with this equipment.   I do not
believe we can.

"Suppose the Chōshū should demand something from us, we would have to yield. Or, suppose the Satsuma should invade us, we could not defend ourselves. We are in a precarious situation. If I put the situation in a few words, it is this: 'A weak clan cannot sin; its armament is the source of trouble.'

"Therefore, I would like to suggest a drastic step, the abolition of all our arms. All the cannon are of Krupp make; they might be sold for three or five thousand *yen*, or may be even ten. And our clan might become a state like the old Ryūkyū. If the Chōshū should come upon us, we would tell them to go ahead and do what they wish, but to go and quarrel directly with Satsuma. If the Satsuma came, we would say the same. Thus we would shift all our difficult problems to other clans and live in peace.

"Then it is clear that the country is going to develop toward a new civilization. So it is most important to establish schools and teach the young men of our clan what the civilization of the future is to be.

"This abolishing of arms would lighten our burden, and would even leave us too 'flush.' So I would suggest another plan. The government of Tōkyō is now finding difficulty in financing its army and navy. You might address a note to them and say that the Nakatsu clan happens to have a certain surplus in its treasury because of the abolishing of its armament. Therefore, the Nakatsu would like to present the amount to the central government to be spent as deemed appropriate. I am sure the central army and navy would be pleased to accept such an offer.

"At present all the clans of the country have different makes of guns and different methods of drilling. One has Krupp cannon, another Armstrong; then there are French rifles and some old Dutch geweren are found elsewhere. I am sure the central government is looking forward to unifying all the armament of the country some time, for with the present variety and conflict, there could be no useful co-operation in time of emergency. And so there could be nothing better than to abolish our armament and to give the money to the central government. This step should yield a double advantage, for the government would be glad of the money and we would be rid of our troubles."

A swordless sa- My suggestion, however, found no
murai? Impos- sympathy among my listeners. Suga-
sible! numa Shingoemon and three or four of
the military officers led a fierce opposition, and the whole assembly agreed
with them. They said my idea would be like ordering a samurai to discard his swords—impossible!

I did not push my argument very far. I simply added, "If you cannot consider my suggestion, please forget it. I merely thought it would be convenient." And I gave up further discussion.

It is a fact, however, that because of my coolness the Nakatsu clansmen were saved from any open conflict and from possible disaster. Moreover, the clan did not reduce the salary of any of its officers; indeed, there were even some increases made. At any rate, the treatment of all the officers proved fair and satisfactory. My wife's family, for instance, which had been receiving two hundred and fifty *koku*, was given a government bond for three thousand *yen* at the disbanding of the clan in the fourth year of Meiji (1871). Her sister's family, Imaizumi, having formerly received three hundred and fifty *koku*, was given a bond for four thousand *yen*. Unhappily these bonds became illustrations of the old adage "Evil money never stays with you," for the clansmen lost all in a short while and now they are all poor again. But it is true, as I have said, that the Nakatsu clan came through the period of the Restoration peacefully.

**Actual business
is foreign to me**

To return now to my reminiscences of money matters—as I have said many times, I was very careful and scrupulous in spending money, but in the art of making money I was indeed indifferent. I do not mean that I was not informed, or that I had no knowledge of the general principles of business, but simply that I had no taste or inclination to engage in buying or selling, lending or borrowing. Also the old idea of the samurai that trade was not our proper occupation prevailed in my mind, I suppose.

When I first came to Yedo, a senior friend of the clan, Okami Hikozō, was engaged in making printed copies of a Dutch dictionary and was selling each copy for five *ryō*. This was a low price for the time and he was making numerous sales. One day I induced a friend of mine to buy a copy, and took the five *ryō* to Okami. To my surprise, Okami handed me back one *bu* wrapped in paper. What did he mean by that? Did he take me for a poor boy to whom one gave money for charity? I felt myself cheapened and had a serious argument with him. I thought that taking any sum of money in the way of a commission was the part of the merchant and never dreamed of it in connection with myself.

**I buy a fire hold-
er and discover
an error in the
monetary system**

My remoteness toward money-making was in the practice of it. As to the theory of economics, I could reason well enough and even surpass many of the merchants of that time. One day I was buying a charcoal fire holder (*daijūnō*) at a hardware store near Kaji-bashi. For some reason I was having a servant carry the money that day as it was in a great number of small coins. I suddenly realized that the weight of those coins which I paid was seven or eight pounds while the weight of the fire holder was only two or three pounds. Yet both the coins and the tool were of the same metal—copper. The coins then were of much less value than the metal object—what a terrible error in our economic system! We could profit by melting down the coins to manufacture the tool. Anyway, this condition could not last long. The value of currency in Japan would surely have to rise sooner or later.

Going further, I compared the actual values of Japanese gold and silver coins which, according to the foreign standard, should be in the ratio of one of gold to fifteen of silver. I discovered that our system of coinage was entirely wrong —terribly wrong. Then I understood the rumor which I had once heard that the foreign traders, ever since the opening of the ports, were profiting heavily by exporting Japanese gold coins. Thereupon I decided to advise one of the rich men I knew to invest in gold coins.

I had no thought of going into this business myself, but I thought it worth-while to tell my friends about it. This was in the sixth year of Ansei (1859) just before I sailed for America, and when I returned some months later, this man told me he had profited a good deal from my suggestion. As a sign of gratitude he put into my hand a pile of silver coins until it overflowed. I did not thank him much or stop to count the sum, but took a poor friend of mine to a restaurant nearby. We had a feast in which I saw to it that my friend had all he could eat and drink. That was about the extent of my exploiting of money or my practice of its science.

In the early years of the Restoration I translated a book on the methods of bookkeeping,[5] and I know that all the current texts follow the example of my book. So I should know something of the practice, if not enough to be an

---

[5] Note on p. 366.

expert. But apparently the brains of a
The first trans- writer of books and those of a business
lator of book- man are different; I cannot put my book-
keeping cannot keeping into use. I even have great
decipher the difficulty in understanding the files
books which other people make. Of course
if I made a special effort to work them
out, I could no doubt decipher them, but I prefer to leave
all these things, including the accounts of my school and my
newspaper, to younger men, my only concern being the final
figures.

Sometimes a student would place some amount with me
for safekeeping, coming every month to take out some for
his pocket money. A member of the present House of
Peers, Takiguchi Yoshirō, did that when he was in the
school, depositing several hundred *yen* at a time. I kept the
money in a bureau drawer and on his monthly calls, I would
take out ten or fifteen *yen* according to his needs, wrap up
the remainder, and put it back in my drawer.

Of course I knew as well as anybody else that it would be
much more convenient to put his deposit in a bank, but
somehow I could not do so. Not only was I unwilling to put
his money in a bank account but I did not feel it right even
to change the bills from the original ones. A queer idea
perhaps—it must hark back to the inborn nature of the
feudal samurai, or to my old habit of student's desk-drawer
accounts.

One day I had a visit with a certain
A million yen big financier and our talk turned to
for my I O U— money matters. He began to describe
if you can find it some of the intricate and, to me, most
bewildering things in high finance. I
said, "Well, you certainly are making things difficult.
Why must you twist things around, borrowing here and

lending there? I know that merchants often do business on
borrowed money, but when you lend, that means you have
at least that much to spare. Then why should you borrow?
Wouldn't it be natural, even for a merchant, to make use of
his own money and avoid going into debt? Your twisting
around seems to me like inviting unnecessary trouble."

My financier friend laughed and began to ridicule me:
"What naïve notions you are trying to preach! A businessman enjoys complicated deals. The more affairs get mixed
up the more chances he finds to make use of his brains. No
one could get along with your unworldly notions. Not only
merchants but everybody in the world must borrow money
some time or other. Where is the man that never borrows?"

On a sudden realization, I replied, "You say there is
nobody in the world that doesn't borrow money. Well, here
is one. I have never in my life borrowed money from anyone."

"Oh, don't be ridiculous."

"No, not once. Since I was born fifty years ago (this
conversation took place fourteen or fifteen years ago), I have
not taken one *sen* of money from other people as a loan. If
you think that can't be true, try and find a receipt—if you
can. Any scrap of paper at all—not only the formal agreement with my seal—if you can bring one, I will buy it for
a million *yen*. But I know there isn't one in the whole Japan.
How is that?"

Then, as if for the first time, I came to realize that I had
never borrowed any money in my life. That had always
seemed natural to me, but it appears it was rather unusual
in other people's eyes.

At present I have some property. But my family finances
are carried on quite simply. I have no debt, nor do I need
to juggle my income around to meet various obligations. I
often keep two or three hundred *yen* at home. It may be

Why bother to deposit money in the bank? profitable to keep that amount in a bank and make use of checks for payments. And I am hoping that all Japan will learn to do so by and by. But as for myself, I prefer the old samurai method of keeping the cash in my bureau drawer. In this respect my wife is no different from me. Our home is like a world apart; the new methods of Western civilization do not enter our household finances.

I can easily understand why people should think I am queer, because in all my life I have never complained how **Never complain of bad times** hard up I was, how troubled I have been because of unforeseen events in my family, or how I could not make both ends meet on account of unexpected disaster in my work. These phrases have no existence in my vocabulary. It seems to me that those who use them are rather odd. I sometimes wonder if they use them as hints for a loan, or because they happen to be currently fashionable. Anyhow, such complaints are beyond my understanding.

One's income ought to be of no concern to others; to go around talking about it is like talking to oneself, which is the most foolish thing in the world. If I haven't much, I don't expect to spend much. Even if I had a fortune, I would not waste it. I certainly would not let anybody but myself have anything to say as to how much I should or should not spend. Rich or poor, I never will go about weeping over my ills. Because of my belief in contentment and my appearing ever in that mood, it may be natural for people to assume that I am rich. But such assumptions are of no interest to me; neither do 1 care whether their guesses hit right or wrong. I live on contentedly.

A few years ago, when the income tax was first instituted,

a certain official in charge came and told me privately that I had property assessed at seven hundred thousand *yen*, and that the government was going to tax me on that valuation. I replied, "Please don't forget what you have just told me. I am going to ask you to give me that seven hundred thousand *yen*, and my whole household will walk out naked from this place, leaving everything—house, godown, all the odds and ends in it, pots, pans, everything. If you have put that valuation on the property, I wish to see that it is really worth it. I don't want any indefinite estimate. I want a cash deal. Then I shall be really a rich man for the first time in my life."

I had a good laugh over it with the assessor.

My private affair is no concern of others If it is due to my inborn nature that I have been so constantly careful of money, at the same time the circumstances of my life have played a part in fixing my nature. I am now sixty-five, but since I left home in Nakatsu at twenty-one, I have been managing my own affairs; and since my brother's death when I was twenty-three, I have assumed the care of my mother and niece. At twenty-eight I was married, had children, and took all the responsibilities of a family on myself. Since then, for forty-five years, except for once imploring and receiving Ogata Sensei's great hospitality in Ōsaka, I have never sought the help or consulted the wisdom of anyone on private matters.

I have worked with energy, planned my life, made friends, endeavored to treat all men alike, encouraged friends in their need, and sought the cooperation of others as most men do. But believing as I do that the final outcome of all human affairs is in the hands of Heaven, whenever my endeavors failed, I refrained from imploring sympathy and resigned myself to necessity. In short, my basic principle is never to

depend upon the whims of other people. I do not remember
when I first felt the guidance of this principle, but it seems
that I have had such a determination, or inclination, since
early boyhood.

I learn the art of massaging When sixteen or seventeen, while
studying under Shiraishi Sensei, I knew
a couple of poor students who were
earning their expenses as masseurs.
Being much impressed by these men, as I was then determined to leave Nakatsu by all means, I learned the art from
them, thinking that if I ran away without a penny, I could
at least earn my food. By hard practice I became pretty
expert at it. I have not since been reduced to using it for a
living, but one never forgets an art once it has been
thoroughly learned. Even now I am a better masseur than
an ordinary professional. Sometimes when we go to hot
springs for a vacation, I massage my wife and children for
an evening's amusement.

This is perhaps one of the tangible results of my principle
of independence and self-help. If this kind of thing were to
be written in a formal biography of the deceased, the writer
would say: "Mr. So-and-So possessed from early manhood
a great faith in the principle of independence. At the age
of such-and-such, while he was a student in such-and-such
academy, he learned the art of massage, etc., etc. . . ."

The biographer would make a great to-do over the massage episode. But in my case I really had not much of an
idea or ambition at that age. I was poor and wanted to
study; I was sure no one was going to help me, so I took up
massage for lack of anything else to help me make my way.
After all, this ambition is a matter of circumstances. Not
everything one may say or think in his boyhood is a guarantee of what he will become in later life. Those who follow
their natural gifts, improving them by education and keep

on going without deviation, are the ones who win in the end.

The one big speculative venture of my life   Though I acknowledge that I have no skill in the actual handling of business, yet once in my life I tried what I may call a speculative enterprise and succeeded in it.

Ever since beginning to write, I had been letting the publishers take care of all the business from printing to selling. Certainly not all the publishers in Yedo were dishonest, but all of them had a tendency to give little thought to the authors. In bringing out a book, the only thing I could do was to write the manuscript. Then the rest of the steps—copying the manuscript, cutting the wood block (which is cut by hand from the copy pasted on the block), making the prints from the blocks, and binding the sheets, or hiring the workmen and buying the paper—all these were done under the management of the publisher. The author would receive a fixed amount of royalty, like the salary portioned out by the feudal lords.

When I saw that my books were selling in large numbers, I felt sure I was losing a great deal because of my dependence on the publishers. After all, the publishers were only merchants with brains not particularly reliable—I could do as well as they. So I decided to take up the business myself. But it was a big venture and difficult to know how or where to begin.

First of all, there were the workmen to secure. The publishers had always been between the workmen and me. The plan which I tried was this:

It was the second year of Meiji when I happened to have some money. Scraping together one thousand *ryō*, I sent a man to Kashimaya, a large wholesale paper store in Sukiya-chō, and ordered one hundred and some bales of paper to be delivered for immediate payment of one thousand *ryō*. Now, a thousand *ryō's* worth of paper was enough to startle the ears and eyes of everyone at that time, for even the biggest of the publishers were not in the habit of buying more than one hundred and fifty or two hundred *ryō's* worth in one installment. It was to be expected that the dealer would give me the best of his stock at his lowest figure.

I really could not tell whether or not the paper was sold to me at a low price, but I took over the order—the hundred-odd bales of paper—and had them all piled in the godown of my residence in Shinsenza. Then I asked a certain publisher to let me have several dozen of his workmen.

Appointing a couple of men from my clan as foremen, I had this large number of workmen put to work in my residence. When the workmen found out how much paper was stored in my godown, they were first of all impressed by the quantity. And believing that they would have employment for an indefinite period, they began to put their trust in me. Also I followed the practice of giving them their wages promptly from the very first day. So a feeling of good faith grew up between the men and ourselves, which soon led to their telling us all the tricks of the trade.

We had begun by pretending to know all about the business, but in reality we were learning it from these workmen. By and by we were able to do all the work of book making under our own management, allowing the publisher only the sale of the finished books at a certain commission. This was indeed something of a revolution in the publishing trade in our country. This is the only instance where I tried my hand in the field of actual business.

XIV

MY PRIVATE LIFE; MY FAMILY

No one is admitted to my inner thoughts

From my early days in Nakatsu I have not been able to achieve what I might call a heart-to-heart fellowship with any of my friends, nor even with a relative. It was not that I was peculiar and people did not care to associate with me. Indeed, I was very talkative and quite congenial with both men and women. But my sociability did not go to the extent of opening myself completely to the confidence of others, or sharing with them the inner thoughts of my heart.

I was never envious of anyone, never wished to become like someone else; never afraid of blame, nor anxious for praise. I was simply independent. To use an extreme expression, I was not taking my acquaintances too seriously. Naturally I had no mind for quarreling. Even in my childhood there was no instance of my getting hurt in a boyish conflict and running home to mother with tears and complaints. I was very active and seemed valiant in speech, but truly I gave little trouble to my mother.

If I boast loudly, I know the limits of propriety

After leaving home and going to Nagasaki and Ōsaka, I went through the usual rough life of the student, laughing and joking, sometimes acting as if I had not much conscience within me. But mine were always boyish pranks, and somehow I knew the bounds of propriety. This was rather from my natural inclination than from conscious effort. I was equal to anyone in loud boasting, but I was never drawn into the line of smutty stories which only the less scrupulous can enjoy.

Sometimes a schoolmate would begin to tell some fresh escapade of the night before in Shinchi. Not moving away as some of the fastidious might do, I would simply break in with a loud counterblast—"Now, you fool, stop your crazy babbling!"

After I moved to Yedo, I came into a wider circle of acquaintances. There were all sorts of men with whom I was going about. Even then no one dared draw me into the talks about the gay quarters of the city, Yoshiwara and Fukagawa. Yet, if I did not talk, I knew quite well the ways of things concealed there, for I could just overhear my friends indulging in their fond talks and learn easily, even intimately.

I had my own weakness in other quarters, however. I was a slave to my mouth and stomach. When there was not enough of good things at home, or when I had an agreeable visitor, I would go out for a feast somewhere, but that was the limit. I would not go to a theater, or even to Ueno to see the cherry blossoms, so far was I from seeking gayety.

How I saw Ueno for the first time In the summer of the third year of Bunkyū, when Ogata Sensei died, I followed the bier from his house in Shitaya to the temple in Komagome where the funeral was held. Then for the first time I passed through Ueno temple grounds. I remember saying to myself, "So this is Ueno where the cherry blossoms bloom." This was six years after I had come to Yedo. It was the same with Mukōjima. I had heard about it many times, but I did not go out there for a long time.

After my fearful illness with typhoid fever in the third year of Meiji, the doctors advised me that horseback riding was the best exercise to take during my convalescence. So I began riding in the winter, and for the first time went to Mukōjima, and then to Tamagawa, thus gradually coming to know the outlines of the city. Mukōjima being particularly attractive for its fine views and good roads, I often rode out there.

One day on returning toward Ueno from Mukōjima, we were passing over a sort of embankment when I suddenly realized that we were near the celebrated Yoshiwara. I suggested to my companions that we ride through that section to see what it was like, but they said it would be too conspicuous to go through a place like that on horseback. So we did not go and I have never had an occasion for going there since.

It may thus appear that I am a queer bigoted person, but in reality I am quite sociable with all people. Rich or poor, noble or commoner, scholar or illiterate—all are my friends. I have no particular feeling in meeting a *geisha* or any other woman. I do not get wrought up as some men do when they find themselves sitting under the same roof with these "unclean creatures."

I offer the cup to a boy Some forty years ago—this is a very old story—when I was in Nagasaki, a chancellor of my clan who was staying in the temple of Kōeiji called in five or six women and had an evening of gay carousing. Though I was holding my drinking habits in check then, I was ordered to take part. When the wine was flowing freely and the room in gay disorder, the chancellor gave me a cup and said, "Drink this, and offer the cup to the one you like best in the room."

Of course he was trying to tease me, for there were several

pretty girls there. If I had offered the cup to any one of them, I should have felt funny; if I had purposely avoided them, it would have seemed funny also. But I did not hesitate at all. I quaffed off the wine and said, "Now, obeying my lord's order, I shall offer my cup to the one I love best. Here, Taka San." And I turned to a little boy who was the youngest son of the head priest of the temple. I showed not a trace of excitement; my lord chancellor seemed displeased.

Last spring when I heard that Yamada Sueji of the Japan Times was going to Nagasaki, I suddenly remembered this incident and asked him to inquire whether the temple was still there and how the little boy-priest named Taka San was getting along. From Yamada's report I learned that the old temple was still standing as before and that Taka San was well. He was not a boy any longer but an old priest of fifty-one years, already retired. Yamada sent me his photograph. I was twenty-one that year; so counting back, I see that little Taka San was then just seven years old. How time runs!

Unafraid of gossip

So even over wine I always knew the bounds within which I must keep myself. But within bounds I was happy to talk and laugh with women or anyone, freely and intimately, for the gossips and suspicions of society were no concern of mine. One need not "turn red when coming in contact with blood." That is how a man ought to be.

The numerous old adages such as "A man and a woman must carry a lantern when they walk together at night" or "When things are being passed, a man and a woman must not pass them directly from hand to hand" are simply amusing to me. What cowards people are to need such rules to keep themselves from mischief! Wouldn't it be a heavy burden on one's memory to remember all those rules? I would rather believe in my own discretion. So I feel no hesitation in paying a visit where there is a young daughter in the house or where the young wife is staying by herself. Or at some feast, if there is a group of *geisha* enlivening the crowd with their antics, I am not put out by the gayety. I would drink with them, drink my fill, and carry on the banter with everybody until I am drunk. Then I should be all the happier. To others, naturally, my ways would seem strange.

I take honor in being gossiped about One day a chancellor of our clan sent for me and gave me a serious advice. "There is a rumor about you," he said, "that you are associating intimately with so-and-so, and that often you stay carousing in his house till quite late. There is a young daughter in that family; also it seems the family has not a very commendable reputation. *Geisha* and women for entertainment are said to frequent the place. It is to be regretted that your name should be associated with the disrepute of that household. Remember the saying, 'A man of high character does not even tie his shoe-laces in a melon field, nor does he so much as touch his hat under an apricot tree.' You are still young. Take my advice and be careful."

I was not in the least abashed.

"Is that true, Sir?" I replied. "This is very interesting. I have often been told that I talked too loudly and that I boasted too much. But I have never been called a gallant in that way. I am certainly honored by this. So I shall not stop visiting my friends. No, I shall go there oftener. I am not such a coward as to change my conduct because of someone's suspicion. I must thank you for your kind consideration. I do feel grateful. But I would rather have this rumor spread further, for it certainly is interesting to know that I am capable of causing such a report."

As I have said, I was such a boor as not to visit Ueno for six years after reaching Yedo, and Mukōjima for fourteen years. So it is quite to be expected that I would hardly be familiar with the theater.

When I was a boy, there was a custom of having local actors give *Kabuki* plays on the *Nō* stage[1] in the feudal castle. I once had the privilege of attending with our lord. Later in Ōsaka, when Ebizō, father of the present Danjūrō, was performing in a theater at Dōtombori, a friend of mine invited me, mentioning that there would be wine to drink during the performances. I suppose I heard the latter part of the invitation, for I went with him eagerly. On our way we obtained one *shō* of wine and the party of two or three friends sat through several acts. That was my second experience.

My first theater going After locating in Yedo, and even after the Restoration, when old Yedo became Tōkyō, I hardly ever stopped to think of theater-going. Then, about fifteen years ago, by an odd chance I went to see some plays and found them interesting. Here is a little poem in the old Chinese style which I wrote for my amusement that evening:

> Famous are the wonders of an actor's art;
> But a scholar, from all such toys far removed,
> Living through fifty springs the one "enlightened" man,
> I wake now in the maze of Pear Garden's magic.[2]

But I have always been fond of music, so much so that I am having all my daughters and granddaughters learn both *koto* and *shamisen* and also, partly for exercise, dancing. To sit and listen to them at their lessons is the chief pleasure of my old age.

---

[1] Note on p. 366. [2] Ibid.

How my boorish- **ness came about**   I do not believe any man is born with bad taste, but probably through various circumstances in life, I have grown this way. First of all, I lacked someone to look after my education and I grew up without learning calligraphy very well. I might have studied it later in life, but then I had already gone into Western sciences, and was regarding all Chinese culture as a mortal enemy. Particularly I despised the false behavior of the Chinese scholars; they would lecture on the four virtues of man—justice, humanity, loyalty, and filial piety—yet when a crisis came, they proved themselves mere weaklings. And among themselves those living a licentious life, drinking freely, composing poems, and skillful in calligraphy were most admired.

I decided that I, a Western scholar, would go in the opposite way. As I had sold off my swords and given up *iai*, which I loved, when swords and fencing were most in vogue, I decided not to compose poems and purposely to remain unskilled in calligraphy.

This peculiar whim of mine was a great mistake. Indeed, my father and my brother were both cultured men. Especially my brother was a fine calligrapher, and something of a painter and sealcutter, too. But I fear I have none of those qualities. When it comes to antiques, curios, and other branches of the fine arts, I am hopelessly out of it. I leave the design of my house to the carpenters, and all the trees and stones in my garden to the gardener's judgment. As for dress, I know nothing of fashion nor do I care to learn about it. I wear whatever my wife gives me.

One day when I was suddenly called out on business, I thought of changing my dress. My wife being out at the moment, I opened the chest of drawers and took out a garment that happened to be lying on top. When I returned, my wife looked curiously at me and said I was wearing an undergarment. She had one more cause for laughing at me.

In this case, of course, my unconcern for dress went a little too near the limit. So I must admit I am missing many of the pleasures that people of finer education enjoy. Nowadays I do go to theaters and occasionally invite actors and musicians to my house, but these have not become my chief diversions. After all, I find my greatest pleasure in seeing my children and grandchildren assembled around me, playing with them, or watching them play music or dance, and in seeing them enjoy the food I can give them. The sounds of their happy voices and laughter, mingled with those of the elders in my living rooms, are the sweetest music I can think of to brighten the days of my old age.

I take a wife and beget nine children Now, about my marriage and the more intimate phases of my family life: In the first year of Bunkyū (1861), through the mediation of a certain member of our clan, I was married to the second daughter of Toki Tarohachi, an officer of my clan in Yedo. And she is my present wife. At the time of our marriage I was twenty-eight and my bride was seventeen. As to our social ranks, her family belonged to the Upper Samurai while mine was of the Lower Samurai. It was a somewhat unusual union, but in both of us there was good lineage; for five generations in both our families there had not been any hereditary diseases. Without question both she and I were perfectly healthy and we have remained so throughout our lives.

In the third year of Bunkyū our first son, Ichitarō, arrived —then Sutejirō, our second son, then a daughter, until finally we had a family of nine children, four sons and five daughters.[3] Fortunately all of them grew up well. The first five

---

[3] Note on p. 366.

children were nursed by their own mother, but after the sixth, we hired wet nurses because we were afraid the mother's health might be impaired.

In caring for the children we gave **Our children's** more attention to their food than to **free activity is** their clothes. They may have worn **never repressed** some shabby outfits at times, but they have never lacked proper nourishment. In training them we encouraged gentleness of mind and liveliness of body, and gave them freedom in most things. For instance, we have never forced a child to take a hot bath. We leave a large tub of cold water near the bath and let them temper the bath water as they wish. They were left quite free, but this freedom did not extend to letting them eat whatever they wanted.

When we decided on encouraging liveliness of body, we had to be content to see a few things broken once in a while. We were not going to scold them for making tears in the paper doors and a few knicks in the furniture. When they were too stubborn in their mischief, a serious look or two gave them to understand that they must stop, but that was the limit of punishment. As to actual beating, it was never known.

We use a certain respectful mode of address in calling our children or our children-in-law. So likewise do the elder children in speaking to their younger brothers and sisters. There is not the usual distinction between strict father and loving mother. In strictness we are both strict; in love we are both loving. We, parents and children, live together like trusting friends. My little grandchild would say, "I am afraid of mother sometimes, but I am never afraid of grandpa."

I may be more lenient than other fathers, but my children and grandchildren do not seem to be particularly spoiled.

Fukuzawa and his wife, Toki Kin (1900). The inscription, in Fukuzawa's hand, reads: "This we took in the thirty-third year of Meiji. Both Fukuzawa Yukichi and his wife were once of the Okudaira Clan."

No secrets in the family In playing with us they are gentle and listen obediently to what we say. So I believe it is just as well that we have not lorded it over them in the sterner way. It is our house rule to have no secrets between any members of the family. We never tell a thing to one child and keep it from another. The parents at times may have to reprimand the children, but then the children are capable of making fun of the parents for something in return.

My family may seem lacking in etiquette So perhaps to the men of the old school, my family appears lacking in the proper etiquette between young and old. When the gentleman of the house goes out or comes in, there is no formal salutation from wife and servants at the entrance. When I go out, I may leave from the front door or from the kitchen. When I return, I come in through whichever entrance happens to be conveniently in my way. Coming home in a *jinrikisha* or carriage, I especially tell the man or driver not to call out "Honorable Return" at the entrance. Even if they should shout, no one would come out to meet me.

I suppose many people—not only outsiders but my own mother-in-law—must be puzzled by this lapse of etiquette. This old woman, reaching seventy-seven years of age this year, once lived in strict convention as the wife of our clan's official. She surely must be feeling that this Fukuzawa family is sadly deficient in the forms of good breeding. Yet she would not be able to point out exactly where the fault lies, so the old lady must be very puzzled over this strange state of things.

Boys and girls are equal Among my family of nine children, we make no distinction at all in affection and position between boys and girls. In our society it is customary to make a great deal over the birth of a boy baby; but when a girl arrives, people say they should perhaps offer congratulations if the baby is strong and gives no trouble to the parents. No such distinction exists for us. I should not have regretted having nine daughters. I am glad, though, that my children are divided evenly among boys and girls.

Some moralists are advocating love for all men in the whole world. I would be a beast not to give my own children equal love and privilege. However, I have to remember the position of my eldest son who will take my place and become the center of the family after my death. So I must give him some privileges. If there is something that cannot be divided, I tell him to take it. Otherwise, there is no difference made.[4]

Once I was visiting a friend in Nihombashi and saw many lovely things piled up in his drawing-room—gold lacquer ware, gilt screens, decorated vases, etc. Learning from him that all these were to be exported to America, I suddenly had the desire to buy them myself. There was nothing I really needed, but they were all lovely things for anyone to own.

I said to my friend, "I don't know how much you expect to make on these things, but I should like to buy the whole lot myself, if you are willing. I have no idea of selling them for profit, but I simply want to keep them."

My friend was not merely a merchant with his eyes fixed on profit. He thought a little and replied, "You give me an idea. These things came from Nagoya, but if I have them sent to America, they will all be scattered and lost. If I sell them to you, they will be kept together and preserved. All right. You can have them."

"Good. I'll take them all."

So for the sum of twenty-two or-three hundred *yen* I came into possession of several dozens of beautiful things. They were carried to my dwelling, but I did not really look at them or count their number. They were simply so much bulk in the storehouse. So a few years ago I told my children to divide the things among themselves.

There was a merry conference and the things were divided into nine equal parts. Then by lottery each child took one of the parts. Some of them, having homes of their own, took their shares away. The rest, belonging to the younger children, are still in my godown. This is about our usual way of doing things. My children are all equal. I am sure they are happy about it.

I disagree with the Western custom in making a will

Recently I drew up a will. We often see in foreign stories an episode of great surprise and wailing at the disclosure of a man's will after his death. I am not impressed by such tales at all. Why should a man make a secret of anything that is to be disclosed after his death? Western people must be doing this only from an unenlightened custom. I declared that I would have my own way about my will, and I have shown it to my wife and children.

"Remember, the will is in this drawer of my cabinet," I told them. "If I change my mind, I'll make another and show that to you again. So read it carefully now and don't quarrel among yourselves after I am dead."

The body must be built first

To continue with my ideas on bringing up children, my chief care is always for their physical health. I have said, "Grow an animal's body; then develop a man's mind." I do not even show them a single letter of the alphabet until after they are four or five years old. At seven or eight, I sometimes give them lessons in calligraphy, but not always. I never give them reading lessons at that age. They are left perfectly free to romp about as they will, my only care being their food and clothing. We do reprimand them a little if they are found engaged in indecent activities or imitating coarse language. Otherwise they are left quite alone, very much in the way we might bring up dogs and cats. That is what I mean by "growing an animal's body."

When they grow well and strong like little animals and reach the age of nine or ten, I begin to give them regular lessons. Then I believe in study at certain fixed hours every day, but even then not at the risk of health. Many parents are liable to be overanxious about their children's studies and praise them whenever they are found sitting at their desks. But in my house no child is praised for reading a book.

Now my own children have grown beyond my care, and I find I am looking after their children. But I care for them in the same way. I reward them when they take an unusually long walk, or if they show an improvement in *jū-jitsu* or gymnastics. But I have never given them a reward for having read a difficult book.

Over twenty years ago I sent my two eldest sons to the preparatory department of the Imperial University. Both of them soon grew ill with indigestion. I had them come home to stay until they were well, but as soon as I sent them back, they again became ill. I tried three times, and each time they grew ill and had to come home. At that time Tanaka Fujimaro was the director of the bureau of education.

I went to him and made a complaint of the inadequate supervision which I could prove by the experience of my sons. I said that if this condition was allowed to continue, many of the students would not live, or if they survived, they would be mentally unbalanced or physically crippled.

"I am keeping my boys in the department," I added, "in the hope that the conditions will improve before they have finished. If you leave things as they are, I shall call your institution a 'slaughterhouse of young men.'"

I spoke as openly as I would to an intimate acquaintance, which he was. But things were not changed as fast as I hoped. My sons were obliged to alternate three months of college attendance with three months of living at home. Finally we were discouraged and I let them take their general education in my own Keiō-gijuku. Then I sent them to America for further education.[5] I do not insist that the discipline used in the Imperial University was wrong, but I feared it was too heavy for my boys. I still believe that physical health is the most important asset in a man's life.

Records of my children's infancy
Any person is interested in knowing, later on in life, something of the facts and nature of his early existence. I am not sure if everybody is as curious as I am, but since this is my feeling, I have been keeping a record of my children—the manner of their births and the exact time to the minute; the condition of their health in infancy; their nature and habits in childhood. I feel sure that my children will enjoy them later just as they would their early photographs, and perhaps find some guidance in them.

Unfortunately I never knew my own father and there is preserved no likeness of his features. I know nothing of my own early childhood except what my mother in scattered occasions has told me. Whenever I hear older people talk of early days, I always listen carefully and regret that there

---

[5] Note on p. 367.

is no way of knowing more. Now that it is my turn to be
an old man, I am writing my reminiscences in biographical
form. Besides, I have already made the notes on my children. So I think I have done pretty well.

Above all, I believe in love and love only for the relation
between parents and children. Even after children are
grown, I see no reason for any formality in the relationship.
In this my wife and I are perfectly of the same opinion. We
are both trying to keep our children as close to us as possible.

Over three hun-
dred letters to my
sons in America
When my sons were in America for six
years, I sent a letter to them by every
mail boat that left—weekly as a rule,
sometimes once in two weeks. Whether
I had any particular news or not, I made
it a rule to write a letter for each mail. Altogether, I sent
more than three hundred letters during those six years.[6] I
would write them; my wife would seal and post them. So
we felt that the letters were from both of us. The boys, on
their part, wrote by every mail. I had told them before
they left Japan:

"While you are abroad, you must write home by every
mail. If you have nothing to tell, write that you have
nothing to tell. Do not work too hard. I don't want you to
come back great scholars, pale and sickly. I would much
rather have you come back ignorant but healthy. Try to be
economical in every way. But in case of illness or such
emergency when money can help you, don't hesitate to
spend any amount you need."

With such instructions my boys came back happily after
their six years of study abroad.

I do not think it is particularly to be commended that I
have a harmonious home and that I am faithful to my wife,

---

[6] Note on p. 367.

A moral life exerts influence in strange quarters

for ours is not the only happy family there is. And I am not fool enough to take pride in living a clean life as if that were the only and final purpose of a man's career. But strange is the reaction of society, for what I take to be simply ordinary behavior proves to be exemplary influence at times, and in unexpected quarters.

In the beginning my reputation in my lord's household was very bad, for I was simply an upstart samurai who had studied some foreign sciences, traveled in strange lands, and was now writing books to advocate very unconventional ideas; moreover I was finding faults with the venerable Confucian teachings—a very dangerous heretic. I can imagine the kind of reports made about me to the inner household.

But when years passed and times had changed, the whole country turning inevitably toward the new culture, my clan came to find that this Fukuzawa was not so dangerous a person as was thought, and that he might really prove useful in some way. A certain influential officer named Shima-zu Suketarō was the first to see the situation and speak well of me in the feudal household.

At that time there was a certain lady dowager in the household whom people called Hōren-in Sama. She was of very noble lineage, having come from the great house of Hitotsu-bashi,[7] and now at her advanced age she was held in particular respect by the whole household.

In conversing with this lady, Shimazu described much of the medicine and navigation and other sciences of the Western lands; also the customs which were very different from our own. The most remarkable of all, he told her, was

---

[7] Note on p. 367.

the relation between man and woman; there men and women had equal rights and monogamy was the strict rule in any class of people—this, at least, was a merit of the Western customs.

The lady dowager could not help being moved by this conversation, for she had had some unhappy trials in earlier days. As if her eyes were suddenly opened to something new, she expressed a desire to make acquaintance of Fukuzawa. When I was admitted to her presence, she found that I was quite an ordinary man—I had no horns on my head or tail beneath my formal skirt. And she gradually began to place confidence in me.[8] Many years later Shimazu told me all about this, and then I learned how I was first admitted to the inner household of the lord.

By this incident I am inclined to think that the doctrine of monogamy does have a great deal of power in society though it usually passes unnoticed. There are people who hold that it is ridiculous to advocate abolishing polygamy in this age. But that is a poor excuse of those who are in the midst of difficulties. The doctrine of monogamy is not pedantic. I am sure that the majority of people in present-day Japan, especially the ladies of the higher society, are all on my side. So I intend to work as long as I live for the abolition of the unhealthy custom. It does not matter whom I may have to encounter. I shall attempt to make our society more presentable if only on the surface.

---

[8] Note on p. 357.

XV

A FINAL WORD ON THE GOOD LIFE

As I look back on the varied but orderly progress of my life, I see nothing particularly unusual. I had some hardships in youth, and now I am enjoying a comfortable old age. All this might have happened to anyone. I am fortunate in that I have reached this age without having done anything that I remember with great shame or regret.

But the world is large. There are many people with different ideas who regard my ways with various interpretations and suspicions. Especially the fact that I have never held a government post while I am not **Why I avoid government service** exactly ignorant of national politics seems to puzzle many people. Everybody in Japan, ten out of ten, even a hundred out of a hundred, is turning toward the government for a career, but why does Fukuzawa alone keep aloof?

Many were the conjectures. Some people have even questioned me directly on this point. Foreigners seem to be no less interested, for a certain American friend of mine has urged me to enter government service.

"Then," he would say, "you can carry on your work more easily. It will be to your honor. And besides, you can make money at the same time."

But I would laugh and give little response to his kind urging.

For a while after the Restoration, many officials of the new government had suspected that I was a supporter of the old, that I was keeping up an allegiance to the shogunate. In every transition period, there are what people call the surviving retainers of the old government. "So, Fukuzawa must be one of those. He lives like a recluse, but he must be harboring a dissatisfaction deep in his heart. A dissatisfied person is always dangerous."

But they ought to remember what this "dissatisfied survivor" did at the time of the Restoration. While all the arguments and conspiracies were going on, I kept quiet and was telling the conspirators that they were fools, for they were surely going to be beaten.

Those conspirators at the Restoration are the ones who should have played the part of surviving retainers. But curiously enough all of them have left off their career in midway, and have turned to offer their second loyalty to the new government. So they, too, have failed to become surviving retainers of the old.

At any rate I was deeply and thoroughly in disagreement with the policy of the bureaucratic shogunate. At the same time I saw no superiority in the imperialists, for they were even more illiberal than the old shogunate which they opposed. Therefore the only course for me was to keep neutral and to serve the country in my own independent way.

By and by it appeared that the new government had changed its policy. An audacious proclamation in favor of the open ports appeared. But such a sudden show of liberalism in the general atmosphere of extreme conservatism could not impress me. I was determined to make a lone stand for the new culture, doing what best I could with my own small power.

Then gradually the new government showed itself true

to the proclamation, bringing about one reformation after another, finally realizing the age of progress that we enjoy today.

So happy and unexpected is the state of things that I have nothing now to find fault with. I might say that my inner desires were all ful-filled. So here again appears a problem in my career. Why not join forces with the government now that its policy has been definitely estab-lished and is being carried out exactly according to my ideas? Yet I have not the least idea of seeking a new career in public office.

A new question arises

I shall relate my reasons now, and for the first time. Even my wife and family would not know them in full, for I have not had an occasion to relate them.

To speak very honestly, the first reason for my avoiding a government post is my dislike of the arrogance of all officials. It might be argued that they need to put on dignity in their office. But in reality they enjoy the bully-ing.

The titles of nobility should have been given up with feudalism, but the men in office were bent on keeping them, thus contriving to place distinction be-tween officials and ordinary men as if the former belonged to a nobler race of people. Anyone joining this nobler group would have to lord it over the commoner as a natural consequence. While he may bully those below him, he must at the same time receive the bully-ing of those above him. This would be a foolish game.

I will not join the arrogant offi-cials

As long as I remain in private life, I can watch and laugh. But joining the government would draw me into the prac-tice of those ridiculous pretensions which I cannot allow myself to do.

The second reason, which cannot but **Their low moral** be distasteful for me to go into, is the **life makes them** low moral standard of the average offi-**a class apart** cials. They live in large houses, dress well, and are often very generous. They may show a splendid spirit in their political activities, clean and courageous. But in private life they have the sad habit of affecting the offhand manners of Chinese "heroes," disregarding the restraint that is a part of a man's moral duty. They keep concubines in their houses and outside, committing the crime of polygamy, but they seem to feel no shame about it; they do not even endeavor to hide it. I must say that these men are promoting the new civilization on one hand and practicing the debased customs of the old on the other. I cannot help feeling that they are in this regard below my standards and practice.

As long as I am keeping these men at a distance, they are not particularly objectionable. I do not mind meeting them for occasional business and social intercourse. But working together under the same roof and becoming really one of them—that is another thing. I may be fastidious and narrow, but again, it is my nature, and I am as I am.

Still a third reason that kept me from **I despise self-** taking office was the sad memory I had **styled patriots** of these men at the time of the Restoration. When the crisis came and the Shōgun returned to Yedo defeated, great was the uproar from all his retainers and adherents—"This great régime of three hundred years begun by the sacred ancestor of the Tokugawa must not be abandoned in a day"—"As loyal followers of the house of Tokugawa, we must not forget the three hundred years of benevolence bequeathed to us"—"Who are these men from Satsuma and Chōshū, now attempting to attack us? Descendants of the men whom our ancestors overcame in the battle of Sekiga-hara.[1] How can we bend our knees before them and bring shame to our proud forebears?"

Spirit ran high. Some advocated throwing up a defence line on the Tōkaidō highway. Others boarded ships of war and withdrew to plan some counter-attack. Many sought audience with the Shōgun to plead for a last stand against the oncoming forces. In the intensity of their ardor some raised their voices and wept. It was indeed like a parade of patriots and would-be martyrs.

But after all, their zealous efforts bore no fruit; the Shōgun decided to surrender and retire. When his government was finally dissolved, some of the still ardent and undaunted escaped north to Hakodate; others led bands of soldiers and carried on intermittent fighting in the northern provinces, while still others concealed their humiliation in their bosoms and went with the Shōgun to his retirement in Shizuoka.

The most ardent of these loyal partisans began to call Tōkyō the "land of the traitors." They would not even eat a piece of cake if it came from Tōkyō. In going to bed at night they would not lie down with their heads pointing toward the capital. They would not even mention the word "Tōkyō," nor listen to it spoken, lest it pollute their mouths and ears. Their actions were much like those of the faithful brothers in Chinese history—Po-i and Shu-ch'i. And Shizuoka seemed to have become the Shouyang-shan of the new era.[2]

But one year passed, then two years—the "Po-is" and "Shu-ch'is" were probably beginning to feel the scarcity of "bracken" on "Shouyang-shan." First they came down to the foot of the "mountain"; then they entered the "land of the traitors." And furthermore, it was not long before they

---

[1] Note on p. 367. [2] Ibid.

appeared at the seat of the new government and were seeking office!

With no apparent embarrassment the once resolute "Po-is" and "Shu-ch'is"and the former vengeful counter-revolutionists, along with nearly everybody else in the empire, calmly presented themselves at the government headquarters and asked for employment. I wonder how they greeted the officials—the one time "traitors." They could hardly have spoken the usual salutation, "For the first time I behold your honored countenance." Probably they composed themselves and said, "I am a humble citizen of Japan whom, we think, you already know."

At any rate, they were received cordially enough, it seems, for in accordance with the old precept, "a high-minded man never speaks of past misfortunes," these regenerated men from the old shogunate were all taken into the new government—all past bitterness forgotten. Now, this would seem a state of things for congratulation; hardly would anyone find fault with it. Nevertheless, I have something to say about it.

First of all, consider the essential basis of the division between them. Suppose it were that the shogunate had held the policy of free foreign intercourse and the imperialist had been opposed to this; then after the imperialists had triumphed, they had come to see their own error and turned to adopt the policy of open intercourse, and the shogunate, seeing their own policy adopted by the new government, had decided to join forces with it—if this supposition were the truth, I should certainly have nothing to find fault with.

But the truth is that at the time of the Restoration there was no one who argued on this point. The conduct of the shogunate party was entirely derived from the ancient doctrine of the retainer's duty to his master and the three hundred years of the Tokugawa régime which they had inherited. Yet when the old régime was lost, the retainers apparently felt that the basis of their stand was also gone. They turned around and offered their services to the new government without the least show of embarrassment.

Of course, among the minor men who did not know the wherefore of the dispute, any change in attitude is excusable, but when it comes to those leaders of troops and commanders of war vessels who had caused disturbances at the time of the Restoration, and those who after the example of Po-i and Shu-ch'i swore eternal allegiance to the Shōgun, I cannot comprehend their logic.

There should be no shame in being defeated in a dispute. I have no mind to accuse a man for having once made an error of judgment. But it seems to me that when a man fails in a dispute, it is his part to take his defeat and retire from active society. But there was nothing like that with these men. They have sought high positions in the rival government and, having obtained them, are proud. After all, the loyalists are not to be trusted; the doctrine of loyalty is a fickle idea. I should be much happier to remain an independent citizen than to associate with this kind of men.

Not that I believe in criticizing the career of others, but knowing the circumstances too well, I cannot help feeling sorry for the shifty, faint-hearted group who once called themselves the loyal retainers of the Shōgun. This, again, may be my fastidiousness or my sensitive temper, but it is one of the reasons why I am free from political ambition.

I would demonstrate the principle of independence myself Now for the fourth reason: Putting aside the matter of political allegiance and doctrine, I disliked that rush and disorderly struggle for office of the new government. Not only the samurai but even the sons of merchants and farmers —if they had any kind of education at all—were swarming together like insects around some fragrant food.   Some who could not be appointed officials sought other connections for profit as if there could be no chance in the world for anyone outside the government.   Nobody seemed to realize there was any virtue in human independence.

Many a time a young man returning from abroad has come to me and asserted his belief in an independent career, saying he would not think of a government post.   I usually listen to his proud declaration with half credulity.   And sure enough, after a while I learn that the same young man has been appointed secretary in a certain department—sometimes he has been lucky enough to be placed in the higher office of a province.

Of course I have no business to be criticizing the choice of a man's career, but I have the feeling that this fallacy of the Japanese people is an evidence of the surviving influence of the Chinese teaching.   To point out this fallacy to our people and lead them in the right way of modern civilization, someone must be an example.   The independence of a nation springs from the independent spirit of its citizens.   Our nation cannot hold its own if the old slavish spirit is so manifest among the people.   I felt determined to make an example of myself whatever the consequence of my endeavor might be.   If I should be the poorer for it, I should live poorer; if I chanced to make money, I should spend it as I wished.   At least I would not depend upon the government or its officials.

In my intercourse with my friends, I do what I can to offer them hospitality, but if it is not sufficient for them, they need not continue my friendship.   I am sincere in my efforts to share what I have according to the means of my household. When I have done my part, it remains with those friends to like me or hate me, praise me or denounce me.   I should not lose my head from joy or anger.

All in all, I am determined to live independent of man or thing. I cannot think of government office while I hold this principle. Then again, I am not particularly anxious to prove that my principle is the right one for the rest of the world. If it proves good, very well; if bad, then that is unfortunate. I have no intention of bearing the responsibility of the result of my stand in the distant future.

From this very full analysis of the reasons for my not taking a government post, it may appear as if I had formulated them in the beginning and proceeded to live accordingly. But that is not so. Truly I have not been tying myself down with any theories. I made this analysis so that there may be some order in my presentation of this survey.

After all, in thinking over the whole of my attitude and my life, I may say that I am at best indifferent to politics. If we divide the world into two groups of men—old topers and teetotallers, the former having no interest in confectionary shops, the latter never entering a bar—I suppose I am a "teetotaller" in politics.

I am a diagnostician, not a practicing physician

Not that I am wholly uninterested in that field, for I frequently discuss the subject and have written upon it, but for the daily wear and tear of its practice I have no taste. I am like the diagnostician in the medical field who can judge a disease but cannot care for a sick man. So people are not to take my diagnosis of politics as any evidence of personal ambition.

The political upheaval of 1881

In the fourteenth year of Meiji (1881) there was an unusual disturbance in the political world of Japan, and in connection with it an amusing incident occurred to me. During the preceding winter I had had an interview with the three ministers—Ōkuma, Itō, and

Inoue[3]—who asked me to take charge of a newspaper, or official bulletin, which they were then planning to start. But at the time they did not reveal its purpose or anything about it. So I refused and left their presence.

After this, certain minor officials kept coming to induce me to consider the matter until finally they revealed to me the secret that the government was going to open a national diet and, by way of preparation, wanted a newspaper. That struck me as an interesting venture and I agreed to think the matter over. My tentative promise was given. But time went on without any definite move being made. The year passed; then the next year was nearly gone. Yet I was still waiting, and there was no particular hurry on my part.

Then it became evident that there was a rift between the principals in high places and subsequently Ōkuma resigned.[4] The resignation of a minister is not a rare occurrence, but on this occasion the resignation had a wider and, I may say, ridiculous effect, reaching even myself. With the consequent shifting of many of the minor officials, many rumors were spread.

One of these stories had it that Ōkuma was a very wilful man, always scheming something, and that behind him had stood Fukuzawa supplying ideas. Moreover, it was said that Iwasaki Yatarō,[5] the head of the Mitsubishi Company, was furnishing funds for us, that he had already given some three hundred thousand *yen*—fitting material for a cheap comedy.

After the resignation of Ōkuma, a general policy for the future was decided upon. Announcement was made for the calling of the national diet in the twenty-third year of Meiji. Many changes were brought about in other departments,

---

[3] Note on p. 368. [4] Ibid. [5] Ibid.

notably in that of education. Here the Western systems were modified and the old Confucian teachings reinstated. Thus the department of education began to do some strange things. I am sure that by now, after more than ten years, the officials themselves are regretting this extremity.

It was really a temporary insanity among the men in office. It must have brought up some very difficult problems for the higher chiefs. I remember being called to Iwakura's[6] residence many times, where he would converse with me in the seclusion of his "tea room" in the rear of the dwelling. He showed his anxiety and said that the present disturbance was even more difficult than the insurrection of the tenth year of Meiji.[7]

To me the whole affair seemed farcical. The government had promised the diet to the people and the date was fixed for the twenty-third year of Meiji. That was the equivalent of an invitation to the people to participate in politics after ten years. But then the government proceeded to impose all sorts of harassing restrictions upon the people. Many persons were arrested and kept in prison; many were banished from Tōkyō. Furthermore, the officials were beginning to give themselves high-sounding titles in imitation of the ancient courtiers and feudal lords. Naturally, the common people were growing irritated, causing more troubles. The situation was as if the host and his expected guests were finding something to quarrel over before the party had really begun.

I took down a full account of the conditions, and have kept it among my private papers.[8] But I have felt that I should not publish anything of so intimate a nature, revealing some very disagreeable circumstances of the time. Once I related the whole thing to my very good friend,

---

[6] Note on p. 369. [7] Ibid. [8] Ibid.

Terajima, and added, "Suppose now I should go around telling people what I know. Don't you think a good many gentlemen in high offices would be embarrassed?"

Terajima, evidently surprised at this revelation, answered with some mischief, "Well, you are right. I always knew that politicians could show a pretty dark interior when it comes to hatching schemes, but this is too much. I think it might be a good lesson to them if you did talk a little."

It was evident he would have enjoyed the results of some disclosures, but I said, "I am now over forty years old, and so are you. Let us remember this and beware of hurting other men."

I have really been looking on, in all this world of politics, erratic and loose as it is, with amusement. But from the other side, in the eyes of government officials, I must appear differently.

The Ordinance of Public Peace and Security One year when the Ordinance of Public Peace and Security[9] was issued, it was rumored that I was to be condemned by this new law and banished from Tōkyō. Ono Tomojirō had heard of it from some close friend in the police department. The report was that Gotō Shōjirō[10] was to be banished along with me. I did not take the story very seriously, for I said, "If I am to be banished, why, I shall just move to Kawasaki, or some other nearby town. After all, they are not going to execute me."

In a few days Ono turned up with another report that the idea of my banishment had been rescinded.

A few years later, some time in the twenties of Meiji, a former pupil of mine, Inoue Kakugorō, was involved in some affairs in Korea[11] and was arrested. There followed a turmoil. The police even came to search my house. Then

---

⁹ Note on p. 369. ¹⁰ Ibid. ¹¹ Ibid.

I was called to the court as a witness, and was asked a number of very odd questions. It seemed as if they were not unwilling to condemn me also.

All of these imputations have been the result of misjudgment on the part of the government officers. I have been simply amused in watching the reactions of other people on these occasions.

Yet on thinking it over, I can see that it is only natural that I should be suspected by the men in politics. First of all, I am conspicuous in avoiding office. Moreover, a man who has no political ambition would usually retreat to the country rather than remain in the capital. But there I was in the midst of the city, associating with all men, expressing myself in speech and articles. I must admit further that I have not been altogether without some experience in causing political movements. For instance, here is an episode which only a few know anything about.

A single editorial moves a whole nation Shortly after the insurrection in the tenth year of Meiji, when the whole country had settled down to peace and people were rather suffering from lack of excitement, on a sudden inspiration I thought of writing an argument in favor of the opening of the national diet. Perhaps some would join in my advocacy and might even stir up some interesting movement.

I wrote an article and took it to the editors of the Hōchi— this was before I had my own newspaper. I said to them, "If you can use this piece as an editorial, do so. I am sure the readers will be interested. But, as it stands, it is too obviously my writing. So change some wording to hide my style. It will be fun to see how the public will take it."

The editors were Fujita Mokichi and Minoura Katsundo, both young men. They took my article at once and began a series of special editorials on the very next day. At that time all arguments in favor of the diet were still pretty feeble. We sat back and waited, curious to see the results of our challenge. For about a week, day by day, the subject occupied the editorial columns. And then Fujita and Minoura wrote further to challenge and agitate other papers.

In a little while an open discussion of the subject had developed in the Tōkyō papers. In two or three months it had spread throughout the country. Finally the bolder advocates of the diet were seen traveling to the capital to present petitions in favor of it. Of course it caused me no slight amusement to see what I had started, but at the same time I felt a little perturbed at the extent to which the movement had gone. For I must admit that my writing was chiefly for my own amusement as there was no personal gain I expected from it. And now that my amusement had brought about a national issue, I felt as if I had set fire to a field of grass and the fire was fast getting out of my control.

There had been anticipation of a national diet ever since the Restoration. I really cannot consider myself the originator of the whole movement. But my long article of several thousand words, which I wrote so carefully that any reader might understand, was the immediate forerunner of the widespread discussion; so I think I am right in believing that I set fire to the fuse that ignited the whole.

Not long ago I met Minoura, and as I could not recall the date of that series of editorials, I asked him about it. He remembered about it very well and lent me the old papers from his files. On looking through it, I found that the discussion ran from July 29th to August 10th in the twelfth year of Meiji (1879). It did not strike me as so badly written on this second reading; and I must confess to a certain glow of pride when I realize that this writing has been instrumental in promoting the Japanese National Diet.

Calling to mind these activities of mine, I must admit that it is not altogether unnatural that I should be suspected of having had some hand in various political disturbances. As my activity in behalf of the new representative government and many other innovations is of value to the country, it is all very well. But if it were to prove detrimental, I should, I fear, be liable to punishment in *Emma's* nether court of judgment even if I may escape the scourge of this world.

All in all, my activities with politics have been that of a "diagnostician." I have had no idea of curing the nation's "disease" with my own hands nor have I ever thought of politics in connection with my personal interest. But behind all I have done, there was a wish that this nation of ours might enjoy the benefit of the new civilization so that she might one day be a great nation, strong in the arts of both war and peace.

I have a number of acquaintances in the political field, but being content in doing what I can with my independent power, I never have a thing to request of them or consult with them. My quiet, contented life may look strange to those officials who have a different way of thinking. But I am without any ill feeling toward the present government or the men in it. Indeed, I feel a real obligation to the present government, for my living safely and comfortably at this old age is entirely due to its good administration. I can easily imagine what might have happened to me in the feudal time, had I persisted in living according to my own ideas as I am now.

I establish a newspaper In the fifteenth year of Meiji (1882) I began to publish a newspaper which I called the Jiji-shimpō. It was the year following the political outbreak which had so stirred the country, and many of my senior pupils had urged me to start a paper.

I could see that our society was rapidly changing. The ever-increasing competition was bringing about more and more of bitter rivalry. Recently the government had experienced a very provoking quarrel inside itself. It was logical to expect similar reactions in subsequent economic and industrial rivalry. The greatest need in such a time is an instrument of nonpartisan, unbiased opinion. But it is easy to make satisfying theories about nonpartisan opinion and not so easy to realize it in practice, for the usual man, conscious of his own personal interests, cannot lightly throw off his partisanship. As I looked about the country, I decided to myself that there were not many besides myself who were independent in living, and who had worth-while ideas in their heads, and who could yet be really free from political and business interests.

With this reasoning I set myself to the task of establishing a newspaper which became the Jiji-shimpō. After I had determined on this project, I paid no attention to certain friends who appeared to warn me of the difficulty. I decided that it should be entirely my own work, no help coming from outside whether the circulation be large or small. As I originated the paper, so could I destroy it. Even if I were to fail, I should not feel any regret or false shame; nor would my family suffer in the least. Thus forewarned and forearmed, I started publication with no regard for outside criticism. The journal has continued to be successful up to this day.

Such was my creed in business, but I must not overlook the credit due my friends and colleagues. These men have done their part as, indeed, their honesty and ability were worthy of the trust I have placed in them.

In the beginning of the paper Nakamigawa Hikojirō had the general management; then for a while Itō Kinsuke; and at present my second son, Sutejirō, is carrying on the responsibility. The first treasurer was Motoyama Hikoichi, then Sakata Minoru; now Tobari Shichinosuke is holding that important office. In accord with my usual nature, I have not entered into the minute accounts of the treasury; I leave all that to the men in charge. Yet not once has any untoward accident occurred, so fortunate am I in having good men with me. And I am convinced that the reason for the continued success of the whole work comes from the worth and ability of these men.

In editing the paper I encourage the reporters to write bravely and freely. I have no objection to severe criticism or extreme statements, but I warn them that they must limit their statements to what they would be willing to say to the victim face to face. Otherwise, they are what I would call *kage-benkei* (shadow-fighters) attacking from the security of their columns. It is very easy for a shadow-fighter to fall into mean abuses and irresponsible invectives which are the eternal shame of the writer's profession.

I am now growing old and I feel that I should be leaving the work to the younger men. I am indeed looking forward to a quiet life with as few duties as possible in my remaining years. The editorials in Jiji-shimpō are now being written by Ishikawa Kammei, Kitagawa Reisuke, Horie Kiichi and others. And I am putting myself farther and farther away from the active work. Occasionally I recommend a subject for their treatment, and when these men submit their work to me, I make such revisions as I think necessary. This is about the extent of my activity with the paper these days.

I always prepare for the worst In looking back again over my life with its varied flow of incidents, the translation and writing seem to stand out as the work which required my greatest effort. I could dwell on it here, but as I have described it fully in the preface to my collected writings

(Fukuzawa Zenshū),[12] the second edition having appeared this year, I shall not repeat. But here are some of my ideas on life and living that I wish to put down.

It has been a habit of mine to be prepared for the extreme in all situations; that is, to anticipate the worst possible result of any event so that I should not be confounded when the worst did come. For every living man there is the possibility of sudden death at all times. To be able to face it with mind at peace is what any man would like to be prepared for always.

And as I decided that I should not die leaving any debt behind me, I could not afford to take much risk in financial ventures. Even when tempted to speculate in something that promised great gain, I hesitated according to my habit of anticipating the worst. I would rather be poor than hold precarious riches. Even in extreme poverty I could be happy making a living as a masseur. I am not a man to be cowed by poor clothes and coarse food. Then why should I endure the worry of possible failure and regret in order to gain some money?

Thus I have been very inactive in financial ventures, but whenever there was nó risk of injuring my self-respect in case of failure, I did not stand back. During the several decades of my work with Keiō-gijuku, I have seen many changes. Sometimes the number of students went up; sometimes it went down. There were times when our financial reserve was so low that I could not employ sufficient teachers.

But at such times I was not in the least dismayed. I have said that if all the assistants should leave me, I would teach by myself as many students as I could handle alone. If all the students should leave, why, I would simply give up

---

12 Note on p. 370.

teaching. This Fukuzawa had not promised anyone that he would found a great institution; there would be no obligation to anyone if I failed in my educational venture. Even from the time I opened the school, I had resolved that I would close it whenever I saw fit. With this resolution I was not to be dismayed by any emergency.

Although I give the best of my ability to the management of the institution and put all my heart into it for its future and its improvement, yet I never forget that all my personal worries and immediate concerns are but a part of the "games" of this "floating world," our entire lives but an aspect of some higher consciousness. And so while I am using my brain in present labor, my mind finds truer rest.

Recently our alumni have started a drive for an endowment for the institution. I should be happy to see their efforts result in a fund collected for our school's future interests. But I am looking on quietly at this enterprise. So likewise with my newspaper, I have never resolved that I must by all means make a success of it. It might prove a failure, but I am always ready for that.

Following the same doctrine, I have never asked anyone to write a preface for any of my books. It is supposed to be an honor to have some prominent man write a preface, but usually it is more of a publicity policy. I naturally wish for a good reception of my books, but again, being resolved that I would not be dismayed by their not selling at all, I could not stoop to begging other men for prefaces which have no intrinsic value of their own.

I am of a very sociable nature; I have numerous acquaintances, and among them I count a number of trusted friends. But even in these relations I do not forget my doctrine of preparing for the extreme—for a friend can change his mind. Then the lost friend must go, but I will let no unpleasantness mar my life. Suppose my friends were thus to be lost one after the other, and at last I were to find myself quite abandoned in the world—even then I would not beg friendship against my sincere feeling. I have been determined on this point since my early days, but fortunately there has been no need to exercise this principle. In the sixty odd years of my life I have been making friends by the thousands, or indeed, by the tens of thousands, but I cannot recall one instance of a quarrel or a lost friendship.

Thus I would go at my work and my personal associations with no selfish ambitions or fear of failure. While on the one hand I do not attach too much importance to all affairs of this world, on the other hand I regard my independence with jealous respect and I endeavor to keep my life from growing stagnant. This philosophy has brought me happily through all the difficult passes of my life.

My personal hygiene Now turning to the subject of physical hygiene, I must admit I have had a very bad and shameful habit of drinking. Moreover, my drinking was something out of the ordinary. There is a kind of drinker who does not really like the wine, and who does not think of drinking until he sees the wine brought before him. But I was of the kind who liked it, and wanted much of it, and moreover wanted good, expensive wine.

At one time when it cost seven or eight *yen* a barrel, my expert taste could tell the better wine from the less expensive if there was a difference of even fifty *sen*. I used to drink a lot of this good wine, eat plenty of nice food with it and continue devouring bowl after bowl of rice, leaving nothing on the table. Indeed, I was "drinking like a cow and eating like a horse."

If I ever got badly drunk, the shame of it might have curbed my habit. But no shame or embarrassment was brought on me by intoxication, for its only evidence was

that I talked with louder voice.   Never was I known to grow
bitter or quarrelsome.   This was rather a misfortune, for I
grew proud of my good drinking habit and at every drinking
bout I would outdrink everybody, take twice or even three
times as much as all the others, calling myself the unrivaled
drinker of the world.   I should certainly be ashamed of
this.

However, aside from this deep drinking, I have always had
healthy habits.   Of course when I was little I had no set
ideas, but even then I had the habit of not eating anything
between meals.   Probably my mother never gave me things
between the three meals.   But even now the same habit
persists with me; especially after supper I cannot put anything in my mouth however tempting the food may be.
Sometimes when I have to sit up through the night when
there is a death in a relative's house, or when there is a fire
in the neighborhood, naturally some food will be brought
before me, but I seldom touch it.   This is a very good habit
left by my mother.

I am generally very quick and pushing in most of my
activities, so much so that my friends sometimes make fun
of me.   But when it comes to eating, three times a day, I
change entirely as if I were a different man.   When I was
little, there was a saying that rapid eating, fast running, and
something else were the accomplishments of samurai.   I was
often admonished for my slow eating.   I, too, wanted to eat
quickly, but it was impossible for me to pack my mouth with
food and swallow it in gulps.

Long afterwards I read in a foreign book of the benefits of
chewing, and learned for the first time that my one-time bad
habit was really a good habit.   Since then I have not hesitated to take twice as much time for meals as other people
do.

I have been fond of wine ever since I can remember, but

while I was in Nakatsu, I was still a child and could not be too free in its enjoyment. While I stayed in Nagasaki for a year, I strictly abstained from it. In Ōsaka I was quite free, but being always in financial straits, I could not satisfy all my greed. So it was not until I came to Yedo at the age of twenty-five and began to have some comfortable reserve in my purse that I could really enjoy myself in this greedy indulgence. I would drink when visiting a friend; drink again when the friend came to call. In entertaining friends I was looking forward to the feast and wine more than my guests were. So, from morning till evening, I was drinking all the time.

When I reached thirty-two or -three years of age, I began to wonder whether I could live the length of life that nature had given me if I went on drinking as I had been. Yet I knew that a sudden break would be impossible—I remembered my sad failure. After all, the only way was to conquer my appetite slowly with a life-long perseverance.

It was as hard a struggle as a Chinaman giving up his opium. First I gave up my morning wine, then my noon wine. But I always excused myself to take a few cups when there was a guest. Gradually I was able to offer the cup to the guest only and keep myself from touching it. So far I managed somehow, but the next step of giving up the evening wine was the hardest of all my efforts. It was impossible to give it up all at once, so I decided to decrease the quantity gradually. My mouth craved while my mind prohibited, and my mouth and my mind were always at war. I think it was after three long years that I felt the outcome to be certain, the mouth being at length overcome.

When I was thirty-seven, I suffered a severe attack of fever and barely recovered from it. At that time a physician friend of mine said that I would never have recovered if I had been the heavy drinker I used to be. Remembering this, I could never again indulge myself. It was during the preceding ten years that I had been most reckless. But since then the quantity has been steadily decreasing, and whereas I was restraining myself in the beginning, nowadays I cannot take much even if I try. Probably this comes from the aging of my body rather than from the restraint of moral scruples.

I know some reckless men who, after reaching the age of forty or fifty, keep on drinking more and more, and finally finding that our rice-wine is not strong enough, begin to use foreign whisky and brandies. There I should like to caution them. They would be wiser to restrict themselves even at the loss of a great source of pleasure. An old toper like myself could master his habit at the age of thirty-four or -five. There are not many in the world who could have coped with me in my full capacity; many hardy drinkers are yet mere striplings to what I was. So I am sure any of these tyros can follow in my steps if they go patiently and slowly.

Physical exer-cise I was born in a poor family and I had to do much bodily work whether I liked it or not. This became my habit and I have been exercising my body a great deal ever since. In winter time, working out of doors constantly, I often had badly chapped hands. Sometimes they cracked open and bled. Then I would take needle and thread, and sew the edges of the opening together and apply a few drops of hot oil. This was our homely way of curing chapped skin back in Nakatsu. Since I came to Yedo, I have naturally been free of any such hardships. One day I was thinking of the old days and wrote a little verse in Chinese form which I repeat here:

In the spring of younger years what varied and lowly toil have I followed;

Having achieved success, I must sit and smile, harming
myself with too much ease.

Here I sit in leisure after a hearty bath, my body clean and
glowing;

Yet I once took stitches with cotton thread in my chapped
and broken hands.

As a youth in Nakatsu I learned the art of *iai* under a
master named Nakamura Shōbei, because then unless one
practised some kind of military art, he was not regarded as
a man at all.   Later, when I left home to take up Western
studies, I took a practice sword with me and often exercised
with it, for I was not doing any hard labor as I used to do at
home.

In Yedo when the anti-foreign sentiment began to run
high and fencing became the fashion of the time, I gave up
iai and took to the pounding of rice for kitchen use, for
which I had had plenty of experience in my boyhood.

In the third year of Meiji when I suffered from fever, I
was very slow in recovering.   A few months later my friend,
Dr. Nagayo (Nagayo Sensai), came to bid me good-bye before
he sailed for Europe in the party of Ambassador Iwakura.
He gave me a small bottle of quinine and said, "Now you
are all well from your illness.   But an illness of that kind is
likely to come back at the same time next year.   So I am
bringing you the very best medicine, quinine hydro-chloride,
which you cannot get in an ordinary drug store.   Keep it;
you will find it useful."

This was kindness itself, but I was not pleased.

"I am all through with illness now," I said.   "Don't try to
keep me an invalid.   I am not going to take that medicine."

Nagayo laughed and said, "This medicine will be useful.
Don't pretend you know so much."

And he left the bottle with me.   He proved to be right, for while he was away, my fever returned many times. I used the quinine every time, finally finishing the entire bottle, and I had not even then returned to my normal health.

From my friend, Doctor Simmons[13] of Yokohama, I learned that it was best to wear flannel next to the body. So I had a complete set of flannel underwear made, even having my socks lined on the soles with flannel. Yet I didn't seem to get any benefit from it. I went on having chills and temperatures at the least provocation. For two years this went on; even in the third year I did not find any improvement.

I will not coddle a disease Then one day I hit upon a new idea: I had been coddling myself too much, almost to the extent of catering to the illness itself. Of course, if really ill, it would be best to follow a doctor's orders, but in the period of recuperation, I should know best how to build up a stronger body.

Originally I was a country samurai, living on wheat meal and pumpkin soup, wearing out-grown homespun clothes. Here I was trying to fit myself into the excessive care of the city-nourished with imported flannel clothes and many nostrums of civilization. It was ridiculous. My poor body must be dismayed by this unfamiliar amount of care and coddling.

I threw off all my flannels and began to wear my simple cotton underwear again. I gave up foreign clothes except for horseback riding. Also I tried using stoves as little as I could. I ceased to worry about the wind and cold, and went out of doors in any kind of weather. But in food I continued to take much of the foreign style cooking for better nourishment. For exercise I returned to rice pounding and

---

[13] Note on p. 370.

wood chopping every day.   Often I found myself perspiring freely and I knew I was growing stronger.

I am now five feet nine inches tall and weigh a little less than one hundred and fifty pounds.   I have not changed much since I was eighteen or nineteen—never having weighed above one hundred and fifty or gone below one hundred and forty pounds, except in time of illness.   This means, I think, a very good state of health.   After that fever I lost much weight and for several years I could not recover it.   However, since returning to my native manner of living, I have regained my former weight, and even now at the age of sixty-five I still maintain it.

I cannot say too surely that this country habit was the source of my return to health.   It may have been that I was recovering anyway, and that I only happened to change my manner of living at that time.   At least, one can safely say that the country habit is not harmful as long as other conditions of living are looked after.   I am not sure whether the wind blowing through the loose Japanese clothes on my body was good for me, or whether I was growing stronger for other reasons and could resist the cold air which is really harmful.   Here is a problem for medical science to investigate.

In general, since that disastrous fever of nearly thirty years ago, I have revised my entire system of living. Instead of the rough and ready habit of the student days and the unreasonable drinking, I have come to adopt the life of a gentleman.   In the beginning I was allowing only a little time from my engrossing work to take care of my body, but as I grow older I am making the care of my body my chief concern.

I go to bed early and rise early, taking a walk of about four miles every morning before breakfast in the fields of Sankō and along the River Furukawa with my young pupils.

Fukuzawa dressed for his morning walk.

一點の寒聲遠く傳う　牛埼の殘月影街お鮮かなり　草鞋竹策秋晩を挿い　歩して三光より古川を渡る　〔早起して學生諸子と散歩す〕

轉句の「草鞋竹策」と訂正されているもの

Fukuzawa's Chinese poem on his daily excursion.

Then in the afternoon I spend about an hour in the practice of *iai* and in pounding rice. I am always regular in my meal times, and in this daily régime I am constant all through the year even when it rains or snows. Last autumn I amused myself writing the following poem in Chinese:

Sword play and rice pounding are my daily exercise

> One slow boom of the temple bell reverberates far away in the still cold air;
> In the sky still shows the half-circle of the waning moon.
> Wearing straw sandals, carrying a bamboo staff, I invade the autumn dawn,
> Passing through Sankō and crossing the Furukawa.

I wonder how much longer this kind of life is going to last. Sixty-odd years is the length of life I have now come through. It is often the part of an old man to say that life on looking back seems like a dream. But for me it has been a very merry dream, full of changes and surprises.

I have come a long way

My life begun in the restricted conventions of the small Nakatsu clan was like being packed tightly in a lunch box. When once the toothpick of clan politics was punched into the corner of the box, a boy was caught on its end, and before he himself knew what was happening, he had jumped out of the old home. Not only did he abandon his native province but he even renounced the teaching of the Chinese culture in which he had been educated. Reading strange books, associating with new kinds of people, working with all the freedom never dreamed of before, traveling abroad two or three times, finally he came to find even the empire of Japan too narrow for his domain. What a merry life this has been, and what great changes!

Were I to dwell on difficulties and hardships, I might easily describe this life of mine as a pretty hard one. The old proverb reminds us, "Once past the throat, the burn (of the food) is forgotten." Of course poverty and other hardships were hard to bear. But as I look backward now, they seem dear among the old glowing memories which remain.

When I first began my studies, all that I hoped for was to acquire some knowledge of the Western culture and then so manage my living that I should not become a burden upon other men. That was my first ambition. Unexpectedly came the Restoration, and to my delight Japan was opened to the world.

Seiyō Jijō (Things Western) and other books of mine published during the old shogunate régime were written with no real expectation that they would interest the public at all. Even if they were to win some attention, I had no idea that the contents of the books would ever be applied to our own social conditions. In short, I was writing my books simply as stories of the West or as curious tales of a dreamland. Then contrary to all my expectations these books were read widely and were even taken for guidance by the people of the day. Moreover, the government of the new age proved itself most courageous in applying the new thoughts. It went far beyond what was advocated in my Seiyō Jijō and began to surprise even the author of the book himself.

In this unexpected turn of events I found that I could not be satisfied with my former ambition. I must take advantage of the moment to bring in more of Western civilization and revolutionize our people's ideas from the roots. Then perhaps it would not be impossible to form a great nation in this far Orient, which would stand counter to Great Britain of the West, and take an active part in the progress of the whole world. So I was led on to form my second and greater ambition.

Consequently I renewed activities with "tongue and brush," my two cherished instruments. On one side I was teaching in my school and making occasional public speeches, while on the other I was constantly writing on all subjects. And these comprise my books subsequent to Seiyō Jijō. It was a pretty busy life but no more than doing my bit, or "doing the ten thousandth part" as we put it.

As I consider things today, while there are still many things to be regretted, on the whole I see the country well on the road to advancement. One of the tangible results was to be seen a few years ago in our victorious war with China, which was the result of perfect cooperation between the government and the people.

How happy I am; I have no words to express it! Only because I have lived long, I have met this wonderful joy. Why, then, couldn't all my friends live to meet it? I am often brought to tears of pity for those who died too soon.

Of course, unimpassioned thought will show this victory over China as nothing more than an event in the progress of our foreign relations, but in the heat of the moment I could hardly refrain from rising up in delight.

After all, the present is the result of the past. This glorious condition of our country cannot but be the fruit of the good inheritance from our ancestors. We are the fortunate ones who live today to enjoy this wonderful bequest. Yet I feel as though my second and greater ambition has been attained, for everything that I had hoped for and prayed for has been realized through the benevolence of Heaven and the virtues of those forebears. I have nothing to complain of on looking backward, nothing but full satisfaction and delight.

However, it seems that there is no end to man's capacity for desire. I can still point out some things I am yet hoping for. Not ideas in foreign diplomacy or developments in our

constitutional government—all these I
There is no limit leave to the statesmen. But I should
to a man's hope like to put my further efforts toward
and desire elevating the moral standards of the
men and women of my land to make
them truly worthy of a civilized nation. Then I should like
to encourage a religion—Buddhism or Christianity—to give
peaceful influence on a large number of our people.[14] And
thirdly, I wish to have a large foundation created for the
study of higher sciences in both physical and metaphysical
fields.

It is these three things that I wish to see accomplished
during the remaining years of my life. A man may grow
old, but while he has his health, he must not sit idle. I too
intend to do all within my power as long as life and health
are granted me.[15]

---

[14] Note on p. 370. [15] Ibid.

NOTES

Numerals in bold type indicate page numbers;
those in small type indicate note numbers.

PREFACE TO THE 1899 EDITION

xiii **1. Sensei.** Teacher, or master, a title given to a venerated person.

xiv **2. the second volume.** This second volume was not written, because Fukuzawa died in 1901.

xiv **3. Ishikawa Kammei** (1859–1943). After studying in Keiō-gijuku, he joined the Jiji-shimpō, Fukuzawa's newspaper, at its establishment and later became its editor-in-chief. After retirement, he wrote the most authoritative biography of Fukuzawa (Fukuzawa Yukichi Den, 1932). Ishikawa is regarded as one of the prominent men who inherited Fukuzawa's spirit.

CHAPTER I

1. **1. samurai.** In the feudal society of Japan, which was changed and modernized at the Imperial Restoration of 1868, there was a strict caste system in which the samurai were the ruling class. This class included the Shōgun who held a position corresponding to the King in feudal Europe, the Daimyō who corresponded to the Barons, and the lesser officials and soldiers. Below the samurai were the farmers, artisans and merchants, forming the so-called Four Castes which comprised the main portion of the population. Above the samurai were the Emperor and his courtiers. The Emperor enjoyed spiritual respect but little political power. Below the merchants were the outcasts, *eta* and beggars. The priests and, to some extent, the scholars stood outside the system. Anyone could become a priest or a scholar and enjoy a relatively free career.

Within the samurai class there was a sharp division between the Upper and the Lower strata (Jōshizoku and Kashizoku).

There were some promotions and demotions within each stratum, but there was hardly any instance of a man passing the
dividing line, nor was there any intermarriage between the two.
Fukuzawa Hyakusuke's position was Chū-koshō, the highest
among the Lower Samurai. His stipend was thirteen *koku*
(about 65 bushels) of rice plus keep for two followers.

1. **2. *hanninkan.*** According to the system created in 1886, *hanninkan* included low officials such as policemen and non-com-
missioned officers of the Army.

1. **3. overseer of the treasury.** In old Japan the chief income
of a feudal lord was the rice which he collected as tax from
the farmers of his province. After larger portion of it had been
distributed among the retainers as salary, the remainder was
shipped to Ōsaka to be sold, for Ōsaka was, as it is now, a
great center of trade. According to the custom of the age,
samurai of higher rank did not trouble themselves with money
matters, but left management of clan's finances to officers of
lower rank.

1. **4. storage office and headquarters.** *Kura-yashiki* in Japanese.
It was an enclosure, usually on a river front, containing the
storage houses and living quarters for the officers and family.

3. **5. Itō Tōgai** (1670–1736). Was a son of another noted scholar,
Itō Jinsai. Living in Kyōto, the two generations of scholars
brought forth a new school of Confucian interpretation called
Kogi-gakuha.

6. **6. Buddhist Abbot.** See note on **samurai**, p. 337. Because
sons of priests usually entered religious career and sons of high
priests generally commanded attention and favor, a priest's career
was not entirely free from feudalism. However, Fukuzawa's
father must have regarded it free in so far as there was no
legal restrictions on promotions.

7. **7. Shiraishi.** Shiraishi Tsuneto (1815–1883). He also called
himself Shōzan. There is an episode to illustrate his self-
respecting character on p. 343, note on **after a quarrel.**

8. **8. Yüan-ming Shih-lüeh, etc.** This list contains books on
history, ethics and poetry which form the basic source in the
study of Confucian classics.

8. ⁹. **Kamei.** Kamei Nammei (1743-1814), a physician and Confucian scholar of Fukuoka. He was recognized as an authority in Kyūshū as against Kaibara Ekken of Yedo.

8. ¹⁰. **Hirose Tansō** (1782-1856). In spite of the disparaging remarks by Fukuzawa, Hirose was a noted scholar and author in Confucianism with disciples numbering over 4000. Born a merchant's son, he was given the privilege of assuming the family name of Hirose and wearing a pair of swords (special privileges of samurai) in 1842 by the Shōgun's government in recognition of his scholarship. This episode proves the factional rivalry among the scholars of the time.

8. ¹¹. **Rai Sanyō** (1780-1832). A noted scholar and poet. His publications on the history of Japan and his political philosophy had much to do in engendering the Imperial Restoration.

12. ¹². **usual corner of the room.** In a Japanese house generally, there is no room set aside for sleeping. All the rooms have their floors covered with thick, mattress-like *tatami*, and people can make comfortable beds on the floor in any room.

12. ¹³. **my brother.** Named Sannosuke (1826-1856). See index for more information on him.

12. ¹⁴. **Rekkō of Mito.** Tokugawa Nariaki (1800-1860), generally known by the name presented to him after his death, Rekkō. A great statesman and administrator. He improved education, industry, the military in his province; advised the Shōgun on coast defence. His House of Mito was one of the three main branches of the Tokugawa family from which an heir was to be selected when a Shōgun did not have a son to succeed him. Therefore, Rekkō commanded a great prestige along with his personal ability. He was made advisor to the Shōgun at the coming of Commodore Perry. Because the House of Mito had a strong tradition of nationalism, he disagreed with Chancellor Ii Kamon-no Kami's policy of concluding treaty with foreign powers, and was ordered to confinement at home.

12. ¹⁵. **Shungaku of Echizen.** Matsudaira Yoshinaga (1828-1890). Lord of Fukui. Great statesman and administrator. Introduced smallpox vaccine in his province by obtaining it from the Dutch. Advocated foreign intercourse at the coming of Commodore Perry. Also advocated alliance between the Shogunate and the Imperial Court. After the Restoration, he assumed several high posts in the new government before his retirement in 1870.

12. 16. **Shōgun.** The actual military and political chief of feudal Japan with his seat in Yedo (Tōkyō). He had been delegated the entire temporal power by the Emperor who lived in Kyōto in seclusion. See note on **samurai** on p. 337.

12. 17. **Egawa Tarozaemon** (1801–1855). His other name was Egawa Hidetatsu. Well known for his leadership in modern gunnery and coast defence which he taught in Yedo to many men who later made themselves prominent in the Restoration. He advocated conscription of farmers for military service. Also, he took the lead in arms development. A foundry which he erected in his province may still be seen at Nirayama on the Izu Penninsula. At the coming of Perry, he proposed and built the *Daiba*, or island fortresses off the shores of Yedo (Tōkyō).

13. 18. **Hoashi Banri** (1778–1852). An unusually versatile man, successful in both scholarship and politics. Studied economics, astronomy, physics, medicine and mathematics besides his chief interest, Confucianism. Taught in the clan school of Hinode clan. Later was made the Chancellor of the clan.

14. 19. **Shin sect of Buddhism.** This sect emphasizes the worship of Amida (the Buddha of Infinite Light) and salvation by his virtue in contrast to the Zen and other sects which emphasize the meditation by which a man is to find his own way under the guidance of Buddha Sakyamuni.

15. 20. *eta.* The lowest caste in feudal Japan, a sort of untouchables. They lived in isolated villages, made a living by slaughter of cattle and curing of leather, which most people thought was repulsive work. The distinction was purely social and professional. Some of them were actually wealthy and cultured, yet prohibited from social contact and intermarriage with other castes. They were liberated by an edict of the Meiji Government in 1871 when it was found that there were some 280,000 of them. Though legally liberated, there still is some social stigma placed on them by conservative Japanese and an active movement is afoot to eliminate it, as a result of which the word *eta* has gone out of use.

17. 21. **god of Inari.** It is one of the most popular deities of Shintoism, the native religion of Japan. Inari is identified by red shrines and red *torii*, and sometimes with a figure of a fox.

CHAPTER II

22. 1. **Nagasaki.** During the Tokugawa period, for over two hundred years, Nagasaki was the one port in Japan where foreign ships (Chinese and Dutch) were permitted to enter and trade under very strict restrictions. There was a small island in the harbor called Dejima where the Dutch had their "factory", or trading post. They were not allowed to come to the main land nor the Japanese allowed to visit them without special permit. Yet Nagasaki was the one window for the Japanese toward the world.

23. 2. **adopted son.** As the eldest son inherited his father's position in the feudal society and also his property, the younger sons were often adopted into other families which had no sons. A younger son who remained in the family would forever be a dependent of his father unless the lord gave him a position which would be a very special privilege. A family without a son, on the other hand, would lose its social position and income at the death of the master of the family. Hence the necessity of adopting a son.

24. 3. **Yamamoto could arrange the visit.** Because the government policy prohibited all Japanese, except for special officials, to have any contact with foreigners, these visits would be limited to looking at the buildings from outside and perhaps a glimpse of Dutchmen from a distance. Even then, these were thought to be enlightening experiences.

25. 4. **all my sisters had married.** The eldest sister O-Rei had married Otabe Buemon, the second sister O-En had married Nakamigawa Saizō, the third sister O-Kane had married Hattori Fukujō. They were all samurai of the Okudaira clan of about the same rank as Fukuzawa.

29. 5. *funayado.* A shipping agency for both freight and pas-

sengers. It often had accommodation for passengers waiting for
the boat.

29.   6. **Yakken.** It was an abridgment and revision of the greater
Doeff's Dutch-Japanese dictionary (cf. **Doeff**, p. 346), compiled by
Fujibayashi Fuzan, 1818.

29.   7. *bu, shu.* The basic unit of the monetary system of that
period was the *ryō* represented in gold coins. One *bu* was one
quarter of a *ryō* and one *shu* was again one quarter of a *bu.*
There was another system represented in copper coins the unit
of which was the *mon.* The rate of exchange between the two
systems varied from time to time, but in 1855 when Fukuzawa
was travelling to Ōsaka, it was fluctuating around 6600 *mon* to
one *ryō.* One may estimate the value of money from the fact
that three *bu* and three *shu* would buy one *koku* (about five
bushels) of rice at that time. This means that one *ryō* was worth
about 9300 *yen* ($ 26) of the present day currency (1965), one
bu about 2330 *yen* ($ 6.50), one *shu* about 580 *yen* ($ 1.60), and
one *mon* about 1.4 *yen* ($ .004). Silver was not used as cur-
rency in the form of coins until a few years later.

29.   8. **the sea of Amakusa.** This is Fukuzawa's confusion with
the Bay of Ariake. A glance at the map will prove it.

33.   9. *gō.* A measure of capacity, about one third of a pint.
Ten *gō* make one *shō,* ten *shō* make one *to,* and ten *to* make
one *koku.*

35.   10. **Ogata.** Ogata Kōan (1810–1863). Born a samurai's son in
Ashimori clan, the province of Bitchū, he studied in Yedo and in
Nagasaki. In 1838 he became a practicing physician in Ōsaka
and at the same time opened a school for the instruction of Dutch
language and medicine. Regarded as an authority of the period,
he translated Dutch books and wrote books of his own and contributed much to the basic study of medicine in Japan. His
school was called Tekitekisai Juku after his pseudonym or simply
Teki Juku. Many men, estimated at 3000, among them many who
distinguished themselves later in all walks of life, studied in this
school at one time or another. Ogata was made personal physician of the Shōgun and his family, and in 1862 moved to Yedo
where he died a year later,

37.   11. **the lord of Satsuma.**   Shimazu Ñariaki (1809–1858).   He was an ardent advocate of progress and the adoption of Western science.   He and his brother, Hisamitsu, who succeeded him as the lord of Satsuma were leaders in the Imperial Restoration movement.

CHAPTER III

44.   1. **all my sisters were married.**   See note 25.4. on p. 341.

44.   2. **forty *ryō*.**   About 370,000 *yen*, or a little more than $ 1000. Biographers of Fukuzawa have long been puzzled how a conscientious man like his brother should have fallen into such a debt.   Very recently, from a pile of casual papers in the Fukuzawa household, an account of the family having formerly lived in a smaller house was discovered.   It is now thought that the debt must have been made in order to purchase the new house. This new house now stands in Nakatsu as a memorial to Fukuzawa.

45.   3. **after a quarrel.**   The cause of his being expelled was that he objected to doing the lowly work of guarding the castle gate which had been assigned to him because of the rank he held in the clan.   This indicates the selfrespecting character of the scholar Shiraishi.

48.   4. **such a book.**   This book was "C. M. H. Pel: Handleiding tot de Kennis der Versterkingskunst, 1852, Hertogenbosch", a textbook written for junior officers, consisting of two parts, field and permanent fortification.   Fukuzawa's translation (cf. p. 51) was not published, because he was still a young student and the idea did not occur to him.   But this book was read widely and later Ōtori Keisuke and Hirose Genkyō published translations.

56.   5. ***jukuchō*.**   A private school in Japan at this time was usually a "home school" in which a group of students gathered around a scholar for personal instruction.   When the number of students increased to require some administration, one of the students was given some responsibility in administration as well as in instruction, and he was called *jukuchō*.   However, he was still a student because the one authority in the school was the scholar.

CHAPTER IV

65.   **1. so the trick was effective.**   These theaters were showing *Kabuki* plays, and it was considered unbecoming and offensive for a samurai to enter a *kabuki* theater, because it was the amusement of the merchant class.   The theatrical art of the samurai was the *Nō* for which the lords would patronize *Nō* masters, or sometimes the lords themselves would perform on the *Nō* stage in the mansion, and the vassals sometimes were permitted to attend the performance.

72.   **2. Nagayo Sensai** (1838–1902).   He later became a very noted man, serving successively as the chief of the Bureau of Public Health in the Meiji government, a member of Genrōin, House of Peers, and advisor to the Imperial Household.   He contributed much to the development of medical practices and public hygiene in Japan.

80.   **3. Grammatica and Syntaxis.**   Maatschappij tot nút van t'Algemeen: Grammatica of Nederduitsche Spraakkunst; Syntaxis of Nederduitsche Woordvoeging.   They were later reprinted on woodblock in Yedo by Mitsukuri Gempo, the Grammatica in 1842, Syntaxis in 1849.

81.   **4. in all about ten books.**   Prof. Tomio Ogata of Tōkyō University, a great grandson of Ogata Kōan, has in his library several books which are known to have been among those "ten books."   Some of them are in book covers of Japanese tanned paper with humorous scribblings by anonymous students.   Prof. Ogata says that Fukuzawa's statement as to the number of books is wrong, for a larger number of books is listed in Kōan's own publications as his source materials.   The students too had access to many more books, some of them hand written copies.   It is conjectured that Fukuzawa was probably refering to the printed books for general students' use.

Here is a list, with no claim to completeness, according to Prof. Ogata, of the major books which are certain to have been in Kōan's library at that time:—Nederduitsche Spraakkunst door P. Weiland.   Uitgegeven in naam op last van het Staatshestuur der Bataafsche Republick Nieuwe door den auteur zelven overzien en

verbeterde druk. Te Dordrecht, Bij Blussé en van Braam. 1846.—
Handwoordenboek voor de Spelling der Hollandsche Taal door P.
Weiland in den Haag, bij Johannes Allart. MDCCCXII.—L. Meyers
Woordenschat, bevattende, in drie deelen, de Verklaaring der
Basterwoorden, Kunstwoorden, en Verouderde Woordens. Laat-
stlyk Merkelyk Verbeterd en Vermeerderd door Ernst Willem
Cramerus, Twaalfde Druk te Dordrecht, by A. Blussé & Zoon.
MDCCCV.—A. Richerand's Nieuwe Grondbeginselen der Natuurkunde van den Mensch. Naar de negende uitgave uit het Fransch
vertaald door A. van Erpecum, Heelmeester te Amsterdam.
Tweede zeer vermeerderde en verbeterde uitgave. Te Amsterdam, bij C. G. Sulpke. MDCCCXXVI.—Handboek der Algemeene
Ziektekunde door G. W. Consbruch. Koninklijk Pruissisch Hofraad enz. Practiserend Geneesheer to Bielefeld, Lid van versch-
eiden geleerde Genootschappen. Naar het Hoogduitsch door F.
van der Breggen, cornz. Med-Doct. de Amsterdam. Te Amsterdam, bij Lodewijk van Es. 1817.—Ziekte-Leer of Algemeene
Ziektekunde, door Ph. C. Hartmann, Doctor en Keizerlijk-Konink-
lijk Hoogleraar in de Geneeskunde, aan de Universiteit te Weelen.
In het Nederduitsch overgezet door M. J. Reynhout. Te Amsterdam bij C. G. Sulpke, 1827.—Encyclopedisch Woordenboek der
Praktische Genees., Heel- en Verloskunde. G. F. Most. Amsterdam. 1835-1838.—Bijzondere Ziekte-en Geneezingsleer Carl
Constatt. H. H. Hageman. Amsterdam 1846-1848.—Enchiridion
Medicum. Handleiding tot de Geneeskundige Praktijk. Erfmak-
ing van Eene Vijftigjarige Ondervinding, door C. W. Hufeland, in
leven Koninklijk-Pruissisch Staatsraad, Lijfarts en Boogleeraar
der Hoogeschool te Berlin. Naar de Laatste Vermeerderde en
Verbeterde Hoogduitsche Uitgave Veetaald door H. H. Hageman,
Jr., Med. Chir. et Art. Obst. Doctor. Tweede, met een Latijnsch
en Hollandsch Register Vermeerderde Uitgave. Amsterdam, bij
H. D. Santbergen, 1838.—Handleiding tot de Verloskunde, door
Gottlieb Salomoṇ, Med. Doctor, te Leyden. Met Platen. Tweede,
Vermeerderde en Verbeterde Druk. Te Amsterdam, bij Johannes
van der Hey en Zoon, 1826.—Grondbeginselen der Scheikunde;
door Josephus Jacobus van Plenck. Uit het Latyn vertaald, door
J. S. Swaan; Apothecar. Te Amsteldam, by J. B. Elwe en J. L.

Werlingshoff. MDCCCIII.—Algemeen Woordenboek van Kunsten en Wetenschappen, voor den Beschaafden stand en ten behoeve des gezelligen Levens, onder Medewerking van een aantal vaderlandsche geleerden Bijeenverzameld, door Gt Nieuwenhuis. Te Zutphen, bij H. C. A. Thieme. MDCCCXX. (seven volumes.)— Nieuw en Volkomen Woordenboek van Konsten en Weetenschappen; Bevattende Alle de Takken der Nuttige Kennis, door Egbert Buys, Hofraad van Hunne Poolsche, en Pruissische Majesteiten. Te Amsteldam, by S. F. Baalde, Boekverkooper. MDCCLXIX.— Geneeskundig Handboek voor Praktische Artsen door G. W. Consbruch, naar het Hoogduitsch, door N. C. Meppen. Derde Druk. Te Amsterdam bij R. J. Berntrop. MDCCCXXXIII. (6 volumes).

82.   5. **Doctor Doeff.** Hendrik Doeff (1777–1835). He became Captain of the Dutch post at Nagasaki in 1801. It was he who, with his courage and ingenuity, preserved the one remaining Dutch concession during the Napoleonic wars. (cf. p. 211) In those days of forced leisure when no ship arrived from home, he wrote the Dutch-Japanese dictionary with the assistance of several Japanese interpreters, completing it in 1817. It was widely copied, but the printing of this dictionary was not permitted until 1858 when Katsuragawa Hoshū put it into print in Yedo.

82.   6. **the Halma.** This was really a Dutch-French dictionary— François Halma: Woordenboek der Nederduitsche en Fransche taalen.

82.   7. **Weiland's Dutch lexicon.** Nederduitsch Taalkundig Woordenboek door P. Weiland.

87.   8. **the present nobleman of that name.** Kuroda Nagashige, Marquis (1867–1939). His grandfather was Kuroda Nagahiro (1811–1887), Lord of Fukuda in Chikuzen.

89.   9. **like separation from an old friend.** Prof. Tomio Ogata of Tōkyō University, a great grandson of Ogata Kōan, has been making a special study of the Dutch studies in Japan and he has come into possession of a copy of an old Dutch book on physics by van der Burg, reprinted in Nagasaki. He thinks it is very likely that this is a copy of the very book which impressed Fukuzawa so much. However, it is not a translation from English:—

Schets der Natuurkunde, ten dienste der Scholen, door P. van
der Burg. Tweede verbeterde en vermeerderde druk. Gounda,
G. B. van Goor, 1855.

CHAPTER V

94. **1.** **Okamoto Shūkichi (Furukawa Setsuzō)** (? —1877). He did
not come from the samurai stock, but after studying under Ogata
and Fukuzawa, he was married into the family of Furukawa, a
hatamoto (retainer of the Shōgun) by Fukuzawa's intercession,
and entered the Shogunate Navy. After he was defeated in the
revolt and pardoned, he served in the Navy and the Ministry of
Engineering (*Kōbushō*) of the Imperial government. Author of
many books and translations. (cf. p. 200 and p. 254)

95. **2.** **stopped....at the river crossings.** Because the Tokugawa
government did not permit building of bridges across certain big
rivers for defence purposes, all the travellers were obliged to ford
them or to be carried across on the backs of the river-men. The
least flood would stop passage for many days until the water
receded.

95. **3.** **Teppōzu.** It is the area now called Tsukiji Akashichō.
The site of the clan estate is now occupied by St. Luke's International Medical Center. In 1958 at the celebration of the
Centenary of Keiō University, a monument was erected on the
street outside St. Luke's to mark the school's birthplace.

97. **4.** **Treaty of the Five Nations.** Treaty of amity and commerce
with the United States, Holland, Russia, Britain and France, 1858.

97. **5.** **Kniffer.** A German trader of the same name, who had
his offices in Yokohama and Kōbe, appears in Japanese newspapers after the Restoration, and it is presumed he is the same
person that Fukuzawa met, but correct spelling of his name or
his initials are not known.

100. **6.** **Mitsukuri Rinshō** (1846–1897). Trained by his grandfather,
Gempo, he was made teacher in Bansho Shirabesho while still
young, later chief of the translation bureau. In the Imperial
government, he was again made chief of the translation bureau
where he gave much attention to the Western civil laws and
contributed much to the formation of Japanese laws. He was

made Doctor of Laws, member of the House of Peers, a Baron.

100. ⁷· **Holtrop.** John Holtrop: English and Dutch Dictionary; Nederduitsch en Engelsch Woordenboek.

101. ⁸· **Kanda Kōhei** (1830–1899). His name should properly be pronounced Kanda Takahira, but generally known as Kōhei. At that time he was teaching in Bansho Shirabesho. He was appointed governor of Hyōgo by the Imperial government. Later made member of the House of Peers and a Baron. A very versatile man, he translated many books on economics, mathematics, government, law, astronomy, archaeology, etc.

101. ⁹· **Murata Zōroku (Ōmura Masujirō)** (1824–1869). Known best as a military strategist and the organizer of the modern army of the Imperial government. Born the son of a physician in Suō, studied under Ogata Kōan in Ōsaka and Siebold in Nagasaki. Practiced medicine at home. Served in Uwajima clan as translator and director of military and naval installations. Later moved to Chōshū clan and modernized its fortification. Although he refused cooperation with Fukuzawa, he began learning English soon after with Dr. J. C. Hepburn of Yokohama. In the war with the shogunate, he showed his talent as a staff of the Chōshū forces. He was made Minister of the Army in the new Imperial government and introduced the ideas of the French system for the Army and the English for the Navy, abolition of the clan forces in order to form a national army, conscription of farmers for military service, etc. His actions were too drastic; he was assassinated by a group of conservative men of the Chōshū clan.

102. ¹⁰· **Harada Keisaku** (1830–1910). He was Fukuzawa's classmate in Ogata's school; taught in Bansho Shirabesho; later studied in Holland and France; served in the Imperial Army; became a general and the chief of the army arsenal, member of the House of Peers, a Baron.

CHAPTER VI

104. ¹· **Kanrin-maru.** According to Katsu Kaishū's Kaigun Rekishi (History of the Japanese Navy), this ship was built at Kinderdijk, Holland in 1856, sold to Japan in 1857 at 10,000 Dollars; a corvette, 165 feet long, 24 feet wide, screw propelled, 12 guns; it was originally named "Japan" by the Dutch. Its tonnage is not recorded by Katsu, but according to Captain Brooke's journal (cf. **Captain Brooke**, p. 350), it was 295 tons. In the wars of the Restoration, Kanrin-maru was among the ships which ran off from Yedo under the leadership of Enomoto, but it was damaged in a storm and captured by the Imperial fleet. In 1869 Kanrin-maru was dismissed from the Imperial Navy. It was used as a cargo boat for several years by some private concerns, but its subsequent fate is not recorded.

104. 2. **envoy's departure to Washington.** The envoys were Shimmi Buzen-no Kami and Muragaki Awaji-no Kami with a retinue of about 80 men. Their mission was to exchange ratification of the treaty of amity and commerce which had been negotiated between the shogunate and the U. S. Consul General Townsend Harris. At the same time they were to study all phases of the Western civilization because this was the very first diplomatic mission sent by Japan to the West. Very interesting journals of the members of the mission and other materials have been published in 1960-'61 by the Committee for the Centenary of America-Japan Treaty of Amity and Commerce; Manen Gannen Kembei Shisetsu Shiryō Shūsei, 7 volumes.

105. 3. **Kimura Settsu-no Kami** (1830–1901). Although Fukuzawa called him the Captain of the ship, he was not a sailor himself. He held a position somewhat like the Minister of the Navy. In San Francisco he was called Admiral Kimura. Katsu Rintarō was the Captain of Kanrin-maru. On this expedition, Kimura was charged with the duty of proceeding to conclude the ratification if anything untoward should happen to the chief envoy. After his return from the voyage, Kimura took several important positions in the shogunate government, but at the Restoration he retired entirely from active life and accepted no invitations from the new government. He wrote many books, "Thirty Year History", etc. His journal of the voyage of Kanrin-maru is valuable.

105. 4. **Katsu Rintarō** (1823–1899). He was among the first group of men to study naval arts under the Dutch in Nagasaki (1855). However sick and inefficient he was on the voyage of Kanrin-maru, Katsu was an able and courageous man. He became Minister of the Navy and erected a Navy Yard and an iron works in Kōbe. He is best remembered as the man who saved Yedo from siege when the Imperial forces were marching upon it in 1868. He went all by himself to the headquarters of the Imperial commander, Saigō Takamori, and negotiated peace. He retired in Shizuoka with the Shōgun for a while, but returned to Tōkyō in 1872 to be made Minister of the Navy in the Imperial government. He was made a Count and a Privy Councillor. He later called himself Katsu Kaishū.

105. 5. **Nakahama Manjirō** (1828–1898). A son of a fisherman of Nakanohama, Tosa. At the age of fourteen, he with a group of fishermen in a boat was blown out to sea by a storm and was rescued by William H. Whitfield, Master of an American whaling vessel. Other men were landed on Hawaii, but Manjirō was taken to Fairhaven, Massachusetts and was reared and educated by the Whitfield family. Called John Mung by the Americans, he shipped on whalers, took part in the California gold rush, finally in 1850 returned home after many adventures. He was at once employed by the Shōgun's government as interpreter, instructor of navigation and general advisor. There is an authoritative biography by his son, Dr. Tōichirō Nakahama—Nakahama Manjirō Den, Tōkyō, 1936.

105. 6. **Captain Brooke.** John Mercer Brooke (1826–1906), an American Navy officer and engineer. He invented the first deep sea sounding apparatus (1853–'4) for which he received a gold medal of science of the Academy of Berlin from the King of Prussia. He made two voyages to Japan, first with the North Pacific Surveying and Exploring Expedition under Commodore John Rogers (1855) during which Brooke sailed a launch from Shimoda to Hakodate and made a minute survey of the coast of Japan. On his second voyage, he commanded the Fenimore Cooper (98 tons) to survey the route from San Francisco to China. While the boat was in Yokohama and Brooke had gone to Yedo, a storm came up and washed the Fenimore Cooper on shore. This is how he came to be stranded in Yokohama and eventually invited to ship on board the Kanrin-maru.

During the Civil War he was with the Confederates; designed
and built the iron-clad ship, the Merrimac; also invented the
Brooke gun, the most powerful gun of the Confederate artillery;
and he became the chief of the Bureau of Ordnance and Hydro-
graphy. But his career was cut short by the defeat of the Confederates. He spent the rest of his life quietly as a professor of
Physics in the Virginia Military Institute. His very interesting
Yokohama Journal and Kanrin-muru Journal (edited by his
grandson, Prof. George M. Brooke, Jr.) have been published as
one volume of Manen Gannen Kenbei Shisetsu Shiryō Shūsei in
1961 by the Committee for the Centenary of America-Japan
Treaty of Amity and Commerce. From his journal we learn that
the voyage of the Kanrin-maru was not made by the Japanese
unassisted as the officers and Fukuzawa boastfully claimed.
Brooke acted as a good teacher.

117. ⁷· **with our obligations unpaid.** According to Kimura Settsu-
no Kami's journal, Captain Brooke too declined compensation of
any kind, declaring that he made the voyage under the order of
the U. S. Navy and that whatever he did during the voyage was
in return for the kindness he received from the Japanese government in Yokohama.

117. ⁸· **Webster's dictionary.** The one Fukuzawa brought back
has been lost, but Nakahama's had been preserved a long time,
and it is known that it was an abridged edition from the American dictionary of Noah Webster by William G. Webster assisted by
Chauncey A. Goodrich, New York, Mason Brothers, 1850, 490 pp.

121. ⁹· **the *rōnin* of Mito.** A *rōnin* was samurai not attached to
a lord. He retained his samurai status with the privilege to wear
two swords, etc. He may have been dismissed from service or
he may have resigned for some personal reason. In the disturbed times of the Restoration, many patriotic or ambitious
samurai became *rōnin* in order to avoid embarrassing their lords
with their revolutionary pursuits. Mito clan being a center of
Imperial cause and ultra-nationalism, it produced many *rōnin* of
particularly violent nature. (cf. **the school of Mito** on p. 364)

CHAPTER VII

124. ¹· **Kaei Tsūgo.** This was a translation of a Chinese-English dictionary of the same title (Hua-ying T'ung-yü in Chinese pronunciation) by Tzu-ch'ing, 1855, which Fukuzawa brought back from San Francisco. It contained about 22C0 words and 500 phrases and short sentences.

124. ²· **the envoys sent by the government.** The purpose of this mission was to negotiate postponement of the opening of the ports of Hyōgo and Niigata to foreign trade and the cities of Yedo and Ōsaka to foreign residence because of opposition within Japan. The envoys succeeded in concluding a five-year postponement with Britain, France, and Russia.

124. ³· **four hundred *ryō*.** The value of *ryō* having depreciated in the past few years, one *ryō* at this time in 1861 was worth about 5000 *yen*, making 400 *ryō* worth about two million *yen* or about $ 5600.

126. ⁴· **free access to English in print.** The list of books purchased in London has not been preserved, but it is presumed that Fukuzawa selected textbooks for High Schools and such elementary materials. See notes for **Chambers's book on economics** on p. 359 and **and every sort I could secure** on p. 360.

129. ⁵· **Alcock.** Sir Rutherford Alcock (1807–1897). He became the first British Consul General in Japan in 1858 and was made the Minister the next year and remained in Japan till 1864. He wrote several books on Japan the best known of which is "The Capital of the Tycoon."

133. ⁶· **Seiyō Jijō (Things Western).** A general description of the West in three books which opened the eyes of government officials, men in business and general scholars to new possibilities. The table of contents includes such subjects as political systems in Europe, methods of taxation, national debts, joint-stock companies, schools, newspaper, library, museum, hospital, poorhouse, insane asylum, steam engine, railway, telegraph, gas light; then there are descriptions of the United States, Holland, Britain, Russia and France each with its historical sketch, government system, Army and Navy, and the incomes and expenditures of the government. The middle book, which is called an interlude volume, was a translation of Chambers's book on economics for the purpose of explaining the Western ideas on man, society, government, law, competition and the natural law of progress, etc.

135. 7. ....**a decision might be postponed**..... The large island of Saghalien, but sparsely settled at this time, had been claimed by both Japan and Russia. A tentative agreement was reached five years later in 1867 and it was decided that the island belonged to both countries. But because of constant troubles among the settlers, the Japanese Minister to Russia, Enomoto Takeaki, in 1875 agreed to give Saghalien to Russia in exchange for the full possession of the Kurile archipelago. At the close of the Russo-Japanese War (1905), the southern half of Saghalien was ceded to Japan, but as the result of World War II, Russia took back Saghalien and occupied the Kuriles also.

136. 8. **Yamatoff.** Actually a man of that description existed. Tachibana Kumezō, a samurai of Kakekawa clan (Tōtōmi), having committed some crime, was wondering about the country as a repentant mendicant priest when he became acquainted with the captain of a Russian ship which was being repaired on the coast of Izu. He went to Russia in the ship. The Russian government found him very useful. In 1857 he wrote a Russian-Japanese dictionary. He did not appear at the visit of the first Japanese envoys in 1862, but he came out to meet Iwakura Tomomi when he came as an envoy in 1873 and he was induced to return to Japan. He lived as a recluse in Zōjōji, a Buddhist temple in Shiba, Tōkyō and called himself Masuda Kōsai; died in 1885 at the age of 65. In Russia he called himself Yamatoff from the Japanese words, Yamato (Japan) and fu (man). It is strange that Fukuzawa did not come to know about him.

139. 9. **which was unpleasant at the least.** There is some doubt about this statement. The Namamugi affair took place on August 21 (Japanese calendar) and the mission left France on the 13th of the following month. Could news travel from Japan to France in that short time when the eastern end of the telegraph line was Shanghai? No mention of the affair is found in the

diaries of the members of the mission nor in Fukuzawa's notebook. Fukuchi Genichirō in his Kaiō Jidan says he did not hear
of the affair until he returned as far as Singapore.

Namamugi is a place between Tōkyō and Yokohama. There
an English trader, Charles Lenox Richardson, was riding a horse
and unwittingly crossed the road in front of the Satsuma Daimyō's
train which was considered intolerable rudeness by the Japanese.
This incident led to the British demand of indemnity and the
battle of Kagoshima (pp. 144–152).

139. 10. **Leap-August.** In the Lunar Calendar which Japan was
using, there were twelve months of 29 days or 30 days in one year.
In order to adjust the months with the season, one extra month
called leap month was added to the regular twelve months seven
times in 19 years.

139. 11. **ten** *chō*. One *chō* is 360 feet. Ten *chō* will be about three-
quarters of a mile.

CHAPTER VIII

141. 1. **anti-Western feeling.....** In spite of the long isolation, the
Japanese people had no personal animosity against foreigners as
attested by the accounts of many Western visitors. However,
among the scholars there were two schools of thought. One of
them advocated isolation because it was dangerous to open intercourse with foreigners before reforming the people's lax morale,
for samurai were lazy and effete after the long peace and the
feudal discipline was in degenerate state. The Western ideas
which gave too much importance to profit and practical usefulness would further degenerate the Japanese.

The other school advocated limited intercourse with the West,
because in their thinking, foreign agression, as proved by the
Opium War of 1840, was too urgent to wait for internal reform.
The country should be opened peaceably in order to learn the
technique of gunnery and seamanship, etc., and thus place Japan
on an equal footing with the West. After the country had been
made secure, it might be closed again if necessary. Both schools
were agreed that the only thing the West had to teach was the
mechanical technique; Japan had superior knowledge in ethical

and social fields, and that technique was a very minor branch of learning though necessary for survival.

The forces which rallied around the Imperial court took to the former school of thought, and the shogunate by force of circumstance took to the latter school. This opposition soon turned into a violent political conflict. "Honor the Emperor and Expel the Foreigners" became the war cry of the imperialists.

In this situation, Fukuzawa and the small group of enlightened scholars had to demonstrate that the West had more to give than the technique, that the Japanese concept of man and society was what retarded the development of their technique, and that the whole Japanese way of thinking must be reexamined.

The great issue was the conflict between the imperialists and the shogunate. The question of foreign policy was being used more as a tool for conflict than as a legitimate question. Therefore, once the shogunate was overthrown, it was easy for the imperialists to forget the former war cry and turn to open intercourse with the West. And the public meekly followed the policy.

143. 2. **my collected works, Fukuzawa Zenshū.** Published in 1898, five volumes. As more materials were collected, a larger collection in ten volumes was published in 1926, and additional seven volumes in 1933 as Zoku Fukuzawa Zenshū. Among the Centenary memorial undertakings of Keiō University is a more ambitious collection (21 vols., 1958–64), which includes letters, memos, scribblings, and even household accounts.

143. 3. **Shinsenza.** In Yedo, Fukuzawa first lived on the clan estate in Teppōzu. He was married in 1861 and moved to a rented house in Shinsenza. The little episode told here occurred at this time. Two years later they returned to Teppōzu. In 1868 he purchased a sizable ground in Shinsenza and moved his school and residence there. Teppōzu is called Tsukiji nowadays and a monument on the street in front of St. Luke's Hospital indicates where Fukuzawa first began teaching. Shinsenza is now called Hamamatsu-chō, but the old site of the school is hardly recognizable.

144. 4. **the battle with the Chōshū clan.** Events of this period are too involved to be explained briefly, but the basic trend was that the nation was losing faith in the Tokugawa feudal government. Their sentiment was drifting toward the Imperial court. Also, the patriotic sentiment of reviving the Emperor as a temporal ruler was mixed with the sectional and personal ambitions and rivalries. Chōshū clan, caught in one of the intrigues, was declared enemy of the Emperor and the Shōgun.

The Shōgun felt that a war would be a good device to rally the Daimyō and the vassals around himself. So a punitive war on Chōshū was declared first in 1864 but it was halted when the Daimyō of Chōshū apologized. War was started again in 1866, this time earnestly, but it resulted in series of victories by the Chōshū army. The shogunate took the death of Shōgun Iemochi for an excuse to ask for Imperial order to end the war. And Chōshū emerged as one of the leading powers.

The best method to harass the shogunate was to insist upon the ancestral doctrine of "close the country." Hence, the antiforeign policy of the Chōshū and other leading clans. They quickly abandoned the policy when the shogunate was overthrown.

146. 5. Enryōkan. Originally a seaside villa of the Shōgun. When Fukuzawa was writing this book, it was being used as place of entertainment for state guests from foreign lands. Since then it has been made into a public park called Hama Rikyū Kōen.

148. 6. St. John Neale. Lieutenant Colonel Edward St. John Neale, deputy Minister.

148. 7. Captain Josling. There are some minor inaccuracies in Fukuzawa's narrative of the battle of Kagoshima though they do not in any way detract from the interest of the story. There were seven ships, instead of six, in the British fleet—Euryalus, Pearl, Perseus, Argus, Race-horse, Coquette, and Havoc. The officers were Rear-Admiral Sir Augustus Leopold Kuper, Commander Edward Wilmot, killed in the battle (Fukuzawa apparently mistook this officer for Commander-in-Chief) and Captain John James Stephen Josling, Captain of the Flagship Euryalus, killed in the battle. There were three, instead of two, Kagoshima ships. Matsuki and Godai were temporary hostages while the battle lasted.

150. **8. Yokohama newspapers.** In 1863, John R. Black (1816–1880), an Englishman, came to Yokohama from Australia and started Japan Herald. This must be the newspaper Fukuzawa refers to. There was no vernacular newspapers at this time except for *kawaraban*, a primitive form of news carrier, printed by woodblock from time to time when there was sensational news, and sold on the street.

151. **9. Shimizu Usaburō** (1832–1878). Though he was a merchant, he had a great interest in Western studies. He learned Dutch under Mitsukuri Gempo; went to France with Tokugawa Akitake in 1867. After the Restoration, he opened a store called Mizuhoya in Tōkyō and imported foreign books, printing machines, medical instruments, etc. He was the first of the merchant class to be admitted to Meirokusha, the first academic society formed in Japan. Fukuzawa's strong argument helped him gain admittance. Shimizu wrote many articles in the periodicals of the society, particularly on the abolition of Chinese characters in Japanese writing. Also he was author of several books on science and history for popular consumption.

151. **10. Alexander Siebold.** Alexander Georg Gustav von Siebold (1864–1911), the eldest son of the German oriental scholar Philipp Franz von Siebold. He served as interpreter to the British Legation. Later he was employed by the Japanese government.

153. **11. Van Reed.** Eugene M. van Reed, an American trader of fortune. Once served in the American Consulate; published a newspaper called Yokohama Shimpō Moshiogusa in cooperation with a Japanese. Following some shady deals, he left the country in 1868.

154. **12. Terajima Tōzō.** For more comments on him, see p. 186. He was later made a Privy Councillor and a Count.

158. **13. Murata Zōroku.** See note for Murata Zōroku on p. 348.

164. **14. the feast of Tanabata.** This is a pretty festival of the stars which originated in China. Two bright stars on both sides of the Milky Way are supposed to be a weaver girl and a young cattle herder, who are very much in love with each other. But the young man is permitted to cross over to meet the girl only once a year on the seventh day of the seventh month, and if there should be a drop of rain, the Milky Way, which is a river, is flooded and he cannot cross over. And so, the young folks on the earth compose poems and hang them on bamboo sprays with proper decorations in prayer for the good luck of the heavenly lovers. In the poems may be expressed some hidden personal sentiments of the poets too.

CHAPTER IX

169. **1. Mitsui Hachiroemon.** The House of Mitsui began business in the 17th century as a draper and moneychanger with stores in Yedo, Ōsaka and Kyōto. It opened many new business ventures such as the transfer of money between cities, etc. It grew to do the Shōgun and the Imperial court financial services. After the Restoration, it developed the great "financial kingdom" of Mitsui. The heads of the Mitsui family traditionally have assumed the name Hachiroemon even to this day. Mitsui is probably the oldest financial families in the world still active.

170. **2. Shinkawa.** It is the Sumida River, which flows through Tōkyō, near its mouth to the sea, for Japanese rivers are called by different names according to their portions. The best wine produced in Nada, near Kōbe, was brought to Yedo in boats by way of Shinkawa. The flavor of the wine was said to improve by being gently rolled in the barrel during the long voyage.

171. **3. all the nightsoil....disposed of to its own profit.** The nightsoil was used for fertilizing, and the farmers used to come into the city to purchase it.

172. **4. whether my argument was sound or not.** The episodes in this chapter make a reader wonder if Fukuzawa had not been influenced by the idea of liberty and equality with slightly detrimental consequence. He was still young (34 years old), very successful in all his undertakings with large income from his books. He must have been too sure of himself which he is here remembering with regret.

174. **5. A Guide to Travel in the Western World.** This was a very practical explanation of foreign travels from the voyage in the steam ship to money exchange. In its preface Fukuzawa said that he looked forward to the time when the Japanese became so familiar with foreign countries that this book need not go on being printed. In the appendix Fukuzawa explains insurance. This is the very first mention of insurance in Japanese literature.

CHAPTER X

178. 1. **retreat....of Shōgun Yoshinobu himself.** Tokugawa Yoshinobu (1837-1913) was the seventh son of Tokugawa Nariaki, Lord of Mito. He was made the 15th and the last Shōgun in 1866 when the former Shōgun died without an heir. A very able statesman, he had seen the inevitability of the times and voluntarily repudiated the Shōgun's authority and returned the temporal power to the Emperor. However, the powerful clans like Satsuma and Chōshū around the imperial court felt that the Shōgun must be defeated on the field of battle in order to demonstrate the power of the new regime. And so, they provoked the shogunate army to a fight at Toba and Fushimi. Yoshinobu returned to Yedo on board a ship and made every show of obedience and humility to the Emperor in order to avoid war. He succeeded in doing so. He was made a Daimyō in Shizuoka where he lived in retirement the rest of his life.

185. 2. **Fukuchi Genichirō** (1841-1906). Having been an interpreter in Nagasaki, he was among the members of the mission to Europe with Fukuzawa in 1862. After the Restoration, he was active in journalism as President of Tōkyō Nichinichi Shimbun (newspaper), also in politics. In his old age he turned to *Kabuki* play writing very successfully, and he is now best remembered by his pen name, Fukuchi Ōchi.

190. 3. **Chambers's book on economics.** Fukuzawa alludes to this book in many of his writings, but the book had been lost and its identity remained a question for a long time. There is no name resembling Chambers among the noted scholars on economics of the contemporary or earlier times. Fukuzawa's biographers have since become convinced that Chambers is not the name of the author but of the publisher. In the 1930's Prof. Seiichirō Takahashi of Keiō University obtained a copy of "Chambers' Educational Course: Political Economy, for use in schools and for private instruction. William and Robert Chambers. London and Edinburgh. 1870." It is a small volume of 154 pages, too insignificant to bear the author's name. This copy is believed to be a later edition of the book which Fukuzawa found most useful in forming his ideas on economics and social sciences.

194. 4. **Katō Hiroyuki** (1836–1916). Fukuzawa disliked him for his bureaucratic attitude, but Katō was the originator of German studies in Japan. He was teaching Dutch in Bansho Shirabesho when the King of Prussia presented a telegraphic machine to the Shōgun and Katō was ordered to study its operations. His contact with the Germans began at that time. After the Restoration, he took various offices in the new government, had the honor of lecturing before the Emperor on political systems of Europe, and he was made the President of the Imperial University, Privy Councillor and a Baron.

196. 5. **Tsuda Shinichirō** (1829–1903). He later called himself Tsuda Masamichi. A career official and a serious student of law. He had been sent by the shogunate to Holland in 1862 with Enomoto and others. He studied in Leyden for two years. He translated and wrote books on law, worked in various offices, became a member of the House of Representatives, the House of Peers, a Doctor of Laws.

196. 6. **a new place at Shinsenza**..... See note on **Shinsenza** on **p.** 355.

199. 7. **and every sort I could secure.** Fukuzawa brought back three or four thousand *ryō* worth of books. The shipment was so large that the customs officers in Yokohama became suspicious and held it until the fall of the Tokugawa government. The list of books has not been preserved, but the following books are known to have been used as textbooks in Fukuzawa's school soon after:— The Elements of Political Economy by Francis Wayland, Peter Parley's Universal History, Elementary History of the United States by G. P. Quackenbos, Natural Philosophy by G. P. Quackenbos, Cornell's Primary Geography, Elements of Moral Science by Francis Wayland, An English Grammar by G. P. Quackenbos. We must concede that Fukuzawa was wise in using these elementary books for his class instruction at this time.

Up to this time, a school usually had only one copy of each book

which each student had to hand copy for his reading. Fukuzawa's large purchase enabled every member of a class to have
exclusive use of an original printed book. This caused a revolutionary improvement in instruction.

Keiō-gijuku's list of textbooks fifteen years later (1882) includes
such titles as An Introduction to the Principles of Morals and
Legislation by Jeremy Bentham, Considerations on Representative Government by John Stuart Mill, On Liberty by J. S. Mill,
The English Constitution by Walter Bagehot, Introduction to the
Study of International Law by Theodore D. Woolsey, The Logic
of Accounts (Theory and Practice of Double-Entry Bookkeeping)
by E. G. Folsom.

200. 8. **Shōgun's men at Ueno.** See note on **the fierce battle of
Ueno** below.

200. 9. **Furukawa Setsuzō.** See note on **Okamoto Shūkichi** on
p. 347.

205. 10. **Mr. Portman.** A. L. C. Portman, Deputy Minister of the
United States.

208. 11. **Keio-gijuku.** The new installation was large enough to
hold 100 boarding students, an amazing number for those days.
More remarkable, however, was Fukuzawa's declaration in Keiō-
gijuku-no Ki that the school was not to be his personal enterprise
but that it was to be maintained by the joint efforts of the men
who came together for the common purpose of learning. Thus
Keiō-gijuku became the first school in Japan with modern organization.

210. 12. **the fierce battle of Ueno.** Shōgun Yoshinobu had surrendered and allowed the imperial forces to enter Yedo without
resistance, but the die-hards, together with *rōnin,* gathered
around Kaneiji Temple in Ueno, where Yoshinobu had retired,
ostensibly for guarding the Shōgun. In order to disband them,
Yoshinobu moved away to Mito, but the band, now 3000 strong
and calling themselves Shōgitai, remained and resisted the order
of the imperial army for peaceful disbanding and a battle became
inevitable. This was the last and the only serious resistance in
Yedo.

210. 13. **an English text book.** From other records this book was discovered to have been "The Elements of Political Economy by Francis Wayland, D. D., late President of Brown University and Professor of Moral Philosophy, Boston, 1866." This day, May 15, was made a memorial day at Keiō University in 1957, called the Wayland Day, and special lectures are given for the occasion every year.

213. 14. **(....organization of the prefectural government).** The Restoration of 1868 was no more than the transfer of supreme power from the Shōgun to the Emperor. The clans remained and the feudal social system of Japan was unchanged. In 1869 several clans voluntarily offered their fiefs (their land and people) to the Emperor, the reason being the moral theory that all belonged to the Emperor and also the clans' difficulty in maintaining independence economically and militarily. The Emperor issued an order that all fiefs in the country should be relinquished but that the lords of each clan would be appointed governors of the same clan. In 1871 a further step was taken to reorganize the 305 clans into prefectures under a centralized government.

214. 15. **Hatano Shōgorō** (1854–1929). Very active in government and in business, he became member of Tōkyō City Assembly, worker in Ministry of Foreign Affairs, President of Nippon Shimbun (newspaper), Director of Mitsui Bank, member of Diet, etc.

214. 16. **laws of "number and reason."** This is Fukuzawa's own way of describing scientific method. On other occasions he used such expressions as *jitsu-gaku* (real or functional learning) and sometimes the English word "science."

217. 17. **my collected works (Fukuzawa Zenshū).** See note for **my collected works** on p. 355.

218. 18. **unoccupied estates of feudal clans.** A *daimyō* used to own several estates in Yedo—his official residence (*kami-yashiki*), second residence (*naka-yashiki*), vassals' quarters (*shimo-yashiki*), rice storage and offices (*kura-yashiki*), etc. But at the Restoration, a decree limited the number of estates to one for each *daimyō*. Consequently there appeared a number of unoccupied estates in the city.

219. 19. **making a book out of it.....** It was entitled *Torishimari·*

no Hō (Laws for Policing) containing police organizations of London, Paris and New York.

224. 20. **establishment of college departments.** Through the kind intercession of President Charles W. Eliot of Harvard University, three American scholars, William Liscomb (Literature), Garret Droppers (Economics), and John Henry Wigmore (Law), were appointed as the first professors of Keiō University, the first private university in Japan, and they began instruction in 1890 with fifty-nine students. The total enrollment of Keiō-gijuku in that year was about 1500.

At Fukuzawa's death in 1901, thanks to its corporate organization the school did not lose its vitality. In 1917 the School of Medicine was established with Kitasato Shibasaburō, Fukuzawa's friend and world-famed bacteriologist, as the Dean. In 1939 Fujihara Ginjirō, an alumnus, established a college of engieering named Fujihara Kōgyō Daigaku with his own private funds and requested the President of Keiō-gijuku to take charge of its operations with the understanding that it should be incorporated with the university in the future, which was done in 1943. In 1957 the Faculty of Business and Commerce was established. At present (1965), the university comprises six faculties with enrollment of some 20,000, including graduate students. Also, there are three Senior High Schools, two Junior High Schools, one Elementary School and a university correspondence course within the Keiō-gijuku organization, bringing the total enrollment to nearly 40,000.

CHAPTER XI

226. 1. **right hand side of the gateway....** This house with the trap door stood on the spot now occupied by the University Library.

230. 2. **my young niece.** O-Ichi, the only daughter of Fukuzawa's brother, Sannosuke. She later was married to Tajiri Takenosuke.

230. 3. **the insurrection around Saigō.** Saigō Takamori (1827–1877) was a great figure in Satsuma clan, one of the leaders of the Restoration, but he was thoroughly a military man often disagreeing with other leaders who were engaged in civil development, and he had been in retirement in Kagoshima since 1873. Those out of gear with the new society and young men of ultra-nationalistic inclination gathered around him and caused an insurrection. Saigō himself had no wish to oppose the government by force, but being a man loyal to his personal friends and followers, he rose to lead the insurrection. When he was defeated and killed, it was a clear demonstration of the power of the government and all attempts to oppose it by force disappeared. Dissatisfied men then turned to the movement for opening the Diet as the one remaining method to oppose the government.

231. 4. **the school of Mito.** The first lord of Mito, Tokugawa Mitsukuni (1628–1700), was a great personality, not only as administrator but also as promoter of learning. His greatest work was in initiating compilation of a history of Japan called "Dai Nihon Shi" by bringing together noted scholars of the country in 1657. His descendants followed in his steps until its completion in 1906. The purpose of this history was to clarify the sacred nationality of Japan. It was natural that Mito should become the center of Japanese studies as opposed to Chinese studies, and also, in later years, of nationalism and ultra-patriotism.

CHAPTER XII

243. 1. **he jumped off the horse.** During the Tokugawa regime, riding a horse in public was the samurai's special privilege. In 1871 this restriction was formally lifted.

247. 2. ....**public speaking**..... The Japanese had been familiar with sermons and story telling, but public speaking and debating as we know it today is Fukuzawa's introduction. The word *enzetsu* (public speaking) is his own invention. It may be said that public speaking was not necessary in a feudal society and it was not developed. Its first public exhibition was given at Keiō-gijuku on May 1, 1875 at the opening of Enzetsu-kan (Hall of Public Speaking). This hall, modeled after a New England Meeting House, is the very first auditorium in the country, now preserved as a monument on the university campus.

247. 3. **the number of copies sold**..... Among Fukuzawa's books,

Gakumon-no Susume (Encouragement of Learning), a series of seventeen pamphlets, had the largest sale. About 200,000 of each number were sold. Of the First Book of Seiyō Jijō (Things Western) some 150,000 copies were sold very quickly and pirated editions raised the number to 250,000.

254. **4. the feeble claims of the shogunate.** At this time, though the Shōgun's government had fallen, there still were some three hundred *daimyō*, or lords of provinces, each claiming autonomy, and the future of the Imperial rule was an unknown quantity Therefore, it was natural for men like Enomoto and Furukawa to seek their own fortune in the still unsettled land of Hokkaidō. Enomoto had a grand, though immature, idea of establishing an ideal state in opposition to the conservative and despotic men who were rallying around the Imperial court.

Enomoto (1836–1908), after being pardoned, was given high offices in the Imperial government such as Minister to Russia, Minister of the Navy, Minister of Foreign Affairs, Privy Councillor, and was made a Count. For notes on Furukawa, see p. 347.

257. **5. ....valuable notes on navigation.....** This was really a hand copied Dutch translation of international marine law from a French book, made by Enomoto's teacher in Holland, J. G. Frederiks, "Internationale Regels Diplomatie der Zee door Thèodore Ortolan". This note is now preserved in the Imperial Household Library (Kunaishō Shoryōbu). The introduction contains Frederiks's greetings to Enomoto, and this is the part that Fukuzawa translated before returning it.

CHAPTER XIII

265. **1. four hundred *tsubo*.** 14,400 sq. ft. One *tsubo* is six-foot square or 36 square feet.

265. **2. three hundred and fifty-five *ryō*.** It was worth about 590,000 *yen* (about $1640), one *ryō* having depreciated again to about 1660 *yen* at this time. One may note the tremendous disturbance in the value of money in these few years. See notes for *bu, shu* on p. 342, and for **four hundred *ryō*** on p. 352.

270. **3. to send my own sons to the United States.** The eldest son, Ichitarō, studied English literature at Cornell University as well as privately. The second son, Sutejirō, was graduated at the Massachusetts Institute of Technology, specializing in Civil Engineering, class of 1888. After coming home, Ichitarō taught in Keiō University, later becoming its *Shatō* (Chancellor). Sutejirō worked as a railway engineer for a while, later becoming President of Jiji-shimpō, his father's newspaper.

273.   4. **relations between the clan and myself were broken off.....** Although the feudal relation was broken off at this time, Fukuzawa's personal interest in the clan and its lord continued as may be verified by the anecdote on p. 234. Also see note for **began to place confidence in me** on p. 367.

282.   5. **bookkeeping.** The translation was made from "Common School Bookkeeping, embracing single and double entry, by H. B. Bryant and H. D. Stratton, 1871". The translation was published in 1873.

CHAPTER XIV

295.   1. **the *Nō* stage.** See note for **so the trick was effective,** p. 344.

295.   2. **Pear Garden's magic.** This is a Chinese poetical expression for theater and theatrical art. The actor here alluded to is Danjūrō who happened to be performing on this day. He later became a frequent visitor in Fukuzawa's home, for Fukuzawa found the actor's personality interesting and stimulating. Danjūrō is a great figure in *Kabuki*, for his efforts caused the public to recognize *Kabuki* as a high form of art, worthy to be performed before the Emperor. Until then it had been regarded as vulgar entertainment fit only for the merchant class.

297.   3. **four sons and five daughters.** The eldest two and the youngest two children were sons and the five daughters were grouped in between. They were Ichitarō (1863-1938), Sutejirō (1865-1926), Sato (1868-1945, married Nakamura Sadakichi), Fusa (1870-1955, married Iwasaki Momosuke who assumed name of Fukuzawa at marriage), Shyun (1873-1954, married Kiyooka Kuninosuke), Taki (1876-, married Shidachi Tetsujirō), Mitsu (1879-1907, married Ushioda Dengorō), Sampachi (1881-1962), Daishirō (1883-1960).

300. 4. **Otherwise, there is no difference made.** It is said that Fukuzawa divided his property into ten parts and gave two parts of it to his eldest son and one part to each of the other eight children. He had provided for his wife with an independent property long before.

303. 5. **to America for further education.** See note for **to send my own sons to the United States,** p. 365.

304. 6. **more than three hundred letters.....** These letters had been preserved and were published in a book entitled "Aiji e no Tegami" (Letters to his Loving Children) in 1953. Fukuzawa reveals himself most intimately in these personal letters.

305. 7. **the great house of Hitotsu-bashi.** One of the main branches of the Tokugawa family. Because its Yedo estate was located at Hitotsu-bashi, it came to be generally called by that name.

306. 8. **....began to place confidence in me.** Hōren-in was the widowed wife of the lord three generations back, a beautiful and very intelligent lady. She must have placed much confidence in Fukuzawa, for in her last days she moved to a small house on the Keiō-gijuku campus which Fukuzawa had prepared for her. The circumstance of her moving there while her family lived in Tōkyō in a fine residence is not known. But she was happy to live like an ordinary woman. Fukuzawa used to invite her to his house for music and other entertainments which had been denied her till then because of her aristocratic position. He took her to *Kabuki* once and she enjoyed it very much.

CHAPTER XV

311. 1. **the battle of Sekiga-hara.** A decisive battle in 1600 which established the Tokugawa supremacy.

311. 2. **Shouyang-shan of the new era.** Po-i and Shu-ch'i were loyal and steadfast followers of the dethroned Chinese king, Chou of Yin dynasty. They retired to a mountain called Shouyang-shan where they lived on wild bracken, for they disdained to receive anything from the new king or from men who surrendered to him. One day someone suggested that the wild bracken might also belong to the new king since all the country was now under his power.   The faithful brothers then decided they could not eat anything and they died of starvation.   Their life is the classic example of loyal men.

316.   3. **Ōkuma, Itō, and Inoue.**   Ōkuma Shigenobu (1838–1922) was one of the ablest statesmen of the period, but being a man of Saga clan, he had difficulty in holding high office above the Chō-shū and Satsuma men who dominated the Imperial government. In the 1881 fiasco, he had advocated the immediate creation of the National Diet.   Soon after he left the government, he formed a political party called Rikken Kakushin-tō (Constitutional Pro-gressive Party) and he had since been on the side of the people and the political party as against the bureaucratic government officials.   Also in the same year (1882) he established a school which later grew into the present Waseda University.   He finally became a Prime Minister in 1914.

Itō Hirobumi (1841–1909) is best known as the man who drafted the Japanese Constitution and he was the most active statesman of the era.   Originally a lower samurai of Chōshū clan, he was sent to England for studies in 1863.   He worked his way to the top by his sheer ability, and after the resignation of Ōkuma in 1881, he was the unrivaled chief of the government.   He went to Europe himself to study constitutions of various countries, partic-ularly Germany, and the Japanese Constitution was promulgated by the Emperor in 1889.   He was made the first Prime Minister and he filled the position four times in his life.   He was assas-sinated by a Korean because he was largely responsible for the annexation of Korea to Japan.

Inoue Kaoru (1835–1915).   A man of Chōshū clan, he was a powerful friend and coworker of Itō.

316.   4. **subsequently Ōkuma resigned.**   This incident, generally called "the Political Disturbance of the 14th year of Meiji", was caused by internal and personal conflict of the officials, not very important in itself, but it marked a turning point—governmental announcement for the Constitution and the Diet in ten years, reaffirmation of Japanese nationalism, etc.

316.   5. **Iwasaki Yatarō** (1838–1885).   He was a great businessman of Meiji era who founded the "financial kingdom" of Mitsubishi which rose quickly to rival the old Mitsui. He was originally a poor samurai of Tosa clan; took part in the trade and transportation activities of the clan and at the dissolution of the clan in 1871, he took the business into his own hands. He was very successful in the Mitsubishi Steamship Company. Then his company, ably supported by his brother and son, spread into all sorts of enterprises.

317. 6. **Iwakura.** Iwakura Tomomi (1825–1883) was one of the few able courtiers who took a leading part in the Restoration movement. At this time he was the *Udaijin* (Chancellor). When the new ranks of nobility were created, he was given the highest rank, *Kōshaku*, which had no equivalent in European titles, and he came to be called Prince Iwakura though he was not of the royal family. cf. p. 218.

317. 7. **the insurrection of the tenth year of Meiji.** See note for the insurrection around Saigō on p. 363.

317. 8. **have kept it among my private papers.** This account is now included in Fukuzawa's collected works (Fukuzawa Zenshū), entitled Meiji Shinki Kiji.

318. 9. **Ordinance of Public Peace and Security.** Called Hoan-jōrei, issued in 1882, it ruled that anyone scheming an insurrection or disturbing the peace of society or even suspected of the same may be banished to the distance of 3 *ri* (about 7 miles) from the Imperial Palace for a term of 3 years. Ozaki Yukuo, one of Fukuzawa's pupils, was among the 570 men condemned by this ordinance. Though it was abrogated in 1889, it has ever since been recalled as the example of an evil policy of an oppressive government.

318. 10. **Gotō Shōjirō (1838–1897).** A man of Tosa clan, he is known for advancing the idea that the Shōgun should return his supreme power to the Emperor, and having his lord suggest it to Shōgun Yoshinobu. He was an active politician and later was made Minister, but being very ambitious and opportunistic, he was at odds with the government at times.

318. 11. **some affairs in Korea.** Inoue Kakugorō (1859–1938) had been in Korea according to Fukuzawa's advice and had been an advisor to the Korean government. He was suspected of involve-

ment in a revolutionary uprising of 1884. Inoue was later very
active in both business and politics in Japan.

324.   12. **my collected writings (Fukuzawa Zenshū).** See note for
my collected works on p. 355.

331.   13. **Doctor Simmons.** Duane B. Simmons (1834–1889) came to
Japan in 1859 as a missionary physician. He and Dr. J. C.
Hepburn were regarded by the Japanese as 2 great doctors.
He helped to establish the Jūzen Byōin hospital in Yokohama,
taught medicine in Daigaku Tōkō and did a great deal to improve
medical practices in Japan. He took care of Fukuzawa during
his illness in 1870 and became a very close friend. Fukuzawa was
particularly struck by his love of his mother, and when he was
retiring because of ill health, Fukuzawa invited him to live in a
house which was built specially for him on the Keiō-gijuku
grounds. Simmons and his old mother lived there until his death,
and the surviving mother went sadly back to the United States.
The house was afterwards used as a club house for both faculty
and students until it was burned in the bombing of 1945.

336.   14. **I should like to encourage a religion.....** Fukuzawa had
many close friends among the Buddhist priests and Christian
missionaries, but he did not take to any of the established
religions. He had the mind of a thorough scientist of the Nineteenth Century. It might be said that he believed in science as
other men believed in religion. This came to him more naturally
than would have been possible with any scientists of the West,
for he had not been brought up in a conflicting religion. He was
most optimistic about the future of mankind, for he believed that
with the basic goodness of man, scientific knowledge would enable him to solve any earthly problems. He believed man was
on the right road to the millennium, though he realized it was to
be a long way. In the meanwhile, he was willing to let "less
enlightened" people enjoy the good influence of the established
religion. Fukuzawa's mind always worked in two ways—according to high ideals and according to immediate purpose. For the
latter purpose, he would follow practical expediency in leading
people step by step.

336.   15. Fukuzawa suffered a stroke in 1898 from which he recovered, but suffered a second attack and died on February 3, 1901. He was mourned by the whole nation. The Emperor sent a special messenger to the bereaved family and the National Diet passed an unprecedented resolution of condolence. His remains are buried in a Buddhist temple, Jōkō-ji, in Ōsaki, Tōkyō.

Appendix I

CHRONOLOGICAL TABLE

Numerals under the years indicate Fukuzawa's age.
Numerals in parentheses after statements indicate page
references in this book.

Dates in this chronology up to the end of 1871 are in
Lunar Calendar unless otherwise indicated. On January 1, 1872, Japan adopted the Western Calendar.

YEAR	FUKUZAWA'S LIFE	GENERAL HISTORY
1835 Tempō 6 (Tempō 5)	Born on January 10, 1835 (December 12, Tempō 5) in Ōsaka (1).	Alexis de Tocqueville's *Democracy in America* is published. Mark Twain is born. (Charles William Eliot was born in 1834.) Ralph Waldo Emerson's *Nature* is published.
1836 Tempō 7 1	Father, Hyakusuke, dies. Mother and five children move to Nakatsu (1, 229).	
1837 Tempō 8 2		Queen Victoria comes to the throne of England.
1838 Tempō 9 3		Ogata Kōan opens his school in Ōsaka.
1839 Tempō 10 4		Michael Faraday's *Experimental Researches in Electricity* published 1839–'55 (88).
1840 Tempō 11 5	(At the age of seven suffers a slight case of smallpox. In early age, was adopted by uncle Nakamura Jutsuhei and had been named Nakamura Yukichi though living in	Opium War.

YEAR	FUKUZAWA'S LIFE	GENERAL HISTORY
	Fukuzawa family) (23–24).	
1842 Tempō 13 6		Hong Kong is acquired by the British.
1848 Kaei 1 12		Communist Manifesto by Marx and Engels.
1852 Kaei 5 17	(Begins attending school at the age of 14 or 15) (7).	Napoleon III is crowned Emperor of France. Hoashi Banri dies (13).
1853 Kaei 6 18		Commodore Matthew C. Perry enters Yedo Bay. Euphimius Putiatin of Russia comes to Nagasaki for treaty negotiations.
1854 Ansei 1 19	February—goes to Nagasaki to study Dutch (21).	March—the first Treaty of Peace and Amity with the United States signed. Crimean War begins.
1855 Ansei 2 20	February—obliged to leave Nagasaki (25–27). March—enters Ogata's school (35).	Instruction of naval arts by the Dutch begins in Nagasaki (104). The shogunate opens Yōgakusho (school of Western studies) in Yedo.
1856 Ansei 3 21	January—brother, Sannosuke, falls ill. March—Yukichi contracts typhoid, recovers in April (40). Returns to Nakatsu to recuperate. August—resumes studies in Ōsaka. Brother dies on September 3. Returns home and is made head of Fukuzawa family. Copies Pel's book on fortification (46). Pays off family debt (44). Goes	The American Consul General Townsend Harris comes to Shimoda in July. Yōgakusho is renamed Bansho-shirabesho. Crimean War ends.

YEAR	FUKUZAWA'S LIFE	GENERAL HISTORY
	again to Ōsaka in November (50).	
1857 Ansei 4 22	Made *Jukuchō* of Ogata's school (56). Tries temperance and fails (75). Translates Pel's book on fortification but it was not published (51).	Henry Thomas Buckle publishes *History of Civilization in England*. Shogunate purchases the war vessel Kanrin-maru from the Dutch.
1858 Ansei 5 23	October—comes to Yedo at the clan's order to open a school (93). On the way stays overnight with Nakamura Ritsuen (229).	June—**Treaty of Amity and Commerce with America signed**. Same treaty with Holland, Britain, Russia and France followed.
1859 Ansei 6 24	Visits Yokohama and discovers the necessity of English language (97). Discovers error in Japan's monetary system (282).	May—ports of Yokohama, Nagasaki and Hakodate are opened. J. S. Mill's *On Liberty* and Charles Darwin's *Origin of Species* published. Alexis de Tocqueville dies. Saigon is captured by the French.
1860 Manen 1 25	January 19—sails from Uraga on board Kanrin-maru; reaches San Francisco on February 26 (March 17 by Western calendar); leaves on March 19 and returns to Uraga on May 5 after a stop in Hawaii (104–123). Engaged by the shogunate as translator (122). August —Fukuzawa's first publication *Kaei Tsūgo* (English-Japanese Dictionary) comes out (124).	January—Japan's first envoy to America leaves for ratification of treaty. March—Ii Kamon-no Kami is assassinated (121). In America the first Pony Express starts on April 3 (Western calendar). Ralph W. Emerson publishes *The Conduct of Life*. Okamoto Shūkichi publishes *Bankoku Seihyō*, the first statistical work in Japan.

YEAR	FUKUZAWA'S LIFE	GENERAL HISTORY
1861 Bunkyū 1 26	Moves to a house in Shin-senza (355). Marries Toki Kin with Shimazu Bun-saburō and his wife as the gobetweens (297). Ordered to go to Europe as a member of a mission (124).	The envoy, Takenouchi Shimotsuke-no Kami and his party are ordered to go to Europe (124). The American Civil War begins. Victor Emmanuel II becomes the first King of Italy.
1862 Bunkyū 2 27	Leaves Nagasaki on January 1 for Europe and returns on December 11 (125).	January—Andō Nobuma-sa is attacked and injured (141). August—an English-man is killed in Nama-mugi (139). In the same month Ogata Kōan comes to Yedo to be made Shō-gun's personal physician. Herbert Spencer pub-lishes *First Principles*.
1863 Bunkyū 3 28	May—fearing British attack, prepares to evacu-ate (145). In the autumn moves back to an apart-ment in the clan estate in Teppōzu (355). First son, Ichitarō, is born in Teppō-zu (297). Burns notes on diplomatic transactions (160).	February—Shōgun Ie-mochi visits the Emperor (144). May 9—indemnity for Namamugi Affair is paid (147). Chōshū clan fires on foreign ships (162). June—Ogata Kōan dies. July—British fleet bom-bard Kagoshima (148). J. S. Mill's *Utilitarianism* published.
1864 Ganji 1 29	March—leaves Yedo for Nakatsu to call on mother. Returns to Yedo in June with six young men. Because of anti-Western sentiment, obliged to avoid Nakamura Ritsuen (229). Refuses conscrip-tion of students for Chō-shū War (184). October	July—Battle of Hamaguri Gomon in Kyōto. August —Shōgun gives the grand order of war against Chō-shū clan (184). Combined fleet of America, Holland, France and Britain bom-bards Shimonoseki, and in September Shōgun's government agrees to pay

YEAR	FUKUZAWA'S LIFE	GENERAL HISTORY
	—made a retainer of the Shōgun (185).	indemnity for the Shimonoseki incident (162).
1865 Keiō 1 30	Second son, Sutejirō, is born.	Katō Hiroyuki publishes *Kōeki Kaitō.*
1866 Keiō 2 31	Begins to curb his drinking (328). In the autumn sells off his swords (164, 240, 247). Publishes *Seiyō Jijō* (Things Western) *Book I* (133, 334, 352).	June—second war against Chōshū. August—Shōgun Iemochi dies and Yoshinobu succeeds. The war on Chōshū is called off. December—Emperor Kōmei dies. Philipp Franz von Siebold dies.
1867 Keiō 3 32	January—sails for the second visit to America with committee for the purchase of a warship and returns in June (166). July —ordered to be penitent, pardoned in October (174, 175). December — purchases Arima's property in Shinsenza (178, 196, 265). Publishes *Raijū Sōhō*, (Rifle Instruction Book) Part I; *Seiyō Tabi Annai* (Guide to Travel in the Western World) (174); *Jōyaku Jūichi Koku Ki* (Our Eleven Treaty Countries); *Seiyō Ishokujū* (Western Ways of Living—food, clothes, houses).	January—Emperor Meiji is enthroned. October— Shōgun Yoshinobu renounces his authority of government and offers it back to Emperor. November—Teppōzu is made foreigner's concession (178). December—The great edict of Emperor's personal rule of the land. Satsuma estate in Mita is burned (265). Michael Faraday dies. Alfred Nobel invents dynamite.
1868 Meiji 1 33	April—removes residence and school to Shinsenza; names his school Keiōgijuku (208). Innovation of charging tuition (208). First daughter, Sato, is	January—Battle of Toba and Fushimi (178). February—Imperial Army is ordered against Yedo. April—surrender of Yedo Castle (196). May—Battle

YEAR	FUKUZAWA'S LIFE	GENERAL HISTORY
	born. May 15—Fukuzawa continues lectures while the Battle of Ueno goes on (210). June—refuses new government's order to serve (203). August—renounces samurai status and becomes a commoner (241). *Heishi Kaichū Benran* (Handbook for Soldiers), *Seiyō Jijō Gaihen* (Things Western, Interlude Part), *Raijū Sōhō* (Rifle Instruction Book) Part II, *Kummō Kyūri Zukai* (Illustrated Book of Physical Sciences), *Keiōgijuku-no Ki* (Pronouncement at the Establishment of Keiō-gijuku) were chief publications of this year.	of Ueno (210). August—Enomoto Takeaki takes seven of Shōgun's vessels to Hokkaidō (254). September—change of the name of era to Meiji announced.
1869 Meiji 2 34	Declines stipend from Nakatsu clan (272). About September, begins to work for the pardon of Enomoto Kamajirō (255). November—joins the Book Wholesalers Guild under the name of Fukuzawaya Yukichi and starts publishing business (288). Declines offer from a wealthy merchant (267). *Yōhei Meikan* (Outline of the Western Art of War), *Shōchū Bankoku Ichiran* (Pocket Almanac of the World), *Eikoku Gijiin Dan* (English Parliament), *Shin-Ei Kōsai Shimatsu*	January—Satsuma, Chōshū, Tosa and Higo offer back their fiefs to Emperor. May—Enomoto surrenders (255). July—English Prince, Duke of Edinburgh, visits Japan (205). September—Ōmura Masujirō is assassinated. Yedo is renamed Tōkyō and is made the Capital. Telegraph line is completed between Tōkyō and Yokohama. J. S. Mill's *Subjection of Women* is published. Suez Canal is opend. Transcontinental railway completed across U. S. A.

YEAR	FUKUZAWA'S LIFE	GENERAL HISTORY
	(Sino-British Diplomatic Relations), *Sekai Kunizukushi* (All the countries of the World, for children written in verse), *Raijū Sōhō* (Rifle Instruction Book) Part III.	
1870 Meiji 3 35	May—suffers typhoid fever for the second time (217, 292, 330). July—second daughter, Fusa, is born. At request of Tōkyō Prefectural government, makes study of Western police systems (218). October—goes to Nakatsu to bring mother to Tōkyō. In Nakatsu speaks before the clan officials (278). Masuda Sōtarō and others attempt to assassinate him (230, 23ℂ) Obtains Shimabara estate in Mita (217). Saves the lives of Ōwara Shindayū and others (249). Begins horseback riding for health (292). *Seiyō Jijō* (Things Western) Part II.	The classes among the Japanese people are abolished, and all are permitted to assume family names. Former American Secretary of State William Henry Seward visits Japan (206). Charles Dickens dies. Franco-German War begins.
1871 Meiji 4 36	March—Keiō-gijuku as well as Fukuzawa's residence is moved to Mita (219). *Keimō Tenarai-no Fumi* (Book of Reading and Penmanship for children).	April—Postal service is established. July—clans are abolished and prefectures are instituted; Ministry of Education is created (213). October—Iwakura Tomomi is sent to Europe (330). Police system in Tōkyō is instituted (218). The Third Republic of France. Wil-

YEAR	FUKUZAWA'S LIFE	GENERAL HISTORY
		helm I becomes Emperor of Germany.
1872 Meiji 5 37	April—sails from Yokohama for Kobe; calls on Mrs. Ogata in Osaka (244); visits Sanda, Arima hot springs, and Kyōto to inspect schools, then to Nakatsu. July—leaves Nakatsu with Okudaira family (234). May—purchases from government the rented Mita grounds (221). *Gakumon-no Susume* (Encouragement of Learning) first essay. *Dōmō Oshie-gusa* (Junior Book of Ethics with many tales from the Western lands). *Katawa Musume* (Deformed Girl, a satire on the current custom of women's shaving their eyebrows and blackening their teeth).	January—Enomoto and others are pardoned. September—railway is completed between Tōkyō and Yokohama. Lunar calendar is abolished and Western calendar adopted; December 3 is declared January 1, Meiji 6th year of the new calendar.
1873 Meiji 6 38	Begins to practice public speaking in his house. Third daughter, Shyun, is born. October—Igakusho (School of Medicine) is opened within Keiō-gijuku, also an annex of Keiō-gijuku is opened in Ōsaka. *Kaireki Ben* (Explanation of the New Calendar, published in January). *Chōai-no Hō* (Bookkeeping) Part I. *Nihon Chizu Sōshi* (Maps of Japan, for children). *Mon-*	September—Iwakura Tomomi returns from Europe. October—Saigō Takamori resigns and leaves Tōkyō after disagreement over invasion of Korea. John Stuart Mill dies.

YEAR	FUKUZAWA'S LIFE	GENERAL HISTORY
	ji-no Oshie (Elementary Reader for Children). *Gakumon-no Susume* (Encouragement of Learning) Essay II, Essay III. *Kaigi Ben* (How to Hold a Conference).	
1874 Meiji 7 39	The Elementary School (Yōchisha) is established in affiliation with Keiōgijuku. An annex of Keiōgijuku is opened in Kyōto. February—begins to issue a magazine, *Minkan Zasshi*. The first meeting of Mita Enzetsu Kai (oratorical meeting) on June 27. Mother, O-Jun, dies. *Gakumon-no Susume* (Encouragement of Learning) Essays IV to XIII; *Chōai-no Hō* (Bookkeeping) Part II.	February—insurrection in Saga; Meirokusha (a scholarly society) is formed. March—Meiroku Zasshi's first issue comes out. April—invasion of Taiwan by Japan.
1875 Meiji 8 40	Mita Enzetsu Kan (Hall of Public Speaking) is opened, May 1. *Minkan Zasshi* is discontinued after June. Keiō-gijuku's Ōsaka Annex is moved to Tokushima. *Gakumon-no Susume* (Encouragement of Learning) Essay XIV. *Bummeiron-no Gairyaku* (Outline of Civilization—considered to be Fukuzawa's most scholarly work).	Alexander Graham Bell invents telephone. Japan abandons claim over Saghalien in exchange for sovereignty over Kurile islands (353). Niijima Jō founds Dōshisha.
1876 Meiji 9	Fourth daughter, Taki, is born. Takes a trip to	February—Treaty of Amity with Korea. Octo-

YEAR	FUKUZAWA'S LIFE	GENERAL HISTORY
41	Kansai area with two elder sons (270). Begins publication of *Katei Sōdan* (Home Journal issued several times a month). *Gakusha Anshin Ron* (Independence of the Scholar's Mind). *Gakumon-no Susume* (Encouragement of Learning) Essays XV, XVI, XVII.	ber—Insurrection in Kumamoto.
1877 Meiji 10 42	April—*Katei Sōdan* is renamed *Minkan Zasshi* and made a weekly. *Bunken Ron* (On Decentralization of Power, advocating less centralized government in Japan). *Minkan Keizai Ron* (Popular Economics). *Kyūhan Jō* (Life in the Old Feudal Clan, a sociological observation, not published at the time). *Teichū Kōron* (Commentary on the National Problems of the Tenth Year of Meiji in defense of Saigō, not published at the time).	February to September —Insurrection around Saigō Takamori (230, 317). Herbert Spencer publishes *Principles of Sociology*. Queen Victoria becomes Empress of India.
1878 Meiji 11 43	March 1—*Minkan Zasshi* is made a daily paper. May—*Minkan Zasshi* is discontinued at 189th issue. December—elected a member of Tōkyō Prefectural Assembly. *Fukuzawa Bunshū* (Collected Essays of Fukuzawa) Part I. *Tsūka Ron* (On Currency). *Tsūzoku Minken*	May—Ōkubo Toshimichi assassinated (239).

YEAR	FUKUZAWA'S LIFE	GENERAL HISTORY
	Ron (Popular Discourse on People's Rights). *Tsūzoku Kokken Ron* (Popular Discourse on National Rights) Part I.	
1879 Meiji 12 44	January—Tōkyō Gakushi-kaiin (scholars' association) is established and Fukuzawa is made its first chairman. January—chosen Vice Chairman of Tōkyō Prefectural Assembly but declines it, very soon after, resigns membership of the Assembly. Fifth daughter, Mitsu, is born. July—*Kokkai Ron* (On National Diet) in Yūbin Hōchi Shimbun under Fujita and Minoura's names (319). *Tsūzoku Kokken Ron* (Popular Discourse on National Rights) Part II. *Fukuzawa Bunshū* (Collected Essays of Fukuzawa) Part II. *Minjō Isshin* (Transition of People's Way of Thinking—influence of new mechanical devices on people's life and the inevitability of the advancement of democracy).	Ryūkyū Clan is reorganized and made Prefecture of Okinawa. Prince Heinrich of Germany visits Japan. General Ulysses S. Grant, former President of the U. S., visits Japan. Gustave Emil Boissonade is engaged to draft civil law. Thomas Edison perfects incandescent electric lamp.
1880 Meiji 13 45	Kōjunsha, the first men's club in Japan, established. Because of financial difficulty *Keiō-gijuku Iji Hōan* (Measure for Financial Support of Keiō-gijuku) is announced. In Decem-	Yokohama Specie Bank opens business.

YEAR	FUKUZAWA'S LIFE	GENERAL HISTORY
	ber urged by Ōkuma, Itō and Inoue to cooperate in starting a government organ, a newspaper (315). *Minkan Keizai Roku* (Popular Economics) Part II.	
1881 Meiji 14 46	January—Inoue Kaoru reveals to Fukuzawa government's secret intention of establishing National Diet; Fukuzawa promises cooperation (315). February—resigns membership in Tōkyō Gakushi-kaiin. July—third son, Sampachi, is born. Two Korean students enter Keiō-gijuku as the first foreign students. Members of Keiō-gijuku gather in Kōjunsha and draw up *Shigi Kempō An* (Private Draft for National Constitution). *Jiji Shōgen* (Commentary on the Current Problems, the necessity of accord within and competition without, Japan's position in the Orient against Western aggression).	October—the political upheaval of the 14th year of Meiji; Imperial rescript for the opening of the National Diet by 1890 (316). A political party Jiyūtō is formed.
1882 Meiji 15 47	March 1—first issue of Jiji-shimpō (321). *Jiji Taisei Ron* (On General Trend of the Times). *Teishitsu Ron* (On the Imperial Household). *Tokuiku Ikan* (On Moral Training). *Hei Ron* (On Armament).	March—Itō Hirobumi and his party leave for Europe to study national constitutions. Ōkuma forms a political party, Rikken Kaishintō. Daiinkun's insurrection in Korea. Ō-kuma establishes Tōkyō

YEAR	FUKUZAWA'S LIFE	GENERAL HISTORY
	These essays were first printed in Jiji-shimpō in serial and later reprinted in book form. Most of the subsequent publications followed the same procedure.	Semmon Gakkō which later became Waseda University. Ralph Waldo Emerson dies. Charles Darwin dies.
1883 Meiji 16 48	June—two sons, Ichitarō and Sutejirō, sail for studies in America (270, 303, 304). July—fourth son, Daishirō, is born. *Gakumon no Dokuritsu* (On the Independence of Learning).	April—the U.S.A. returns to Japan the indemnity for Shimonoseki Incident. July—the first issue of Kampō (Official Gazette). Iwakura Tomomi dies. France makes Viet Nam its protectorate. Britain occupies Egypt. Karl Marx dies.
1884 Meiji 17 49	*Zenkoku Chōhei Ron* (On the National Conscription). *Tsūzoku Gaikō Ron* (Popular Discourse on Foreign Diplomacy.)	Five ranks of nobility are created. Kingyokukin's insurrection in Korea.
1885 Meiji 18 50	*Nippon Fujin Ron* (On Japanese Womanhood) *Hinkō Ron* (On Moral Conduct). *Shijin Shosei Ron* (On Men's Moral Life).	The government is reorganized and the Cabinet system is instituted; Itō Hirobumi is made the first Premier. Iwasaki Yatarō dies.
1886 Meiji 19 51	Takes a trip to Kansai in March and April. *Danjo Kōsai Ron* (On Association of Men and Women).	The Imperial University is established. Mitsukuri Shūhei dies.
1887 Meiji 20 52	March 21—sees Kabuki play for the first time in Shintomiza theater (295). October—Keiō-gijuku is reorganized and Koizumi Nobukichi is made President (Sōchō).	December—Ordinance of Public Peace and Security (Hoan Jōrei) (318).

YEAR	FUKUZAWA'S LIFE	GENERAL HISTORY
1888 Meiji 21 53	March—called to the court as witness on Inoue Kakugorō (318). November—two sons, Ichitarō and Sutejirō, return home from America through Europe. *Nippon Danshi Ron* (On Japanese Manhood). *Sonno Ron* (On Reverence for the Emperor).	January—Inoue Kakugorō is arrested for involvement in Korean insurrection of 1882 (318).
1889 Meiji 22 54	January—begins financial campaign in preparation for university departments in Keiō-gijuku (224). Makes a long tour of Kansai area with the whole family in September and October.	February 11—the National Constitution is promulgated. Mori Arinori assassinated. July—railway from Tōkyō to Ōsaka completed.
1890 Meiji 23 55	January 27—Keiō-gijuku opens its university departments (363). Emperor grants 1000 yen to Keiō-gijuku in support of the new university departments.	January—Niijima Jō dies. July—the first election for the National Diet. October—Imperial Rescript on Education. November—the first National Diet convenes.
1891 Meiji 24 56	*Yasegaman-no Setsu* (Spirit of Manly Defiance, criticizing the conduct of Katsu and Enomoto at the time of the Restoration. Not published at the time).	February—Sanjō Sanetomi dies. March—Itagaki Taisuke is made head of Jiyūtō. May—Russian Crown Prince on visit to Japan is attacked and injured in Ōtsu.
1892 Meiji 25 57	May—makes a trip to Kansai. November—takes up the work of building a laboratory for infectious diseases for Dr. Kitasato Shibasaburō.	

YEAR	FUKUZAWA'S LIFE	GENERAL HISTORY
	Kokkai-no Zento (Future of the Diet). *Chian Shōgen* (A Word on the Public Security). *Kokkai Nankyoku-no Yurai* (Origin of the Difficulty in the Diet). *Chiso Ron* (On Land Tax).	
1893 Meiji 26 58	September—Dr. Kitasato's laboratory for infectious diseases, called Yōjōen, is opened. October—Fukuzawa's bronze statue is unveiled at Keiōgijuku. *Jitsugyō Ron* (On Business).	Terajima Munenori dies.
1894 Meiji 27 59	February—goes to Nakatsu with Ichitarō and Sutejirō to visit graves.	March—Kingyokukin assassinated in Shanghai. July—new treaty with England as the first instance of treaty revisions. August—declaration of war against China.
1895 Meiji 28 60	March—takes a trip to Hiroshima with family. December—celebration for reaching the age of 60.	April—Peace Treaty with China; intervention of Russia, Germany and France. Wilhelm Konrad Roentgen discovers X rays.
1896 Meiji 29 61	April—visits Ise Grand Shrine with family. November—trip around Shinano, Echigo and other provinces with family.	
1897 Meiji 30 62	Campaign for Keiō-gijuku endowment (325). November—trip to Kansai and Sanyō with family. *Fukuō Hyakuwa* (One Hundred Discourses of	Nishi Amane, Gotō Shōjirō, Mitsukuri Rinshō die.

YEAR	FUKUZAWA'S LIFE	GENERAL HISTORY
	Fukuzawa). *Fukuzawa Zenshū Chogen* (Foreword to the Collected Works of Fukuzawa) (143, 217, 323).	
1898 Meiji 31 63	May 11—manuscript for *Fukuō Jiden* (Autobiography of Fukuzawa Yukichi) completed. September 26—suffers stroke. *Fukuzawa Zenshū* (Collected Works of Fukuzawa). *Fukuzawa Sensei Ukiyo Dan* (Fukuzawa Sensei's Talk on the Worldly Life).	Pierre and Marie Curie discover Radium. Spanish-American War. Tsingtao leased by Germany. Port Arthur and Dairen leased by Russia. The Philippines and the Hawaiian Islands are annexed to the U. S. A. Bismarck dies. The Ordinance of Public Peace and Security abrogated. Kensei Kai is formed. Kanda Kōhei dies.
1899 Meiji 32 64	Recovers from the effects of the stroke gradually. June—*Fukuō Jiden* (Autobiography of Fukuzawa, published in book form). *Onna Daigaku Hyōron* (Reproof of "The Essential Learning for Women"). *Shin Onna Daigaku* (The New Essential Learning for Women).	Katsu Kaishū dies. Foreigners are given freedom to live among the Japanese. Boer War begins.
1900 Meiji 33 65	*Shūshin Yōryō* (Moral Code), compiled by his senior pupils, published. Emperor grants 50,000 yen in recognition of Fukuzawa's work in education and writing; Fukuzawa donates it to Keiōgijuku.	Wedding of the Crown Prince (later Emperor Taishō). Kuroda Kiyotaka dies. Itō Hirobumi forms Seiyū Kai. Boxer rising and siege of legations in Peking.
1901 Meiji 34	January 25—second and fatal stroke. Fuku-	Queen Victoria dies on January 22.

YEAR	FUKUZAWA'S LIFE	GENERAL HISTORY
66	zawa dies on February 3. Funeral on February 8. After his death three new books were published. In April, *Fukuō Hyakuyowa* (More Discourses of Fukuzawa). In May, *Teichū Kōron* (Commentary on the National Problems of the Tenth Year of Meiji, in defense of Saigō, 1877) and *Yasegaman-no Setsu* (Spirit of Manly Defiance, criticizing the conduct of Katsu and Enomoto at the time of the Restoration, 1891) both of which Fukuzawa had shown in manuscript only to his closest friends.	

ENCOURAGEMENT OF LEARNING

The First Essay, 1872

BY FUKUZAWA YUKICHI

INTRODUCTORY NOTE. This essay was Fukuzawa's first attempt at expressing his own ideas and its influence on the thinking of the Japanese people was unprecedented. Because newspapers and magazines had not yet gained wide circulation, this essay was brought out in pamphlet form, and the public took to it "like the thirsty to water." Some 200,000 copies were sold. Happy with the success of the first essay, Fukuzawa went on to publish a series of seventeen essays, all called "Encouragement of Learning," between 1872 and 1876.

Previous to this essay, Fukuzawa had written some widely read books, such as *Seiyō Jijō* (Things Western), and he had already been recognized as a man well informed on Western civilization. But with the publication of "Encouragement of Learning," Fukuzawa established himself as a thinker and an intellectual leader of new Japan. There followed a torrent of publications from his pen which led the nation in its great evolution to modernity.

It is interesting to note that this first essay contains practically everything that Fukuzawa was to discuss in his subsequent works, such as the meaning of education and learning, the dignity of an individual, freedom and independence, etc. And, very significantly, the very first line of the first essay, "Heaven never created a man above another . . . ," is the most quoted of Fukuzawa's sayings.

The language used in this essay is very quaint. For instance, the word Heaven as used here has no religious meaning at all. Today the word Nature would be used, but in 1872 the Japanese word for Nature had not come into general use. Also, Fukuzawa was not writing for the intellectuals alone but for the general populace of Japan as well. Fukuzawa once said that he always tried to write so clearly that an uneducated woman from the countryside would understand the words when they were read to her from the next room through the paper door. And so he chose to use everyday expressions of that time in order to reach the general people who knew nothing other than feudalism.

In spite of the quaintness and the outmoded expressions, the basic ideas in this essay are as fresh and virile to men of today as they were to those of 1872. There were many other scholars who advocated new thoughts, but Fukuzawa was foremost in force and clarity of expression and above all in reaching a wide circle of people. It is certain that there has never been in all the history of Japan an essay which compares with this one in its influence on the Japanese people.

February 20, 1960   EIICHI KIYOOKA

Encouragement of Learning

"Heaven never created a man above another nor a man below another," it is said. Therefore, when men are born, Heaven's idea is that all men should be equal to all other men without distinction of high and low or noble and mean, but that they should all work with body and mind, with dignity worthy of the lords of creation, which they are, in order to take all things in the world for the fulfillment of their needs in clothing, food, and dwelling, freely but without obstructing others, so that each can live happily through life.

However, taking a wide view of this human world, we find wise and ignorant men, rich men and poor men, men of importance and men of little consequence, their differences like those of the cloud and the slime. Why should all this be? The reason is apparent. In the *Jitsugokyō* it is said, "If a man does not study, he will have no knowledge. A man without knowledge is a fool." The distinction between the wise and the foolish comes from whether they have studied or not.

In society there are difficult tasks and easy tasks. Those who undertake difficult tasks are called men of high standing and those who undertake easy tasks are called men of low standing. All the tasks in which one must use his mind and which involve much worry are difficult, and those in which one labors with hands and legs are easy. And so, physicians, scholars, government officials, or big merchants and big farmers who employ many serving men are to be called men of high standing and importance.

When a man is high in standing and importance, his house will naturally be wealthy and, from the viewpoint of lowly people, he will appear to be high beyond their reach. But looking into the root of it all, we will find that the difference comes merely from whether the man has learning or not, and that there are no Heaven-made distinctions. The proverb says, "Heaven does not give riches to men, but gives it to the labor of men." Therefore, as I have said before, a man is not born with rank or riches. Only those who strive for learning and are capable of reasoning will become men of rank and riches while those without learning will become poor and lowly.

Learning does not mean knowing strange words or reading old, difficult literature or enjoying poems and writing verses and such accomplishments, which are of no real use in the world. These accomplishments give much pleasure to the human mind and they have their own values, but they are not to be valued and worshiped as much as the usual run of scholars has tried to make out. Since time immemorial, there have been very few scholars in Chinese classics who were good household providers or merchants who were accomplished in poetry and yet clever in business. For this reason merchants and farmers become concerned when their sons take to learning seriously, thinking that their fortunes will eventually be ruined. This is natural in anxious parents, and proves that this kind of learning is far removed from and quite useless to daily life.

Therefore, this kind of learning without real use should be left to other days and one's best efforts should be given to real learning that is near to men's everyday use—for instance, the forty-seven letters of the alphabet, the composition of letters, bookkeeping, the abacus, and the use of scales. Advancing farther, there will be many subjects to be taken up: Geography is a sort of story of and guide to Japan and all the countries of the world; Natural Philosophy is the study of the nature and the function of all things under the heavens; History is a detailed chronology and studies the conditions of every country in the world, past and present; Economics explains the management of a household and of a country and of the world; Ethics gives the natural principles for a man's conduct of himself and with his fellow men and shows how he should behave in society.

For the study of these subjects, one should read the translations of Western books. In writing one may let the Japanese alphabet suffice in most cases. If there should be a youth with a promise in scholarship, let him learn the "letters written sideways" and let him grasp the fundamentals in even one field or one subject, and according to these let him investigate the principles of things near him, and thus let him fulfil the need of every day. Such is Jitsugaku (Scientific Knowledge or Real Learning) for all men, which should be generally imbibed without distinction of high or low in society. Only after this, should men pursue the separate ways of samurai, farmer, artisan, and merchant, and the household business of each. In this way a man may attain his independence, a house its independence, and the nation too will attain independence.

In the pursuit of learning, the important thing is to know one's proper limitations. The nature of a man as he is born is not bound or restricted; a man as an adult man and a woman as an adult woman should be free and unrestrained in their actions. However, by stressing freedom alone without regard to one's proper limitations, one is most liable to fall into waywardness and licentiousness. What is meant by limitations is to conform to the reason of Heaven and humanity and to attain one's own freedom without infringing upon that of other men.

The boundary line between freedom and waywardness lies in whether one infringes on others or not. For instance, when one is using one's own money, it may seem that one is free to indulge in wine and women and to abandon oneself to licentiousness. But it is not so by any means. One man's licentiousness will become the temptation of many men, causing the general degeneration of the society and the disruption of education. Even if the money he spends is his, his sin cannot be pardoned.

The problems of freedom and independence exist with a nation as much as they do with an individual man. Since ancient times, Japan has been an island country far to the east of the Asian continent, not associating with foreign countries, living on its own produce, and never being sensible of want. But since the Americans came in the Kaei Era, foreign trade and intercourse began and developed to the state we see today. There have been arguments of many kinds even after the opening of the ports, some advocating loudly the closing of the ports and the expulsion of foreigners. However, these arguments take a very narrow point of view like that of the proverbial frog at the bottom of a well; they are not worthy of our note.

Take Japan, take any nation of the West; every nation is under the same heavens, illumined by the same Sun, enjoying the beauty of the same Moon, sharing the same ocean, breathing the same air, possessing the same human sentiments. Therefore, whatever we have in excess we should give to them, taking to us whatever they have in excess, teaching each other and learning together, never ashamed nor boastful, each fulfilling the needs of the other, mutually praying for the happiness of all. So, according to the reason of Heaven and the ways of man, a nation should hold mutual intercourse with all others, and when reason is against it, it should bow even before the black natives of Africa, and when reason is on its side, it should stand in defiance of the mighty warships of England and America, or when the honor of the country is at stake, every man in the whole nation should throw down his life to defend the glory of the country. Such should be the picture of a free and independent country.

But some people are like the Chinese, who thinks there is no nation in the world except his own, and whenever he meets some foreigners, he calls them barbarians as if they were beasts walking on four legs, despises and detests them, and simply endeavors to keep them out, never thinking of the real strength of his own country, with the result that he is subjected to humiliation by those "barbarians." All this indicates that he is ignorant of the proper limitations of a nation, exactly like a man who, not know-

ing the true meaning of freedom, falls into the evils of waywardness and licentiousness.

Since the return of the Imperial rule, Japan's system of government has come to be much changed. Externally she associates
with the world under international law; internally she guides the
people to an understanding of freedom and independence, permitting
the plain people to take family names and to go on horseback, which
one may consider the finest act of all times. One may say that the
movement to make the four classes—samurai, farmer, artisan, and
merchant—equal has here been placed on a firm footing.

Therefore, henceforth among the people of Japan there will be
no such thing as the rank to which a man is born. Only by his
ability and the position he holds will a man's rank be determined.
For instance, it is proper to pay respect to a government official,
but this is not the respect of the man himself. We should pay
respect to the fact that he holds his position because of his ability
and administers the precious laws for the benefit of the people. It
is not the person that one is to respect; it is the law that one is to
respect.

All people remember that during the Shōgun's regime the August
Jar of Tea used to be carried along the Tōkaidō Highway. Not
only the Jar of Tea but a hawk in the Shōgun's household was
more precious than an ordinary man; when a horse of the Shōgun's
household came by, all the travelers on the highway stood aside.
Everything, even a piece of stone or tile, appeared awesome and
precious when the words "belonging to the Shōgun" were attached
to it. Though disliking it for many centuries, people had become
used to it, and thus the ugly custom came to be. After all, this
did not come from the dignity of the law, nor from the value of
the things themselves; it was simply a cowardly device of the government to show off its power and to restrict the freedom of the
people. One may call it an empty pretense without substance.

Nowadays, as such miserable laws and customs are to be dis-
continued throughout the country, people ought to set their hearts
at ease, and if there should be the least complaint against the government, they should never hold it against the officials in secret, but
they should seek a proper channel to present the case and to argue
about it quietly and without hesitation. If the case should be in

accord with Heaven's reason and with humanity, one should fight for it even at the risk of one's own life. Such shall be the lot of a man who calls himself a citizen of a civilized nation.

As I have said before, an individual man and an individual nation are free and unrestricted according to Heaven-made law. And so, if this freedom of the nation is in jeopardy, one should not fear to stand against all the nations of the world; if one's individual freedom is in jeopardy, one should not stand in awe of even the government officials. Moreover, at the time when the equality of the four classes has been established, all men should feel secure in giving free rein to their activities as long as they follow the ways of Heaven. However, as every man has his position in society, he must have ability and virtue appropriate to his position. In order to give ability and virtue to oneself, one must learn the logic of things. In order to learn the logic of things, one must study his letters. This is the reason for the urgent need of learning.

As we look around today, the position of the three classes— farmer, artisan, and merchant—has advanced a hundred fold, and soon will be on a level with the samurai. Even now, the way has been opened for drawing talented men from among the three classes into government service. Therefore, all men must reflect upon themselves and realize that they now occupy a high position, and therefore must behave in a manner worthy of that position.

There is no one more pitiful and obnoxious than the ignorant and the illiterate. In the extreme of ignorance, they lose the sense of shame. When they grow poor and hungry because of their ignorance, they do not blame themselves, but they envy the rich, sometimes banding themselves to force a petition or even taking to armed rioting. Shall I call them shameless, or shall I call them lawless? They owe their security to the law of the nation and they carry on their household business under the law. They take advantage of it when they may. Yet, when their personal greed dictates, they break the law. Is this not an outrage on fair reason?

It sometimes happens that a well-established man with some means knows only how to accumulate money but is entirely ignorant in educating his children. Uneducated children will be foolish, which is not to be wondered at, and they will become lazy and licentious, finally squandering away like a wisp of smoke the fortunes inherited from their ancestors. To rule such foolish men, reason will not do; the only way will be to keep them in order by the show of force. A proverb of the West says, "Over foolish people, there is a harsh government." It is not that the government is harsh of itself; it is the foolish people who bring harshness upon themselves. If the government over foolish people is harsh, reason requires that the government over wise people should be good. Therefore, in our country, too, we have this kind of government because there is this kind of people.

Should our people ever sink into deeper ignorance and illiteracy, the government will become even severer than today. Should people turn their minds to learning, acquire an understanding of logic, and advance toward civilization, the government will move toward freedom and leniency. The severity or leniency of the government are natural consequences of the worth or unworthiness of the people themselves. Who in the world would prefer harsh rule to good rule? Who would not pray for strength and fortune for his own country? Who would welcome humiliation from foreigners? These are human sentiments common to all.

In this age, for those who have the mind to serve their country, there are no problems urgent enough to worry the mind and torture the body. The important thing for everyone for the present is that he should regulate his conduct according to humanity, and apply himself earnestly to learning in order to absorb a wide knowledge and to develop abilities worthy of his position. This will make it easy for the government to rule and pleasant for the people to accept its rule, every man finding his place and all playing a part in preserving the peace of the nation. This should be the only aim. The encouragement of learning that I advocate, too, takes this for its aim.

INDEX

Adoption, importance of, in feudal Japan, 341

Age, reckoning of, in Japan, 21n

Akamatsu, Daizaburō, 105

Alcock, Sir Rutherford, 129

Anchor, of ship Euryalus, 148–57 *passim*

Andō, Tsushima-no Kami, 141

Anti-foreign sentiment, Japanese, 121–22, 141–65 *passim,* 188–206 *passim,* 225 ff; *See also* "Expel the Foreigners" movement

Asano Bizen-no Kami, 147

Assassination, 225 ff.

Atsumi, Teiji, 250

Azuma-kan (ship) 168, 254

Ban, Tetsutarō, 105

Bear, dissection of, 63–64

Bellecourt, de (French minister), 145

Bizen, Sukesada, 240

Black, John R., 357

Books: copying of, 81–84; Dutch, used in Ogata's school, 80–85, 344–46; English, importation into Japan, 126, Japanese government's plan to import for profit, 171–72, purchased in America by Fukuzawa, 199–200

Bowl, china, as treasure on voyage to America, 107

Brooke, John Mercer (Captain), 105–18 *passim,* 350–51

Buemon, Otabe, 341

Buhachi, 34

Bullying, of street merchant, by students for amusement, 66–67

Calligraphy, 296

Carpet, 113

"Chambers's book on economics," 359–60

Charms, disrespectful treatment of, 17

Chemistry, student experiments, 84–87

Chie (beggar woman), 15

Children, rearing of, 298 ff.

China, future of, 277

Chinese learning, Fukuzawa's criticisms of, 206–7, 213–17

Chōshū clan, 191; and anti-foreign movement, 355–56

Classics, Chinese, 7–8

Cloak, crested, as gift of honor, 182–83

Coins: carried by Japanese on first mission to America, 108; given to American officer, 116–17

Colorado (ship), 167

Culture, Western, Japanese difficulty in comprehending, 133–35

Currency, Japanese, 281–82, 342, 365

Customs, American, strangeness of, 112 ff.

Dancing, American, 114

Danjūrō, 366

Diet, student, 60